Fatal Decisions

Fatal Decisions

Errors and Blunders in World War II

Edmund L. Blandford

CASTLE BOOKS

This edition published in 2001 by Castle Books
A division of Book Sales, Inc.
114 Northfield Avenue, Edison, NJ 08837

This edition published by arrangement with and permission of
Airlife Publishing Ltd
101 Longden Road, Shrewsbury, SY3 9EB, England
E-mail: airlife@airlifebooks.com
Website: www.airlifebooks.com

Copyright © 1999 Edmund L. Blandford

First published in the UK
by Airlife Publishing Ltd

British Library Cataloguing-in-Publication Data
A catalogue record for this book is available from the British Library

ISBN: 0-7858-1366-7

Typeset by Phoenix Typesetting, Ilkley, West Yorkshire
Printed by Biddles Ltd, Guildford and King's Lynn

Foreword

The margins between negligence, incompetence and simple error that result in tragedy can be slim. Miscalculations by those involved in the international game of power politics can bring about national setbacks, while in war, mistakes by generals and battlefield commanders cost lives. At the other end of the scale, errors by rank-and-file soldiers and civilians alike can bring both farce and death.

Wrong turns and misjudgements on a strategic scale are not the stuff of this collection. None of the events recorded in this book made any great impact on the overall direction of World War II: none of the great climacterics of that conflict are included here. What the reader will find are just a few of the lesser-known incidents involving humans caught up in the struggle that completely changed, and in some cases ended, their earthly lives.

Edmund L. Blandford

Contents

Triton *on Target*

No matter how 'phoney' the British public thought the first months of World War II were, the truth was the Royal Air Force and Royal Navy were in action from the first days. The public attitude was perhaps typified by a comment in a letter to the skipper of HM Submarine *Spearfish*, when a relative wrote: 'We hardly know there's a war on.' True, the relative concerned lived in the country, but apart from the false alarm air-raid sirens in the first hours of the war and the blackout, the town and city dweller on both sides also remained largely unaffected.

The submarines of both Britain and Germany were already in position before war broke out; *Spearfish* was almost sunk by a U-boat just four minutes after receiving the Admiralty signal 'Total Germany', which meant 'Commence hostilities against Germany'. At least that is how the official account, *HM Submarines* (HMSO, 1945), tells it; this is counter to German records, which speak of a similar signal being despatched not at 11.15 a.m., but an hour later. Whatever the timescale, *Spearfish* is recorded as having chased the enemy boat for six hours, even trying to ram it – without success. The episode is not mentioned in German accounts of this period. Another early wartime story tells of HM Submarine *Ursula* encountering a U-boat in the North Sea, the enemy boat evading the spread of torpedoes loosed by the British sub, which then pursued the enemy vessel and fired a further torpedo, which resulted in an explosion. There is, again, no German record of any U-boat being lost in such circumstances at that time.

Spearfish was finally caught and damaged by enemy craft in the eastern North Sea before the end of September 1939, and only just escaped after the arrival of British destroyers. Other British submarines were encountering similar dangers, including deadly minefields; losses in both the Royal Navy and *Kriegsmarine* over the next year would be heavy, and not only in terms of submarines, at the time the most hazardous branch of naval service. For the British, the loss of the two aircraft carriers *Courageous* and *Glorious* was the worst, though in a sense a loss involving far fewer lives was the most grievous, particularly since it involved human error.

In World War II the 'silent service' took up a far more aggressive stance from the start, its main area of operations the enemy waters of the North Sea. But in 1940 the emphasis was switched to the coastal seas off Norway in an attempt to disrupt German sea traffic involved in the vital ore supply trade with Sweden. In fact, the war reached fever pitch in early spring when the British destroyer *Cossack* sailed into Norwegian waters to rescue Allied seamen prisoners aboard the German ship *Altmark*, whose captain had anchored in a fjord before sailing on to Germany. The incident caused an international furore; the enemy was outraged and the Norwegian government protested strongly to the British.

At the heart of the matter in those tense days was the Norwegian government's submission to Hitler's demand that German ore ships routed from Sweden via the northern port of Narvik be allowed to sail through Norwegian territorial waters on their way to Germany. This safe passage of war materiel to the *Reich* was anathema to the Chamberlain government, and especially Winston Churchill, who urged that action be taken to stop it. Initially, this action took the form of a Royal Navy submarine 'blockade' set up off the Norwegian coast, waters that were very difficult for submarines on account of currents and enemy patrols. By April 1940 the British had gone much further, persuading their French ally to join in a military expedition to Norway itself, the principal target the German-used port of Narvik.

But it was far to the south that the Navy's subs were stationed, their crews' chances not high as they manoeuvred between British and German minefields to reach their patrol stations, a journey made even more hazardous by German sea and air patrols. The losses speak for themselves: HMS *Thistle* was sunk by U-boat on 14 April; HMS *Tarpon* and *Sterlet* were sunk on 22 and 27 April respectively; and HMS *Seal* was mined and captured on 5 May. Three S class boats also went missing during those weeks, and in all around six British submarines were lost during the weeks of that ultimately abortive campaign, even though on land, despite the enemy's total air supremacy, the Allied forces around Narvik almost persuaded General Dietl to quit. None was more amazed than he when his opponents began evacuating their forces from the base. The *Kriegsmarine* also suffered crippling losses in the campaign, which from their point of view proved a disaster. For all the successes scored by the Royal Navy's surface warships and submarines, for the crews of the latter their trade amounted almost to suicide. Yet despite this, and the paltry extra 'danger money' given to them, they were a highly dedicated band of men, all volunteers at that time. Every man soon learned what the initials 'DD' meant: Discharged Dead, as marked on the paymasters' rolls.

Submarines had come a long way since the amazing day in 1620 when a Dutchman in the service of King James I of England successfully navigated a submersible craft along the Thames for some miles. But in the Victorian era, the weapon developed in America as the 'Holland boat' was seen not only as a potential menace to the supremacy of the world's most powerful navy, but cowardly, 'unfair' and likely to be taken up only by those nations envious of Britain which possessed smaller navies. Indeed, Admiral Sir Arthur Wilson advocated treating all submariners as pirates, to be hanged if caught. Nevertheless, the submersible warship had come to stay, its power amply demonstrated in 1901 when the French submarine *Gustav Zede* 'torpedoed' a battleship of the same fleet as it left harbour. The Admiralty in London was among various naval authorities around the world who took note of this sensational event, which was reported in the press. Little time was wasted commencing experiments with submarines, the Royal Navy at first using a few of the American Holland boats before having British designs drawn up and built. It was Captain R.H.S. Bacon who invented the periscope, though the early models produced upside-down and reversed images when viewed from astern or from one side.

By the outbreak of World War I Britain possessed seventy-four submarines, and these did good work over the next four years helping to maintain the Dover Patrol, which denied use of the Channel to German shipping. Some boats even penetrated the Baltic where Swedish ore traffic to the Kaiser was stopped. But submarines were very vulnerable to accident: the *A1*, *A5* and *A8* were lost long before war came, and when submarines joined the Grand Fleet in a North Sea sortie one night to try to intercept the Kaiser's High Seas Fleet a series of disastrous collisions occurred: two large submarines were sunk, two more and a light cruiser badly damaged. And wartime conditions also helped produce several cases of misidentification that resulted in more losses. By that war's end British submarines had sunk 54 enemy warships and 274 other vessels, losing 54 boats out of a force of 203.

Early in World War II the Royal Navy's submarine force was organised into five flotillas; the Germans had fewer, but expanded rapidly as the war progressed, until the *Kriegsmarine*'s U-boat force totalled thirty-two flotillas. The British utilised more types than the enemy, from the U class of only 540 tons displacement through to the older, smaller H type and the S and T classes of 670 and 1,090 tons. The P class displaced 1,500 tons and was used as a supply boat; HMS *Porpoise*, for example, made the run to beleagured Malta in 1941–2. The design of giant subs of nearly 3,000 tons, such as the French *Surcouf* and the USS *Argonaut*, did not lead to any real success; both vessels were lost in the war. Neither was the earlier, experimental British M type carrying a huge twelve-inch gun perpetuated.

During these patrols in Norwegian coastal waters, HM Submarine *Salmon* sank *U-36* in December 1939 and *Porpoise* sank *U-1* on 16 April 1940, but the Germans' anguish over losses was not as great as the chagrin brought about by faulty torpedoes, a problem which had vexed the British in World War I. Grand Admiral Raeder suggested, sarcastically, that Doenitz try using some of those torpedoes captured with HMS *Seal*, whose crew were fortunate to survive having been sent to a German

POW camp, their captain to face a searching Admiralty inquiry after the war as to how he came to surrender his boat. *Seal*'s crew were unlucky to fall foul of an enemy mine; elsewhere, early Allied disasters led one German historian to remark post-war that 'In the first weeks of the war the record of the British Navy had not been exactly creditable.' He was, in fact, referring to certain weaknesses in the British side at sea, inevitable ones and more than matched by the Germans' own errors. But the worst blunder on the British side was concealed (not unnaturally) at the time and is rarely heard of today: the sinking of one Royal Navy submarine by another.

As related, British submarines were at the ready even before war was declared and either near their designated patrol zones or within reach when the Admiralty signal was sent. Their crews had set off from the depot ships in Rosyth or the Moray Firth, keyed up and anxious to be first to get a crack at the enemy's warships, especially the vaunted 'pocket' battleships. For the boats sent to watch off southern Norway there existed a peculiar hazard that would tax navigators and skippers: fresh water rushing in from the Baltic to the North Sea created difficulties of buoyancy in submarine handling due to greatly fluctuating water density. HMS *Oxley* arrived off Norway during the night of 10 September 1939, about to begin a ten-day patrol in a designated zone, on watch for German shipping. Other British submarines were allocated adjacent patrol areas – five boats in all, among them HMS *Triton* (the enemy also owned a ship of the same name), the subs ordered to remain five miles apart. The *Oxley* was assigned Sector 4, *Triton* 5, and owing to the prevailing currents all five boats experienced difficulties maintaining their correct stations. One account tells of 'irregular sets' (wireless communication) and the unwillingness of commanders to surface to fix their position owing to the danger of German patrols (this could be done via two lights ashore, as well as – presumably – by noting the position of the nearest well-lit Norwegian townships).

Despite the communication problems, both *Oxley* and *Triton* had been in contact by VHF radio several times. At 20.04 hrs (8.04 p.m.), *Triton* surfaced, her captain, Lt Commander H.P. de C. Steel, managing to obtain a position fix via the Oberstad light (067 degrees) and Kvasseim (110 degrees), which meant that *Triton* had drifted south-west of her billet. The captain, mindful of the darkness and drizzle, ordered a patrol course of 190 degrees to the south. To reach this, the helmsman steered 170, the sub zig-zagging fifteen to thirty degrees each side of this course line at only three or four knots. The boat trimmed down and charged its port engine, with land just visible eight miles off the port bow. Satisfied with progress, Lt Commander Steel went below, after ordering his OOW (Officer of the Watch), Lieutenant Stacey, to keep clear of a merchantman visible off *Triton*'s port quarter and steering a similar course. Lieutenant Stacey suggested a slight course change that would

HM Submarine *Oxley*, lost to torpedoes from HMS *Triton* (below),
itself lost in the Adriatic, December 1940. (Photographs courtesy of Royal Navy
Submarine Museum.)

bring the boat to starboard of the steamer, which was still stern on to the
submarine. The skipper concurred with this.

Suddenly, the conning tower bridge lookouts reported a light closer
to them, quite distinct from what would have been the steamer's own
navigation lights. Stacey at once ordered a slight turn to starboard and
informed the captain. It was 20.55 hrs. On training his binoculars Stacey
made out what appeared to be another submarine to starboard. Despite
the gloom, he was able to pinpoint and identify the vessel as definitely

a submarine, now apparently one mile distant off the starboard bow.

The urgent summons brought the captain to *Triton*'s bridge, but it was some minutes before he was able to discern what his second officer pointed out to him. When at last he could confirm Lieutenant Stacey's view, he ordered Nos. 7 and 8 torpedo tubes made ready, the alarm sending the whole crew to action stations. The skipper also ceased charging the boat's starboard engine, and *Triton* proceeded on its main motors. Confirming the other vessel as a submarine, Steel ascertained it was proceeding on a north-westerly course, but when he thought about whether it could be the *Oxley* he at once dismissed the notion (as he explained later), as they had been in touch earlier and had confirmed their respective positions.

One of the two telegraphists on *Triton*, Leading Seaman Eric Cavanagh, had just relieved his shipmate and gone forward for some food when he was called back to the bridge and handed the signal lamp. The captain told him to stand by to make the challenge, and to be sure to use the correct letters. *Triton* was then lined up, bows on to the other submarine, and the signaller flashed 'IFO'. After twenty seconds without the necessary response 'DY', the *Triton* challenge was repeated. Still no reply came. By then, Steel was almost positive they had found a U-boat, but as a last try he ordered Able Seaman John Day to make ready a rifle grenade, the standard procedure in such a situation. Day had been studying the other sub's conning tower and believed it to be unlike *Oxley*'s. The skipper then ordered a third challenge to be flashed by Cavanagh's lamp, and when no response came he ordered Seaman Day to fire the grenade, which he did. The charge shot up over the sea and exploded into three green stars. Incredibly, even this failed to elicit any visible response from the other boat.

Some fifteen seconds later Lt Commander Steel ordered *Triton*'s torpedoes fired, but before any result was seen and after about thirty seconds had elapsed, the bridge crew saw 'an indeterminate flashing' from the other boat's tower. If it was a signal, it was quite unreadable. Whatever the flashing light signified, it was not in Morse, and *Triton*'s crew were convinced it had to be a U-boat trying to fox them. In any case, it was too late for further obfuscation. *Triton*'s torpedoes exploded on target, just as Lieutenant Stacey fixed his boat's position by the Egero and Oberstad lights as four and a half miles inside their own sector.

As the noise of the explosion faded, *Triton* headed for the spot, and on reaching the other boat's last known position the bridge crew could see no sign of wreckage or survivors. Suddenly, they heard cries for help and presently saw three men in the water. Four of *Triton*'s crew, led by Lieutenant Guy Watkins, went with lines to help the survivors out of the oily sea. Two were hauled to safety, one of them the captain of HMS *Oxley*, Lt Commander Bowerman, the other an able seaman who, it transpired, had just begun his bridge watch when the torpedoes struck.

The third survivor, Lieutenant Manley, was swimming towards *Triton* when he suddenly sank from view – for good. A continued search for more survivors failed to find any.

HM Submarine *Oxley* was the first ship of the Royal Navy to be lost at sea in World War II. Fifty-three of its crew were lost. When *Triton*'s turn came, fifty-four sailors died.

In the inquiry that followed, blame for this terrible blunder was laid squarely on the captain and subordinates of *Oxley*. Although remaining at periscope depth throughout the day, *Oxley*'s crew had fixed their position as one and a half miles inside the eastern limit of their sector, eight miles south of her patrol position and seven miles from *Triton*. Therefore, *Oxley*'s captain took his boat north for two hours before surfacing at 20.30 hrs, whereupon he learned *Triton*'s current position, given by his subordinates. This he queried, 'as it seemed very improbable'. Yet his HTD (higher telegraphist detector) insisted the data given was correct, adding that fading on the radio equipment made confirmation and indeed communication with *Triton* impossible. Lt Commander Bowerman was still of the opinion the latest position given him did not conform to the information provided by *Triton* earlier, so he decided to proceed on a course which, he thought, was divergent to the other boat. In evidence, the captain stated: 'I was very surprised I was as near the edge of my area as my fix gave me.' Bowerman hoped to obtain final confirmation of his true location on surfacing, but when he did at 20.30 hrs he became confused by the 'misty rain over land' when trying to observe the Ebero and Oberstad lights. The lights had been reduced by the weather to a vague glare, yet this hardly explains the fact (which emerged clearly in the inquiry) that *Oxley*'s true position at that moment was not two miles inside its own sector, but four miles inside *Triton*'s.

A quarter of an hour after *Oxley* surfaced, Lieutenant Manley arrived on the sub's bridge, to be informed by his skipper the course was 330 degrees at five knots, which he believed would bring them to their proper patrol position. After warning the OOW to keep alert for *Triton*, the captain went below, but had barely checked the boat's position on the chart and made for the wardroom when he was summoned to the bridge, where Manley informed him of another submarine off the starboard beam, adding that a grenade signal had been fired towards *Oxley*. A reply had been sent, but had failed to explode. When Bowerman asked Manley if the signal lamp had been used, he told him yes, but his hesitant manner caused the captain to order a repeat flash.

By then it was too late.

'I saw a flash immediately beneath me and heard a dull explosion', Bowerman recounted. 'The ship shook and seemed to list to port and break in two in the centre.'

There was no chance of escape for the crew trapped below.

The inquiry ascertained from the evidence given that *Oxley* was indeed well out of its appointed sector, while *Triton* was within hers. The range given to Bowerman by his HTD of seven and three-quarter miles (from *Triton*) was incorrect. Yet surface observation at 20.30 hrs failed to convince the captain he was well off course and had drifted far eastwards. A submarine remaining beneath the surface in the prevailing sea conditions needed very careful handling, especially with four other boats in the area. The fact that *Oxley* remained under observation for some time by *Triton's* bridge lookouts, and that its own watch failed to see and respond to the repeated challenges, pointed to dangerous slackness. Allowing for the tiredness and boredom that inevitably accompanies such night watches at sea, the officers should have remained vigilant in circumstances where surprise could mean death. No blame whatever was attached to Lt Commander Steel and his crew whose conduct was considered 'praiseworthy'. Nevertheless, Steel was moved on to instruction duties at the submarine training school at Fort Blockhouse. *Oxley's* unfortunate skipper was given command of a destroyer, a task he apparently carried out with success.

As for the public, they learned of the loss when BBC news and the Fleet Street papers made it public soon after, via the soon familiar lines of an Admiralty bulletin: 'HM Submarine *Oxley* is overdue and must be presumed lost.'

With a new commander, and following Italy's entry into the war in June 1940, *Triton* sailed to Gibraltar and soon commenced operations in the Mediterranean before moving on to the Adriatic, where it vanished in December 1940, just one of the twenty-five Royal Navy submarines lost in the first sixteen months of the war.

Athenia *Torpedoed*

Whatever assurances Hitler received and believed from his Foreign Minister, Joachim von Ribbentrop, that Britain would never go to war over Poland, Commodore Doenitz's U-boats made the necessary preparations for hostilities by despatching 80% of their force to the Atlantic in August 1939, in good time to beat the Royal Navy blockade Doenitz knew would be put into place. Twenty-one ocean-going submarines took up station in the north-west Atlantic, having cut through the English Channel which at that time was still completely clear of minefields and without hostile British warship patrols. Among these U-boats was *U-30*, one of ten Type VIIs built between 1934 and 1936 by Germania of Kiel and A.G. Weser of Bremen. These early Type VIIs displaced about 915 tons loaded, were 64 metres long (less than 200ft), and armed with five torpedo tubes, one 88mm deck gun and two MG34 machine-guns; the crew numbered forty-four.

By that fateful Sunday, 3 September, this German submarine force was strung out in a line of interception ready to sink British shipping, and, as it turned out, French vessels too. Their captains were also empowered to surface and stop neutral ships in order to inspect papers and cargoes that might be destined for Britain. The German naval signal to commence hostilities with Britain was sent at 12.56 hrs, no mention being made of France, which did not declare war until 17.00 hrs. Before long, the 'Phoney War' had set in on the Western front, but things were different in the air and at sea.

At noon on Friday, 1 September, as German troops fought their way into Poland, the 13,581-ton liner *Athenia* left Glasgow, heading for Belfast and Liverpool to pick up more passengers. Taken aboard the ship in Britain were those people stranded in French ports by the cancellation of various sailings by other ships due to the threat of war, mostly Americans and Canadians anxious to get away from the danger areas. The *Athenia*, built in 1923 by the Fairfield Shipbuilding Company of Glasgow and operated by the Donaldson Line, finally set sail from Britain on the evening of 3 September.

At this early stage the Admiralty had not started up its convoy system, and was in fact waiting to see what developed in the war at sea. In the meantime, ships crossing the Atlantic were advised to sail singly on a zig-zag course at best speed, though along the east coast routes convoys were arranged. Twenty-three German U-boats had actually left Kiel and Wilhelmshaven in August 1939 over a ten-day period, a further ten subs being sent into the Baltic, but these were soon withdrawn. At 14.00 hrs on 3 September a further signal from Commodore Doenitz to his U-boat commanders in the Atlantic read: 'Commence economic warfare according to operations order until further notice.' The two German pocket battleships *Graf Spee* and *Deutschland* had already slipped into the Atlantic and would begin their own independent anti-shipping raids.

As the light began to fade on that first evening of war in September, *Leutnant* Lemp, the twenty-five-year-old captain of *U-30*, raised his periscope, anxious to take one last searching look around the horizon before darkness fell. Suddenly, he saw a shape looming up over the north-eastern horizon, barely visible in the gathering gloom. Within seconds his first officer had called 'Alarm!' and the whole crew rushed to action stations, something they had practised over and over again, both in waters close to their bases in the North Sea and in the Baltic, which was free of potential enemy patrols. The planesman did his utmost to main-tain the submarine on an even keel as Lemp endeavoured to identify the vessel becoming larger in his periscope lens. Shortly, Lemp realised without doubt that the ship approaching *U-30* on a quarterly course from England was a liner. Excitement grew in him, and it soon passed to the crew as the captain made known his observations: a large, unescorted vessel, almost certainly British, about to enter torpedo range!

A few concise orders were rapped out, a slight course correction was given, and the forward torpedo tubes were loaded and readied for firing as the first officer thumbed through a ship identification manual in an effort to place the silhouette, or at least obtain some kind of reasonable description for the boat's war log. *Leutnant* Lemp decided the ship had to be an armed merchant cruiser; even if it was a liner, it would only be sailing alone if armed. And, if mounting weapons of any description, it fell outside the orders governing U-boat warfare, even though Lemp did not feel such restrictions applied, for if armed the merchantman or liner at once became in effect a man-of-war and could legitimately be attacked without warning. There were no cautions or restrictions from Commodore Doenitz with regard to enemy warships. This target was too good to miss; here was a chance to show what the new breed of U-boat mariners could do. In any case, Lemp reasoned, this large ship seemed to be off the normal shipping routes, and it was zig-zagging, most likely for a very good reason. It was probably carrying troops or armaments. He did not stop to think to where. There is no way of knowing if Lemp's second-in-command advised caution, or if any discussion or even argument broke out within the close confines of the control tower in *U-30*.

Two feet of the U-boat's periscope cut a feathery wake in the grey Atlantic waves, a slightly phosphorescent trail that would have spelt doom to the Germans beneath the waves had any British warship or plane spotted it – but there were no escorts anywhere near the *Athenia*. The forty-four men aboard *U-30* waited and waited in great tension as the final moments ticked by; men licked their lips and throats became dry as the great vessel loomed ever nearer in the captain's periscope lens. Every man was waiting for the sharp '*Los!*' from their commander that would bring the slight thud and jar through the boat as the first torpedoes were expelled from the bow tubes. And when at last the order came and the deadly missiles went on their way, not one German seaman aboard that boat had any idea of the furore they would cause, or the fact that presently the *Kriegsmarine*'s torpedoes would themselves be virtually useless junk, like those of the US Navy during its early days of combat in the Pacific.

The first officer and mate glued their eyes to their watches as silence again reigned through the boat. The seconds passed with agonising slowness, until at last came a double thump – a hit! The radioman on listening watch confirmed the explosions and the whole crew cheered wildly until he signalled for silence. The stricken liner was sending an SOS. In another moment the radioman handed a scribbled message to the captain, and Lemp learned he had torpedoed the liner *Athenia*. The first officer began running through his manual once more as Lemp read the message again: 'SOS . . . SOS . . . ATHENIA TORPEDOED . . . SOUTH-WEST ROCKALL.' The exact position of the attack was given. It was just after 21.00 hrs.

The liner *Athenia* goes down in the Atlantic, first of the U-boat victims,
sunk in error by *Kapitanleutnant* Fritz-Julius Lemp.

Lemp stood aside to allow some of the bridge crew to view the stricken
vessel, which was listing but not sinking too rapidly; the lifeboats
appeared to be lowering in good order. Then the radioman reported
more signals as other vessels responded to *Athenia*'s distress call. The first
officer on *U-30* handed his captain the ship manual, pointing to the
silhouette and details of their victim, Lemp's eyes scanned the lines and
black shape; there was no doubt, it was *Athenia*. Taking another longer
look through the 'scope, he searched more carefully, unable to be certain
if guns under covers or even troops were visible. Some, even many, of
the figures he could see crowding the decks and climbing into lifeboats
could well be military personnel. Lemp knew it was impossible to tell.
More thoughtful now, he half decided to order the boat surfaced in order
to get nearer and at the very least look for a name on one of the lifeboats,
even perhaps interrogate some survivors – or take some prisoners? In the
event he did nothing.

'We've stirred up a hornets' nest! Let's get out of here!'

Rapidly giving orders, Lemp had his boat move away from the area,
his decision partly brought about by the receipt of more intercepted
signals indicating warships coming at high speed.

By next morning the news had broken worldwide, and an Admiralty
bulletin at 05.00 hrs gave news of the sinking which had occurred 200
miles west of the Hebrides. Many newspapers had already set up their

front pages in Britain; these were hurriedly changed, the boldest type-faces being used to announce the first bout of Nazi atrocity against the Allies in World War II. 'U-BOAT TORPEDOES BRITISH LINER – 100 AMERICAN GIRLS ON BOARD' ran the Daily Express headline, and the newspaper went on to quote Prime Minister Chamberlain's earlier statement. 'We fight against evil things, brute force, oppression and perse-cution – and against these I am certain right will prevail.' The papers reported that there were 1,470 passengers on *Athenia*, most of them American, and in due course all but 112 were said to be safe. Not sur-prisingly, the newspapers reminded their readers of the *Lusitania* sinking in 1917, when American lives had also been lost, this outrage precipi-tating the USA's entry into that war.

From this angle alone, *Leutnant* Lemp had committed a gross blunder. His submarine slunk away, maintaining radio silence, so that all Doenitz and the German people at home knew of the disaster came via the Allied and neutral news services. Dire as the news was for Hitler and his entourage, it was even more serious for Doenitz, whose specific orders appeared to have been flouted, though until Lemp and his crew returned to base no exact details from the German side could be known. As an ex-U-boat skipper, Doenitz, was well aware of the difficulties faced at sea by U-boat crews, especially under the restrictions imposed by him at that early stage of the war. But that one of his brave young lions should have been stupid enough to sink an ocean liner on the very first day of the war seemed inexcusable. Doenitz had some explaining to do, not only to his superior, Grand Admiral Raeder, but to the *Führer* who was outraged by the news – as indeed was Propaganda Minister Goebbels, who now excelled himself by producing perhaps his most outrageous and absurd lie, that Winston Churchill had arranged for a bomb to sink *Athenia* merely in order to inflame American opinion against Germany. The world at large was not deceived, except for one or two fascist rulers who preferred to believe such fantasy.

For the Germans it was a propaganda disaster; it now appeared the U-boats had not waited before opening up unrestricted submarine warfare. Indeed, in that very same week three more ships were sent to the bottom of the sea: the *Bosnia*, *Royal Sceptre* and *Rio Claro* were lost on 5 and 6 September, all important vessels to the British. But proof that neither Doenitz nor Hitler believed in Goebbels' propaganda came with more radio messages flashed to all U-boats at sea: 'EXISTING ORDERS FOR MERCANTILE WARFARE REMAIN IN FORCE'. This signal was sent out at 16.55 hrs on 4 September, followed by another at 23.53 hrs when a further clarification was made, on Hitler's orders, that no passenger ships were to be attacked at all, even if in convoy. As a result, no more ships of the kind were torpedoed in the period, though in fact very few liners continued to sail the Atlantic.

The twenty other U-boat skippers observed these rules, though obvious troop ships and freighters sailing under warship escort were excepted. It was not, however, too hard a war for the German sub captains who, despite the vastness of the ocean, found targets enough, though the troop ships conveying Commonwealth soldiers to the mother country escaped attack, probably because of their heavy escorts. Despite the restrictions, it was Otto Schuhart in *U-29* who had sunk the three British ships mentioned in the first week of the war. It was also *U-29* that had sunk the first major Royal Navy warship lost in World War II, the carrier *Courageous*, sunk in the north-east Atlantic while under destroyer escort. Its aircraft patrols had just been taken aboard again after searching for a merchantman reported to be under U-boat attack; of the 1,250 men aboard the carrier, about 500 were drowned. The carrier *Ark Royal* had just missed such a fate when a salvo of torpedoes launched by *U-39* missed. The submarine was promptly traced and sunk by the destroyers *Faulkner, Foxhound* and *Firecracker.*

Leutnant Lemp and his crew returned to base. The captain was placed under virtual arrest and his crew were quarantined while the investigation by Doenitz went ahead. Doenitz always had a soft spot for his captains, and since they were comparatively few in number he had got to know them all. Lemp was not incarcerated, though his log was impounded and, according to one source, altered in an attempt to conceal the truth, even though *U-30*'s record described only an armed merchant cruiser being attacked. In his memoirs, Winston Churchill referred to 'the confession of the U-boat captain', citing one of the Nuremberg documents. Whatever the truth of Lemp's 'confession', it is fair to assume he genuinely believed the liner *Athenia* to be an armed merchantman and therefore liable to attack. Lemp sank seventeen ships with *U-30*, and was awarded the Knight's Cross in August 1940.

His career would come to an abrupt end in circumstances which hugely favoured Britain the following year.

The Battle of Barking Creek

Such was the threat of terror from the air in Britain that even before the *Wehrmacht* struck against Poland on 1 September 1939 very many thousands of people were suffering the first inconveniences of war. Not only were large numbers of militiamen and reservists called to report for full-time duty, large numbers of children and adults were evacuated from major cities considered most vulnerable to German air attack.

That such an assault was possible and indeed probable was something Britain's leaders had convinced themselves of. Neville Chamberlain's government were at one with opposition parties and military experts in assessing the chances of annihilating air raids that would bring a great weight of bombs on the civilian population as almost a certainty. In 1937 the Air Raid Precautions Sub-Committee of Imperial Defence reported that based on World War I experience every ton of bombs dropped would cause fifty casualties (seventeen killed, thirty-three injured). Therefore, a total *Luftwaffe* offensive using gas, explosive and incendiary bombs would bring 200,000 casualties in one week, 60,000 of those fatalities. In the event, though some night raids on cities caused more casualties even than those suffered by the Germans under far greater RAF assault, overall casualty figures were lower than expected: almost 30,000 were killed in London throughout the war, for instance, 60,000 in all. Most of the great numbers of cheap coffins quietly made and stored before the war were not needed.

Nonetheless, in 1937 the government was correct to make ARP (air raid precautions) a compulsory matter, as were the Germans. Through an Act of Parliament local authorities were compelled to take action in setting up appropriate organisations to deal with air raid emergencies. How they coped is beyond the scope of this work; what is relevant is the 'knock-on' effect which resulted from the fear of air attack at the top, leading to widespread anti-raid propaganda through various effective means such as cigarette cards. And when war finally came, the nervous state of the government resulted in the immediate closing of all places of entertainment, a panic measure that brought a depressing loss of morale and was soon rescinded. In fact, Nazi propaganda – and, of course, the terrible bombing of Guernica by the German Condor Legion Heinkels during the Spanish Civil War – had helped to establish the air raid neurosis in British leaders, especially Winston Churchill, who felt that in certain circumstances the Germans would be unable to resist using mass air terror to cow the enemy. All of these prognostications were not upset simply because the *Luftwaffe* failed to show up when war was declared. The false alarm sirens of 1 September did nothing to alleviate matters; the Lord Chancellor's declaration in December 1938 that Hitler's air force was capable of delivering 3,000 tons of bombs in one day was still taken seriously. News of the swift subjugation of Poland and the *Luftwaffe*'s part in it, including the blitz on Warsaw, simply amplified such notions.

Preparations in ARP begun in 1938 included the digging of deep trenches in public parks; these were abandoned to the elements following Chamberlain's 'triumph' at Munich which 'solved' the crisis over Czechoslovakia. As soon as the real thing came a year later the workmen were turned out again to drain the trenches and turn them into proper air raid shelters.

In the armed forces, while the Royal Navy had always been seen as Britain's first line of defence, in the modern age the comparatively new Royal Air Force protected our skies from aerial incursion, though judging by the experts' views on probable air raid casualties the government held little faith in the RAF's ability to hold back enemy bombers. Aiding the 750-strong fighter force were the 'barrage' balloons of a command only set up in 1938, plus a woefully inadequate Anti-Aircraft Command. Fighter Command was organised into thirty-nine front-line squadrons, with 400 planes in reserve. Of its first-line strength 347 were Hurricanes and 187 Spitfires, the rest made up of obsolete biplanes and the new twin-engined Blenheim Mk 1s. Among the biplanes were seventy-six Gladiators, some of which would be called upon to combat the modern Messerschmitts of the *Luftwaffe* in the Norwegian campaign the following year. Air Chief Marshal Sir Hugh Dowding estimated that forty-six fighter squadrons would be needed to combat German air attack on Britain, but soon after war came he was obliged to despatch some of his Hurricane units to France.

The RAF's fighter interception force relied on a system of ground control, at the heart of which lay advanced warning of attack by the new and secret radar system: eighteen Chain Home (CH) units covering the east and south coasts of Britain, from Aberdeen to Portsmouth. The Germans also had radar (radio detection and ranging), but had so far failed to develop it into a fighter control system. British radar posts, in theory, would give warning of incoming raiders up to 100 miles distant at whatever height except low level. Aiding the existing anti-aircraft lookout posts were the highly skilled volunteers of the Observer Corps. The system was much more extensive in coastal coverage than that eventually organised in World War I when the Army and police were the chief planks of defence warning, but the radar sets themselves were untried in war and crude by later standards, and of course the operators were inexperienced. Fighter pilots, too, were quite naturally inexperienced, and would take time to learn the techniques and skills necessary for defence and survival in air combat.

It was these shortcomings that led to the so-called 'Battle of Barking Creek'.

Belief that fear of air attacks was justified came early. The crowded streets of central London emptied quite rapidly when, not long after Prime Minister Chamberlain's sombre announcement of war, the eerie cadences of the air raid sirens began to howl across the capital and southern England. Thousands hurried to the nearest shelter; the few who through bravado tried to remain, gawking in the streets, were bullied away by harassed and nervous policemen. As a demonstration of how the British public would behave under threat from the air it was admirable, and when soon afterwards the single wailing note of the 'All Clear' came, the crowds emerged relieved and smiling into the Sunday morning sunshine. The cause of the alarm had been an unidentified civil plane crossing the Channel, but that night other areas along the East Anglian coast suffered more alarms as jittery defence posts made more errors. A further alarm followed the next day.

Then, soon after six a.m. on Wednesday, 6 September, the CH radar station at Canewdon near Southend-on-Sea, Essex, began recording 'enemy aerial activity' over the North Sea. It appeared that groups of up to twenty German aircraft were heading in towards the Thames estuary. Fifteen minutes were needed to confirm that no RAF planes were in that area, so the plots were accordingly marked as 'hostile' and the air-raid sirens began to wail in the zones to be affected. It looked as if the first, expected, mass enemy air attack was becoming a reality.

Then, AA units on the Essex coast reported aircraft near West Mersea, and the whole British defensive system swung into action. The 11 Group sector controller, Group Captain Lucking, alerted the Hurricanes at North Weald to scramble a flight of fighters to investigate, put the adjacent 12 Group on alert and advised the Observer Corps of his actions. Contrary to orders, the station commander at North Weald promptly ordered his entire fighter strength into the air; twelve serviceable Hurricanes of 56 and 151 Squadrons scrambled, soon followed by two more excited pilots who flew after the main formation but trailed behind one thousand feet lower. It would be this luckless pair who suffered as the episode took on fiasco proportions.

The Hurricanes began patrolling the line Harwich–Colchester, the eyes of every pilot straining to catch a glimpse of the enemy they fully expected to see at any moment. In the meantime, at 06.45 hrs twelve Spitfires were scrambled from 54, 65 and 74 Squadrons based at Hornchurch and flew east to intercept the 'enemy' raiders. As they reached the mouth of the Thames they spotted their 'prey' and the cry 'Tally-ho!' was given by 74 Squadron pilots, who at once went into the attack. The future Air Commodore Donaldson, then the leader of 151 Squadron, watched in disbelief and then horror as immediately after he called 'Bandits!' and ordered his pilots to await verification, he realised the 'enemy' coming at them were Spitfires. Two of the latter, flown by Flying Officer Byrne and Pilot Officer Freeborn, attacked some of the Hurricanes, this despite having the rising sun in their faces which had prevented positive identification. Pilot Officer Hulton-Harrop was struck in the head by a bullet and died; his Hurricane went down in a gentle glide, over Essex and into Suffolk, to crash on Manor Farm, Hintlesham. Had his fighter been fitted with head armour it is most likely he would have escaped injury. His fellow airman, Pilot Officer Rose, escaped injury, but was forced to land at Whetstead in Essex.

More confusion occurred when AA gunners opened fire on 65 Squadron Spitfires off the coast, this despite the pilots flashing the correct recognition signal in Morse. In the subsequent inquiry, it was found that the ground gunners were young, unable to read Morse, and woefully ignorant in aircraft recognition. Indeed, the Observer Corps personnel were far from being up to standard themselves. During the episode, these watchers had received reports from the radar post of

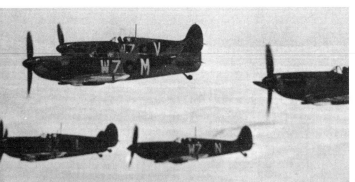

a

b

c

d

The 'Battle of Barking Creek', September 1939, and another incident early in the war when Spitfires (a) attacked Hurricanes (b) and Hampdens (d). Pilot Officer Hulton-Harrap was the first RAF Fighter Command fatality (c).

incoming enemy planes, but had been unable to see or hear any at all.

Group Captain Lucking was relieved of his command the same day and taken under close arrest to Air Vice Marshal Keith Park's HQ. The offending Spitfire pilots were also placed under arrest, while Pilot Officer Rose flew to Hornchurch the same day to give evidence.

Reports that twin-engined Blenheims had been responsible in the first instance for this episode, a story published long after the war by one eminent researcher, seem to be untrue. As for the radar crew at Canewdon, their records, if any, have long since vanished. In his history of Hornchurch fighter base, *Raiders Approach!*, Squadron Leader Sutton OBE commented that it was 'unsurprising' Spitfire pilots and AA gunners should have been so trigger-happy in the first days of the war, when it seemed 'inconceivable' that Hitler would refrain from launching mass air attacks on Britain. Fighter pilots were by nature aggressive and quick off the mark, but Sutton states it was AA bursts around Hurricanes which alerted the Spits and brought about the attack. The early usage of ground-to-air radar at Canewdon had resulted in a fluke: echoes from the west were somehow reflected as if from the east and not filtered out. The incident led to better practice and the introduction of identification, friend or foe, devices in RAF aircraft.

And this was by no means the only mêlée of the war between friendly fighters of either side. The *Luftwaffe* indulged in the Battle of Koepernick, and four days after Christmas 1939, the British defence system erred again – with serious results. Spitfires of No. 602 (City of Glasgow) Squadron were scrambled from their base at Drem, east of Edinburgh and near the sensitive Firth of Forth, after a warning of 'bandits' heading in from the sea. Although only just after three p.m., dusk was falling and there was sea mist, neither helping visibility. Despite these conditions, the intruders were spotted and the RAF pilots zoomed in for a first attack. One after another the Spits roared in, each pilot thumbing his gun button to set his eight .303 machine-guns chattering, sending streams of lead at the alarmed crews of the twin-engined, twin-tailed machines now trying to escape only one thousand feet above land. Only as the Spitfires broke away past their targets did the terrible truth dawn on their pilots: the 'bandits' were RAF Hampdens. By then it was too late; two of the friendly bombers were going down. The survivors were almost out of fuel and made emergency landings on the fighters' own base at Drem, their crews soon facing their chastened attackers. It seems liaison between Bomber Command – who had despatched the Hampdens on an exercise – and the defence system was not as it should have been.

Next morning the fighter pilots rose, went to attend to their ablutions and found all the toilet rolls gone. The bomber boys had already taken off, but soon roared back over the fighter field – to bomb it with toilet rolls.

By July 1942, the officer commanding the famous Biggin Hill fighter station in Kent was Group Captain 'Dickie' Barwell. Misidentification in air combat had become a problem: twenty-five Allied aircraft had been shot down in error. Group Captain Barwell promoted recognition contests to help counter the situation, only to become a victim himself. When a 'bogey' was reported over the sea, Barwell took off in a Spitfire Mk VI, despite the fact he had broken his back and was still in plaster; he was accompanied by Squadron Leader Bob Oxspring. They failed to find the enemy plane but were themselves attacked by two Spitfires from Tangmere. Hampered by his plaster cast, Barwell was trapped in his blazing fighter and fell into the sea.

The Third Eagle Squadron of American volunteer pilots trained on Spitfires had unfurled their flag at Biggin on 3 May in the same year. By September, these pilots were about to transfer to the US Army Air Force, and in the middle of that month flew what was to have been their final operation before donning American uniforms. It proved more than that. In one of the most incredible episodes in the history of air warfare, the whole squadron of twelve Spitfires was blown wildly off course over the Channel by a vicious headwind, and the pilots failed to realise this until they emerged from cloud to find themselves over Brest. Taken on by the heavy German flak defences, the Spits were damaged and, out of fuel, were forced to make emergency landings. The French Ile de France Group would never take over the Eagles' mounts: the aircraft and the American pilots were captured by the enemy. Only one of the pilots managed to escape. He headed north towards Cornwall, only to crash into the cliffs at the Lizard.

The Hero of Scapa Flow

On the night of 17 October 1914, just two months after the start of World War I, a U-boat alarm was raised in the Royal Navy's main fleet anchorage at Scapa Flow in the Orkney Isles. The great warships of the Grand Fleet hurriedly raised steam and fled the harbour while destroyers and other small craft scoured the waters of the bay for the intruder. A quarter of a century later, almost to the day, *U-47* was able to navigate the narrow sound where a gap still existed between two blockships to torpedo and sink the battleship *Royal Oak*, which went down in the bay with heavy loss of life. How could the British have permitted such a blunder?

Although not possessing a Fleet Air Arm as such, the German Navy under the Nazis did have *Luftwaffe* squadrons specifically designed to co-operate with it: the *Kustenflieger*, or coastal patrol units, rather on the lines of Britain's RAF Coastal Command squadrons but ranging less far over the North Sea. Beyond this arrangement, the *Kriegsmarine* also on occasion achieved co-operation with the regular units of the *Luftwaffe* bomber force, which in the first months of the war were KG26, the

Heinkel 'Lion' group, so-called because of its use of a lion rampant insignia, and the newly formed KG30 comprising a small number of the new 'wonder bomber', the Junkers 88. It was these two groups that were enrolled into a Navy plan to try to trap heavy units of the Royal Navy's Home Fleet based at Scapa.

Constrained by Hitler's order that only shipping and naval base targets could be bombed, the *Luftwaffe* endeavoured to strike at the warships at Scapa and around the Firth of Forth. These early raids caused much headline news on both sides, futile though they proved in terms of results. The Germans' problems were manifold: ships were notoriously difficult to hit with aerial bombs, especially on the move, while those in bases were protected not only by the warships' own AA guns but by Army guns and RAF fighters. Despite these hazards, which applied equally to RAF bombers trying to hit German warships at Kiel and Wilhelmshaven, a plan was hatched to lure the British ships into a trap.

A small force comprising the battlecruiser *Gneisenau*, the cruiser *Köln* and nine destroyers left their north German bases and sailed up the Norwegian coastal waters as far as the Utsire Light where, as expected by the Germans, they were spotted by the crew of an American-built Lockheed Hudson of Coastal Command. The Admiralty relied heavily on the RAF to keep them informed of German warship dispositions, and this they did. So far the German plan had worked to perfection. The Hudson's radio operator sent off a sighting report: one German battleship, one cruiser and nine destroyers – heading north! At the Admiralty operations room the telephones jangled urgently; was this the first German attempt to break out into the Atlantic via the Faroes Passage south of Iceland? If the British acted quickly the enemy vessels could be trapped by superior forces and annihilated.

British supremacy at sea and especially in the North Sea had long been established, and was maintained against the new fleet of the Kaiser in World War I, decisively demonstrated in the Battle of Jutland. The new German Navy had nothing like the same number of battleships; Hitler's rashness in going to war several years too soon had upset Grand Admiral Raeder's plan for a great and well-balanced surface fleet that could really challenge the Royal Navy. The Home Fleet was based permanently at Scapa for the twin purposes of denying the enemy ships free use of the North Sea and stopping him from slipping into the Atlantic to cause havoc among Allied shipping lanes. The pocket battleship *Deutschland* had got into the Atlantic easily before the war started by passing through the English Channel, as had the *Graf Spee*, which had yet to be hunted down and eliminated.

Admiral Forbes hurried out of Scapa with his battleships, cruisers and destroyers; men on leave had to be left behind. The hunt was on. The British ships headed east at top knots, but what happened next was quite unexpected. The hunters became the hunted. For once out of range of shore flak protection and above all the short-range RAF fighters, the bombers of KG26 and 30 went into action. Bomb after bomb rained down on the British ships from the swooping *Luftwaffe* eagles, whose squadrons flew 148 sorties that day, the war ships twisting and turning as best they could to avoid being struck, mostly by 500lb bombs, a proportion of which never exploded. Despite the German aviators' best efforts, the British escaped. Nevertheless, Nazi propaganda went into top gear; great fanfares announced the routing of the British fleet and the downfall of Albion.

The Admiralty's fears of *Luftwaffe* attack were thus redoubled, and since the base at Scapa was still lacking sufficient protection, as soon as Admiral Forbes returned, his fleet and all those heavy units remaining in that zone were ordered to remove themselves to the western side of the Scottish coast at Loch Ewe, where the German bombers could not reach them. That is, with one exception: the old but still powerful and fully manned battleship *Royal Oak* stationed between Shetland and the Orkneys, its 800 or so sailors as bored with their existence as sailors could be in such latitudes, where shore leave meant little and the isles were barren, usually cold and rainy, and totally lacking in facilities. For whatever reason, the *Oak* was not sent off to join its sister ships but was ordered back into Scapa's main anchorage where its crew remained, most of them below decks in the fairly miserable and spartan accommodation available. There was very little to do, not much drill, only the usual morning rounds of inspection; the men yarned, played the Navy board game 'uckers' and other pastimes, wrote letters, slept, and attended their respective 'messes' for meals.

Far away, behind the German base at Kiel, lurked a U-boat whose skipper had received a very special kind of briefing from his chief, Commodore Doenitz. *Leutnant* Gunther Prien had been one of the most successful U-boat captains of the early months of the war; with *Leutnant* Herbert Schultze of *U-48* he had accounted for fifty-one Allied (mostly British) ships totalling 310,000 tons. Doenitz had dreamed up a plan to penetrate Scapa and deal a most humiliating blow to the Royal Navy. As a submarine skipper himself in the Great War, Doenitz had been captured by the British and for whatever reason been locked away as unbalanced. Now, with the right man for the job and, he judged, a fair chance of success, the U-boat chief had decided it was the best time to gamble one small boat against the might of the British Navy. Doenitz knew all his sub skippers; he met them, talked with them, got to know their strengths and weaknesses, and could see which commander had sufficient experience, skill and, above all, nerve to try such a dangerous operation.

Prien set off with his crew in *U-47* on 8 October, a bright autumn day, passing through the Kiel canal and into the sea, his course north-north-west. It took five days of cautious sailing to reach a point opposite the

Orkneys where, at 04.00 hrs, he submerged his boat, safe from patrolling RAF planes, to wait for dusk. At 19.00 hrs that evening, as darkness fell, Prien ordered his boat to periscope depth and set course for the narrow inlet that would take his crew into the lion's mouth that he thought must be Scapa. As it grew dark the U-boat was surfaced, its hull almost invisible in the grey waves, its conning tower a speck on the ocean. As the boat's bows cut along west, the bridge lookouts could see no other vessel in sight. Tension mounted, the whole crew well aware they were now approaching the time of greatest danger, every man below wondering why their captain had kept the boat on the surface – surely some lookout ashore must spot them? Were the British asleep? Were there no well-manned flak posts or marine shore batteries where men continually swept the sea with high-powered glasses, watching out for the enemy?

The bridge watch heard only the faint swish of the U-boat's slim hull as it cut through the sea; they saw not a light of any kind, no searchlights suddenly stabbed the gloom and not a shot was fired as Prien sighted his boat at the narrow channel of Holm Sound. The dark cliffs seemed to envelop the little boat as it entered the passage. Ahead, Prien could just make out the masts of the two blockading blockships which largely barred the way through the water of the mainland and its nearest island. It was all new to him: he had never navigated in such circumstances, and with some sudden uncertainty, fearing British mines or some other under-water barrier, he ordered a swing to port before returning to his original course. There were the obstructing masts, and certainly there must be little depth of water between either of the wrecks and the opposing shore-lines. It would be folly to try to submerge. With stomachs taut, the bridge crew crouched as the boat eased its way very slowly between the little they could see of the two blockships.

Then they were in the clear and steering acutely to port, into the vastness of the main bay of Scapa; next, a swing back to starboard, all this time the boat stressed by the strong currents that persisted in and out of the sound. But with nerve and skill Prien gave the courses and had his helmsman below keep the U-boat reasonably steady as he and his first officer, Engelbert Endrass, trained their night-vision binoculars on a darker mass low against the land across the bay. With a muttered ex-clamation, delighted by the fact that at last some vessel could be seen, Prien pointed his fellow officer to dead ahead where he felt sure he could now see the tall foremast of a ship of some size silhouetted against the sky. Good fortune lay with the Germans, for at that latitude the Northern Lights, otherwise known as the Aurora Borealis, were a common sight; the fantastic blue flickering across the northern sky helped Prien to see the unmistakable mast of a large warship, probably a battleship, appar-ently at anchor less than two miles in front of *U-47*.

Prien had his boat perfectly trimmed, although the surrounding land-scape cut out much of the sea winds. There was a breeze, but above all

Probably the last picture taken of HMS *Royal Oak* (a) before its sinking by Gunther Prien of *U-47* (b), who received a tumultuous reception in Berlin (c).

the strong current still affected them. He now had the boat moved nearer, hull down, the water swirling over the casing until both he and Endrass confirmed the enemy ship was indeed the fat target they had hoped for – and the only one available. There was no point in waiting. Endrass set up the bridge sights while his captain ordered the four bow torpedo tubes made ready. At 00.58 hrs, all was set.

Less than a minute later three torpedoes hissed out of *U-47*'s bow tubes; somehow the fourth became stuck. The officers on the bridge and those below counted off the seconds on their watches, until at last they

23

heard not a shaking blast but a small, muffled explosion that did not seem to emanate from the hull of the battleship; no tell-tale spout of water gushed up from its hull. Prien could not understand it. Three torpedoes fired at a sitting target from little over a mile away, and no hit? What was the noise they had heard? They waited, but no more explosions came; all they saw was a cyclist's light moving along a clifftop path, and this soon vanished. There was no alarm, no warnings the U-boat had been spotted, yet surely the explosion must have alerted the British? Were they all fast asleep on the ship?

In fact, every man awake on *Royal Oak* had heard the noise, everyone believing there had been some kind of internal explosion in the bows, and ratings were sent forward to investigate. Only much later would an inquiry determine that Prien's first torpedo had grazed the ship's anchor chain, exploding harmlessly. His other two missiles had either missed completely or struck the hull and failed to detonate. The time would come when the *Kriegsmarine* would discover the truth concerning its dud torpedo detonators.

Still under great tension and very disappointed, Prien had his boat reversed and loosed off a single torpedo from the stern tube, again with no result. Pale and greatly baffled, he next had the sub move off a few hundred yards while the sweating torpedo room crew began reloading the bow tubes. Then, refusing to wait any longer, Prien had the U-boat slip back to its target position. Still it did not occur to the British on board *Royal Oak* or those ashore that an enemy U-boat could conceivably be among them. It was now 01.22 hrs, and the two missiles prepared were fired. Again the Germans waited with even greater anxiety for some result. After twenty seconds a great double explosion came and a vast waterspout rose up from the hull of the battleship. A series of internal blasts followed aboard the stricken warship, and shortly after the German bridge crew on *U-47* saw the great ship turn over and sink with considerable noise both above and below the water. The *Royal Oak* took 833 Britishers with it, including Rear-Admiral Blagrove who commanded the Second Battle Squadron.

Aboard the U-boat all was elation. Prien and his officers took one last look at the disturbed waters where the battleship had sunk, and then their boat crept away, past the blockships and out of the sound to the safety of the open sea where the men really let fly their roars and songs of triumph. Every man downed some schnapps and looked forward to a great welcome back at Kiel. When they reached home, Prien was handed the Knight's Cross by Grand Admiral Raeder, while Doenitz received his promotion to Vice-Admiral on the deck of *U-47*. At Scapa it took twenty-four hours to close the gap used by the enemy sub. A third blockship was used and many more AA guns and balloons were added to the harbour defences.

The loss of the *Oak* immediately raised a hue and cry on security grounds. At first it just did not seem possible to the British that a German

U-boat could have perpetrated such an act without 'inside help'. Thus the myth of a German spy ashore at Scapa was born and perpetuated; at the time, and quite extraordinarily, the blame for the lapse was laid at the door of the head of MI5, Colonel Vernon Kell, who was put out of office. In fact, the fault lay primarily with the Admiralty for failing to make secure their main fleet base. When Winston Churchill, as First Lord, got together with the military chiefs, they decided that eighty-eight heavy and forty light AA guns were the minimum requirement for the defence of Scapa, plus controlled minefields and other traps to deter future enemy attempts. A third blockship was also used to close the gap *U-47* had slunk through. Quite clearly, they were slamming the stable door shut after the horse had bolted.

Gunther Prien went back to the Atlantic with his crew in *U-47*, having been fêted in every fashion; they even had a song dedicated to them and their 'little boat' that had so humbled the British. In March 1941 they were lost in action, as were two other U-boat aces, Joachim Schepke in *U-100* and Otto Kretschmer in *U-99*, the latter captured with thirty-nine of his crew. The 'grey wolves' of the early war years were vanishing fast.

Incident at Venlo

During the reign of Elizabeth I, Francis Walsingham contrived to build a network of spies, both at home and abroad. England had good reason to be suspicious of its continental neighbours, whose allegiances fluctuated between rulers, while at home plots and conspiracies were constant among rivals and against the Crown. Yet the Queen, however aggrieved and unnerved by such goings-on, and increasingly reliant on good intelligence, adopted a two-way attitude in her dealings with Walsingham. On the one hand she found his doings repulsive, yet on the other she knew his worth, and this ambivalence was reflected in the scale of funds allowed him – paying his agents often proved difficult.

Despite Walsingham's efforts, the defensive network at home, and to some extent abroad, was allowed to wilt, largely due to government indifference. It was an unknown Army officer named Kell who, in a later era, managed to resurrect Britain's intelligence service at home, while that designed for service overseas continued to operate on a shoestring budget. It proved expedient to use diplomatic cover abroad to control spies; often the 'passport control officer' in embassies would perform a dual function, while military attachés and their aides came to be recognised by the host country as spies in their own right. The expansion across the world of British influence led to the setting up of a proper organisation at home to control the Secret Intelligence Service – MI6 (Military Intelligence Department 6), which unlike MI5 and the Special Branch confined its activities exclusively to overseas spying. Its controlling officers and staff overseas were largely of the upper and intelligentsia classes, men whose loyalty to King and Empire were unquestioning, yet possessed of a certain deviousness and with a zest for intrigue. To speak at least two languages was essential, to be capable of ruthlessness an asset, though not a prerequisite for spying which often required endless patience and rarely led to danger or combat.

The typical MI6 man could be ex-Army or ex-university, even ex-government, but rarely middle-class, certainly not a grammar or high school type. Hand-picked and belonging to a narrow band of 'club types', the overseas spy for Britain was confined to the old boy network through its system of recruiting, which began to fall apart (unknown to its bosses) in the 1930s as a result of the influence of ex-university corruptibles Burgess, Maclean and others. In the 1930s the ex-War Office Army officer no longer on regimental or corps payrolls seemed as ideal a recruit as the upper-crust professional with several languages; a blameless career in the King's service and a natural interest in military matters seemed to make him ideal for trying to ferret out secret information overseas. Certainly such men, even former military bureaucrats rather than combat officers, filled the bill in foreign assignments.

Into this category fell two British officers whose singular exploit in 1939 helped to break the monotony of the so-called 'Phoney War'. Captain Best and Major Stevens dabbled not in military intelligence, but politics at the highest level; in getting their fingers burnt they also highlighted Britain's dangerous vulnerability to a new force opposing them: the SD, or *Sicherheitsdienst*, the security service of the Nazi SS. The British officers bungled, and their falling into the German trap brought great discredit and embarrassment to the British and the Dutch.

Before relating the 'Venlo Incident', as it came to be called, it is useful to take a glance at the more established spy system threatening Britain after the Kaiser took power in the time of Edward VII and his successor, George V. Irrationality and power lust drove the Kaiser to enter an arms race against Britain, irrespective of his royal ties with this country, and this was chiefly accomplished through the mad 'battleship race' which saw both sides spending vast sums to try to outweigh the other's 'dread-nought' fleet. The Kaiser's growing hostility drove him to have his spy chief activate agents in Britain, but when war came in August 1914 twenty out of twenty-one persons spying for the Germans were rounded up. The defeat of Germany in 1918 did not, as in the much later case of the collapse of the Soviet Union, result in the demise of the fallen state's spy organisation, so when Hitler finally achieved power in 1933 the *Abwehr* stood ready to serve a new master. This it did, in ways naturally un-publicised, its chiefs, in particular Admiral Canaris, figures who by preference and profession, like their counterparts outside Germany, remained shadowy or unknown.

Hitler, and especially Himmler, admired the organisation and methods of the Soviet secret police, and having assured his *Führer* he could do even better, the SS chief was permitted by Hitler to take over every German police agency, including the *Gestapo*. Himmler had by then installed Reinhard Heydrich as head of a quite separate SS security service, the SD. Initially designed to watch over the Nazi party, the SD spread itself to infiltrate all Germany, and by the outbreak of war had become involved in activities beyond Germany's borders, especially in Czechoslovakia. Himmler's protégé, Heydrich, nursed along his own fledglings, allowing them some initiative and setting in train his own projects, always expanding his personal frontiers. Eventually, Heydrich would be regarded as the most sinister and dangerous man in Nazi Germany.

During the build-up to war, in the latter part of the 1930s, the British, including MI6, allowed themselves to be deluded by the naïve belief that the conservative elements in the German military-political set-up were amenable not only to trying to restrain their new *Führer*, but actually to toppling him by a coup. While it is true there were such elements among the German conservative crust, no organisation or will to act against Hitler existed. The 'reactionary', hierarchical Prussian set of career generals and their feeble political counterparts were anathema to Hitler and his Nazi cronies, and were watched very carefully by both *Gestapo* and SD.

Along with Hitler's own great admiration for the British and their Empire existed a German belief in the capabilities of that country's spy system, and while not amounting to paranoia, fears of British penetration and intrigue on the continent were rife. The National Socialists badly needed British approval of their new Germany, but while this seemed to come via the smiles of certain dignitaries such as Lloyd George and the Duke of Windsor, the basic reaction to Hitler and his regime was hostile. For Hitler's part, a friendly or at least quiescent West was essential to his plans for eastern expansion; for the British, subversion was the name of the game, since they were militarily weak. By the autumn of 1939 the British were pinning their hopes, in order of preference, on a collapse of Nazism from within, aided by the conservative elements within Germany; the gradual tightening of economic screws via the Royal Navy's blockade at sea; and lastly, a stalemate on the Western Front, leading to Hitler asking for a parley. It was the first of these MI6 tried to foster.

Heydrich, a clever and cunning man, far more devious than the British allowed for, and in any case virtually an unknown force to them, had recruited into his SD not only toughs of animal cunning, but men of some intellect whose talents lay via the mind rather than through pistols and fists. One such man was Walter Schellenberg, a young fellow with law training – like a few more of Heydrich's crew, a real personality with a

27

brain – by 1939 flattered to find he had, to his amazement, been groomed by an unseen mentor at high level who had him tutored through the *Gestapo* and SD. Schellenberg was one of the thoroughly Nazified opportunists, the kind whose careers burgeoned very suddenly once the new regime took power, men who but for Hitler (and Heydrich) would most certainly have remained unknowns, closeted away in minor posts of the German civil administration or armed forces. He had the same mind for intrigue and plotting as any spy anywhere, but being part of Heydrich's gang he had at his fingertips the kind of armed roughnecks more usually found in works of fiction.

Having performed most satisfactorily in Czechoslovakia, Schellenberg entered the war as part of Himmler's security staff on the SS *Reichsführer*'s special train that entered Poland in September 1939. Once the campaign ended he was taken back by Heydrich to act out a rather different role, that of *agent provocateur* in the field against the British Secret Service. He had now, after less than five years' service in the SD, risen to become his chief's right-hand man. As an assistant he could call on Alfred Naujocks, an ex-boxer turned fixer and sometime adjutant for Heydrich, responsible on the ground for arranging the 'incident' at the radio station at Gleiwicz on the German–Polish border in order to enable Hitler to launch World War II. That kind of 'in the field' activity was not in Schellenberg's line; much more to his liking was the excitement of matching wits with British agents across the border in neutral Holland.

By October 1939 he had advanced into Heydrich's circle of friends, a friendship which would be enhanced by the triumph at Venlo. Schellenberg had learned of the astonishing extent of his master's guile and activities, which included a desire to get even with 'the gentlemen across the street' – a reference to the *Abwehr* offices nearby, and in particular to Admiral Canaris, a representative not only of the old order, but more specifically the German Navy, whose chiefs had thrown the then Lieutenant Heydrich out following his seduction of a shipyard owner's daughter. It was that affront that had propelled the young Heydrich into the Nazi movement, with the accompanying feelings of bitterness and desire for revenge which would begin, so he hoped, with his new SD intelligence system usurping the role of Canaris's *Abwehr* and showing it up for what he believed it to be: an old-fashioned, amateurish organisation. There was some truth in this notion: the *Abwehr*'s performance against the British Isles in World War II proved pathetic, whereas the SD pulled off some spectacular successes.

Schellenberg also learned how his chief had carried out the fantastic General Tukhachevsky affair, the forging of documents proving the connivance of the Soviet military man with German officers. These forgeries were very cleverly passed to Stalin through intermediaries, the result a massive public purge by the Soviet dictator which saw the demise of hundreds of Red Army officers, including generals, almost fatally weakening Stalin's officer corps before the German invasion of 1941. Yet, though the success was enormous, how Heydrich managed the actual forging was even more cunning. Having requested Canaris to co-operate in providing some original documents for the purpose of forging signatures, and having failed to get them, Heydrich had the *Abwehr* chief's offices burgled by SD agents and the papers stolen. The culprits were obvious to Canaris, a man of part-Italian background which had resulted in a greater attraction to the Mediterranean area.

The Heydrich masterpiece operation against the Soviets in peacetime guaranteed him Hitler's admiration and the *Abwehr* chief's very considerable detestation. These feelings would be amplified when Heydrich went on to claim new plaudits for his organisation through Venlo and MI6 bungling. As for Schellenberg, his advancement had been so rapid it certainly added to his already considerable ego. Heydrich intrigued and amazed him, a married man but rapidly becoming well known to every plush restaurant and nightclub door-keeper in Berlin as the most ruthless stud of all. His activities on the sex front in the German capital seemed insatiable – what woman dared refuse the advances of the most powerful man in the *Reich*? Heydrich's wife soon learned of the 'Knight of the Kurfurstendamm' and storms erupted in the family household. To a British author after the war she complained there were 'Girls, girls, girls!', while one German source stated the number of females taken by Heydrich must have been 'incalculable'. Heydrich took both his wife and Schellenberg out to the swish night spots, but it was without *Frau* Heydrich of course that his sexual activities took place. Yet, despite all this frenetic activity, the SD chief still found time to entertain guests on 'family evenings' at home, when among his accomplishments he would serenade on his violin. There was more: Heydrich excelled at sports, horse riding and fencing, became a fighter pilot and was photographed with his Messerschmitt 109 bearing the SS flash insignia.

Heydrich learned, through his own agents in Holland, that the British had set up a secret service network in that country and were hopeful, through Dutch helpers, of trying to contact the 'German Resistance'. Heydrich decided to enter the game, and instructed Schellenberg to play the part of a German Army officer in contact with conspirators against Hitler, the idea to draw out the British simply to learn of their plans, then perhaps embarrass them by disclosures. There was no more to it than that – at first. It was all very exciting for Schellenberg, who was required to don a disguise and assume the identity of an actual officer on whom (naturally) Heydrich held a file. Captain Schammel of the German Army transport service was employed in Poland. Heydrich instructed Schellenberg that Schammel wore a monocle and was the spokesman for a group of dissident officers who wished to be rid of Hitler. This, so Heydrich explained, was just the kind of news the British wanted to hear.

For the SD chief it was merely a game, with no real end target, save that of making fools of the enemy.

To set up his trap Heydrich made use of two agents known to be working for the Czech and French secret services. When Czechoslovakia was overrun in 1938 its spy chief, General Moravec, fled to England with some of his staff, continuing to operate from London as best he could. Heydrich's men had discovered a Czech officer and former motor racing champion who had been persuaded to work for the SD on the continent, using the name Geullert. The second agent coralled by the SD was German, an ex-policeman from Hamburg called Morz, who operated under the names 'Michelson' or 'Fischer'. Heydrich proposed using these two men as the link to London via two known British spies working in Holland, a Captain Best and Major Stevens, who were harboured by and working with Dutch Intelligence.

One French writer on such matters has commented that by this time, perhaps echoing the national sentiment of apathy in Britain, the Secret Intelligence Service was 'in a bad way', its recruits not up to par, its days of triumph in the past. That may have been the case, but the same commentator has stated that under Colonel Claude Dansey ('Uncle Claude'), MI6 did 'magnificent work' between 1940 and 1945. This may also be true, but it could be their reputation took such a terrible knock through the Venlo affair that drastic steps were taken to ensure such an event never happened again.

Schellenberg was not the only man on the German side to come into actual contact with the enemy. Another SD agent, Dr Helmut Knochen, suitably disguised, fed the same tale as that passed to the British agents by Morz and Geullert (the latter SD agent No. F479). It was the new Czech set-up in Britain that first alerted the British to the trail in Holland. One Major Burtill had gone over to meet *Herr* Morz-Mortenson, but smelled a trap and broke off contact. Not so Best and Stevens, who had already swallowed a few titbits of information given by the SD agent F479. Coming from two different sources (Knochen and Morz), Best and Stevens believed in the possibility of a revolt by the German generals, with whom Knochen claimed to be in touch.

By then, Walter Schellenberg was receiving his orders direct from Himmler and Heydrich. The former had sent him on various jobs. These included (so he later claimed) a tour of the *Reich* during which he unmasked several spies in Dusseldorf and Dortmund. For the Dutch job Heydrich briefed him personally, the junior wearing his usual civilian clothes as he listened carefully to his smartly uniformed chief in the head-quarters in Berlin. The action that unfolds here naturally relies on the later testimony of three of those most closely involved, three men each of whom had his own reasons for colouring or amending his part in the play.

On 21 October 1939, after calling at a house in western Germany run by the SD as a staging post and equipment store, Schellenberg travelled to the Dutch frontier with SS Colonel Christensen, the border police on the German side instructed to ask no questions. The two Germans took precautions, carrying little luggage and ensuring no article of their clothing bore tell-tale linen marks. (Before leaving, Heydrich had sent them a telegram advising of the *Führer*'s approval of the operation, and cautioning them to take extreme care.) The Dutch border police proved awkward, insisting on inspecting the Germans' car thoroughly. Then they drove on, reaching the appointed meeting place at Zutphen where a black Buick car awaited them. Inside it sat the two British officers. Schellenberg was startled to see that one of them, who proved to be Captain Best, also wore a monocle. This bit of the disguise had bothered him, for Schellenberg was short-sighted and found it difficult to use the glass. Best spoke excellent German and soon struck up a good rapport with Schellenberg, largely through a love of music, the Britisher giving the impression he was a good violinist.

So the four men, ostensibly enemies, sat together in the American-built car chatting amicably on general topics before Schellenberg finally reminded the Britishers of the matter in hand. He then claimed to speak for a group of German officers aiming to overthrow Hitler by force; in that event, what would the attitude of the British government be? The Britons responded by assuring the Germans their government was greatly interested and would 'contribute powerfully' to stop the war spreading. The Britishers were not in a position to offer binding agreements there and then, but if a further meeting could be arranged to include the German general representing the dissidents, then HM Government would be prepared to make a binding agreement. The two SD men were gratified to hear that the British agents were in direct contact with both the Foreign Office in London and 10 Downing Street. The four men then took lunch in a nearby café before breaking up in general bonhomie, arranging to continue the discussions at the Hague on the last day of the month.

As soon as the two Germans returned to their base, Schellenberg telephoned his report to Heydrich in Berlin; the SD chief was very excited, confidence in his protégé justified. Heydrich's star was still in the ascendant. Hitler had approved his scheme as it fitted in nicely with his own idea of lulling the Allies into the 'Phoney War' stupor before smashing them out of the game with a great offensive. The Western powers needed to be deluded into passiveness beforehand, to sit back behind their fortifications while they awaited the German generals' coup against the *Führer*.

As evidence of their good intentions, the British sent via a contact in Berne, Switzerland, extracts of a Chamberlain speech made on 12 October in which strong hints were given of support for any faction that overthrew the Hitler regime. Curiously, and by extraordinary chance, there really was a scheme to get rid of Hitler, though the feeble-minded generals were not part of it. A competent yet naïve German communist had made a time bomb which he managed to conceal in the Munich beer hall where the *Führer* was scheduled to make his appearance and speech on the anniversary of the failed *putsch* of 9 November 1923.

Heydrich's plan reached its climax on 30 October, when not two but three Germans set off to meet the two British agents. Without doubt a likeable personality, Schellenberg had used his charm on a friend at Berlin University, a professor and Austrian holding dual rank as a colonel in both the German Army medical branch and the SS. Schellenberg's inspiration was to persuade the professor to join the adventure in Holland as the 'general' heading the anti-Hitler plot. With Heydrich's full agreement the Austrian, by the name of Max von Crinis, intrigued and amused by the game he had been invited to join, accompanied Schellenberg and Christensen on 30 October to the German–Dutch border, his assumed name 'Colonel Martini'.

This time the Germans motored to Arnhem to meet the two Britons, but after three-quarters of an hour there was no sign of them. Had they been warned off, or smelt a trap? Worse was to follow. The Germans' car was approached by two Dutch policemen who, after questioning them, made them drive to the nearest police station, where they were politely searched, Colonel Martini's toilet case especially being minutely examined. Schellenberg, alarmed and nervous, refused to answer the Dutchmen's questions without a lawyer being present, so after ninety minutes stalemate resulted. Then, a lieutenant entered the room, showed the Dutch policemen some papers and the Germans were released with apologies. Once outside they found the black Buick with the two Britons awaiting them. They apologised profusely, saying they had been to the wrong place, the Germans guessing they had arranged the whole thing with their Dutch collaborators.

The five then drove to the Hague where the British agents showed them into a building obviously used as their spy HQ. Captain Best then explained British terms: the overthrow of Hitler must be followed by the signing of a peace treaty with the Allies and the restoration of Czech and Polish territory to its rightful owners. The return of former German colonies in Africa was also discussed, something the British saw as a sop and bribe to Hitler, seemingly unaware he had little or no interest in such a deal. After further talk the two sides drew up an *aide-mémoire* which Major Stevens then telephoned to London. The Foreign Secretary Lord Halifax was to be consulted and a formal agreement drawn up.

Three hours later, Schellenberg complained of a migraine, brought on, he said, by smoking too many strong English cigarettes. He withdrew to the washroom to freshen up, and Captain Best followed him, saying, 'Do you always wear a monocle?' Schellenberg, quick-witted, responded with, 'I was going to ask you the same question!'

Major Stevens stayed at the MI6 haven while the rest of the friendly party drove off to a nearby villa owned by a Dutch general who happened to be the father of the Nazi Dr Werner Best's wife. Best would become well known as a Nazi boss in Denmark after that country's occupation by the *Wehrmacht* the following spring. Then Major Stevens joined them, announcing he had obtained full agreement from London, whereupon Schellenberg told him he and von Crinis would set about arranging matters with the conspirators in Berlin. At that moment an agitated agent F479 arrived, Morz showing nerves and tension, Schellenberg trying to reassure him with the promise of putting in a good word for the renegade German in Berlin – if he wished to return to the *Reich*. The whole group then went to dine with their Dutch host who had arranged for 'the most succulent oysters' Schellenberg had ever tasted, the conversations round the table proving very enlightening and entertaining for the pseudo-conspirators as the two Britons freely told them of British attitudes to the war. The Austrian 'general' played his part to the full, using his Viennese charm as part of his role as the university professor with a part-time job in the *Wehrmacht*. To the Germans, the two British officers appeared to fall for it all completely.

After a comfortable night at the villa the party drove off in two cars to the Commerce Bank which the Germans discovered also seemed to double as a British spy outpost. In the bank office the most ludicrous part of the German scam took place: the presentation to the German of a transceiver radio and code book. These items were actually handed over by the same Dutch lieutenant who had secured their freedom at the police station. The radio was the means by which the Germans could arrange the next meeting. After this little ceremony the German party regained their car with the loot, driving off for Germany with great glee.

It was Schellenberg who, on reporting his triumph in Berlin next day, suggested to Heydrich that he further the plan by actually travelling to London. This fantastic idea finally unnerved the normally ice-cold SD chief, who drew back in alarm, fearing it was all really a British trap. He told his agent it seemed too good to be true, cautioning him to do nothing until Himmler and the *Führer* had been consulted. For the adventurous and vain Schellenberg it was disappointing; he had conjured up visions of being wined and dined in the enemy's capital. Despite this, Heydrich allowed his three men actually to establish radio contact with the British agents, and over the next week Best and Stevens asked the Germans three times to fix another meeting. Obviously, the British were anxious to set the German officers' plot rolling, though naturally not a whisper of this ongoing farce reached the public on either side.

By 6 November Schellenberg's own patience had expired, and without calling Heydrich he arranged another meeting with the Britons, to take place at the Café Backhus near Venlo and the river Meuse. In this scenario other watchers became apprised of the British plan, no matter how embroiled and earnest they were; the Czech Intelligence chiefs in

London were now even more suspicious. Colonel Alois Frank knew his British counterparts had a working spy system in Holland, a country he visited often himself. He then met Captain Best who disclosed the 'tremendous job' he had in hand with German military dissidents, obviously expecting much to come of it. Before he left the Czech officer, he promised to divulge details later, and in a café in Utrecht the Britisher told how his job would, he hoped, ensure peace between Britain and Germany. In fact, Best disclosed that a deal would come about at Venlo next evening. When Frank expressed doubts, suggesting a change of venue, away from the frontier, Best assured him everything was arranged – the Dutch were helping by providing full security.

When 7 November came, the day of the arranged meeting, just two days before the attempt on Hitler's life in Munich, Schellenberg decided to play safe, informing the British by radio that the 'opposition general' was unable to leave his duties in Berlin. Major Stevens responded by telling the Germans they must make more effort and produce their man by the following day. Schellenberg wired Heydrich urgently; the SD head replied to Schellenberg's base in Dusseldorf that he must exercise caution. The *Führer* was now uninterested in taking the matter further; clearly he disliked the idea of sending even a bogus dissident general into Holland. Nevertheless, Heydrich seemed willing to allow his man some leeway, permitting Schellenberg to meet the British to find out more. In fact, the British had but one thought: to transport both Schellenberg and his 'general' to London so that final negotiations could be made before the supposed military *putsch* took place in Berlin.

During this period, Alfred Naujocks had been enjoying leave, his reward for the triumph at Gleiwicz and work at the SD forging factory in Dellbruckstrasse. Heydrich's fear that his men could in fact be walking into a British trap led him to recall Naujocks and brief him fully on the situation pending on the German–Dutch border. Naujocks would go there himself to ensure Schellenberg's safety, taking a dozen hand-picked and armed SS men. Heydrich was fearful that his envoys might themselves be kidnapped and paraded in London as a grand propaganda coup. Such an event could conceivably cost him his job. In any case, Naujocks must retrieve Dr Knochen and the agent Morz before the British and Dutch could arrest them. It has also been suggested that Heydrich did not entirely trust Schellenberg, who could have been intoxicated by the taste of good living provided by the Englishmen; if he reached London he might decide he preferred the good life there. Well, Naujocks was a tough guy who could haul Schellenberg back home if need be. When Schellenberg met Naujocks, he guessed what was afoot. The two men mistrusted each other; indeed, it has been suggested that Schellenberg received favoured treatment after his capture by the British in 1945, intimating that he may have actually co-operated with them in October and November 1939.

a

b

c

d

e

Walter Schellenberg (a) was Reinhard Heydrich's (b) executive in kidnapping the two British Secret Service agents, Major Michael Stevens (c) and Capt. Sigismund Best (d), at the Café Backus (e) in Holland in November 1939.

On the day of the next meeting, and following a restless night, Schellenberg read in the papers how the King of the Belgians had offered to intercede to try to bring peace to the warring nations. Schellenberg felt relieved; he could now tell the British he preferred to wait and see what came of this development. By this time he had secured the help of yet another bogus 'conspirator', an industrialist and member of the reserve army with high rank and corresponding status as an honorary member of the SS.

When the German party arrived once more at the same café rendezvous near Venlo they were again kept waiting, this time for forty-five minutes, clearly under surveillance by men trying to pass themselves off as innocent civilians. Then, at last, Captain Best and Major Stevens arrived and the two parties enjoyed a convivial meeting, with no sign of anything untoward. But when this meeting broke up nothing concrete had been arranged, and back in Dusseldorf Naujocks irritated Schellenberg when he disclosed his role. The latter tried to explain to the SS tough how completely the British had swallowed the bait, telling Naujocks bluntly he did 'not need a nurse', whereupon Naujocks tried to flatter him by saying he was providing a dozen armed men for Schellenberg's personal protection – Heydrich had no wish to lose such a valuable agent.

Then, dramatically, during the night of 8/9 November, Schellenberg's slumbers in the SD building in Dusseldorf were rudely interrupted by the jangling of the telephone. It was *Reichsführer* Himmler himself informing the agent of the bomb explosion in the beer hall at Munich. Himmler insisted the '*englische Geheimdienst*' (Secret Service) were responsible. The *Führer* – who had left the beer hall unexpectedly early – now ordered the kidnapping of the two British agents in Holland. Schellenberg's objections were brushed aside. He had to obey. But when he woke Naujocks and the head of the SS squad they too voiced doubts; they knew the frontier at Venlo was crawling with Dutch security men. As a result, a revised plan was hatched to ensure Schellenberg's safety.

The last meeting took place under a leaden November sky amid falling temperatures. Before leaving Dusseldorf, Schellenberg inspected the SS squad, ordering them to look him over well; he wanted no mistakes of identification, especially since Captain Best also wore a monocle. The Schellenberg party left before one p.m. and arrived at the frontier an hour later, the 'general' left on the German side in the customs police post. By three o'clock the two British agents had still not arrived, the Germans again under watch by Dutch security men, some strolling the street with dogs. The café seemed much too crowded for such a location and the Germans grew more anxious, wondering if they had walked into a trap. Finally, at 3.20, the Britishers arrived, driving up at speed in a grey car. Schellenberg and one of his colleagues went out to meet them. The drama was now about to reach its climax.

Alfred Naujocks had left Dusseldorf three-quarters of an hour after Schellenberg, and on arriving at the frontier he instructed the elderly customs policeman not to intervene. Then the barrier was raised and very slowly the two carloads of SS men edged across the border into Dutch territory, concealing their vehicles behind a building. There the SS squad waited, watching the Dutch police and a gang of workmen apparently erecting barbed wire and what looked like a concrete anti-tank barrier. (Several months later an SS army would crash through those very obstacles when Hitler decided to invade Holland and the West.) Naujocks had used a convertible with the top rolled back ready for action, and he had the men in the second car crowd into and around his own vehicle. They were poised, with weapons at the ready, rather like a bunch of gangsters in a Hollywood film.

As soon as Naujocks saw the two British officers speed up in their car he leapt into action. Defying Dutch neutrality, he ordered his two cars forward. The driver rammed his foot down and the convertible raced along and jammed itself against the Britons' own car, right outside the café. It all happened in seconds – a flash of rushing figures, shouts and pistol shots as the SS men sprang from their car before it even stopped. At that moment a Dutch Intelligence lieutenant pulled out a pistol and fired, his bullet shattering the windscreen of Naujocks' car, his second aimed at Schellenberg. Naujocks, already out of his car, fired his own weapon and the Dutchman collapsed. Naujocks shouted to Schellenberg to take cover, which he did with alacrity, running off to hide behind the building the SS men had themselves used. When he looked back he saw the SS men hauling the two Britishers out of their car. In that instant he was suddenly seized by a large SS lieutenant he failed to recognise and a pistol was shoved under his nose. Despite his protests, the SS man struggled with him and was about to pull the trigger of his pistol when a fist thrust forward violently to knock the gun aside. The SS lieutenant's deputy had saved his life. Schellenberg now ran to his own car with Christensen, driving back over the frontier to leave Naujocks and his men to close up the operation behind them. As they did this, according to his later account, Dutch civilians shook their fists at them and cursed them. The old customs officer on the German side was fearful of trouble and begged Naujocks to leave some men to protect him. Back at Dusseldorf, Naujocks's men unloaded a third prisoner, who proved to be one Lieutenant Dirk Klop of the Dutch General Staff. He was wounded and died in hospital that night.

The exploit was not reported in the papers, which were full of the attempt on the *Führer's* life. Heydrich listened to Schellenberg's report, but only seemed interested in pinning the guilt on the British Secret Service and the great manhunt for accomplices of the thirty-six-year-old communist Georg Elser, who was himself arrested during the night of 8 November as he tried to escape across the frontier into Switzerland.

That the British showed 'astonishing naïvety' seems justified comment. Major Stevens was chief of MI6 intelligence operations in Holland, which were directed against the *Reich*. 'Like a child falling into the hands of brigands' was how one historian viewed it. Much later, having survived German captivity, Major Stevens denied any incompetence, or that he had disclosed anything concerning the arrangements with the bogus Germans.

The blunder by Best and Stevens of allowing themselves to be kidnapped in a neutral country and taken as prisoners into Germany raised curious issues, apart from great embarrassment for MI6. The two officers had not been spying in the *Reich* and were proved, after exhaustive *Gestapo* and police investigations, to have no connection with Georg Elser, the bomb maker. Protests flew from the Dutch side; the violation of their frontier by armed Germans and the shooting of personnel was a grave affront. But the most important fact to emerge from the Venlo incident was the emergence of the SS–SD as a potent intelligence agency, as was proved even more damagingly to the British and Dutch later in the war.

Both Captain Best and Major Stevens survived the war in German captivity, only to face more embarrassment and inquiry at home following their repatriation. The SIS chiefs had assumed both British agents had died in enemy hands, and were surprised to find they had survived. By then it was known through captured German documents that both had 'sung' quite freely to their SD interrogators. In defence, both pleaded the Germans seemed to know almost everything anyway, having bribed Dutch plainclothes police sympathisers to keep them informed of the British set-up in Holland. Furthermore, the *Abwehr* and SD had photographed everyone using Major Stevens's offices. Stevens was dismissed from the service, but following the death of Claude Dansey in 1947, Best pressed the SIS chief Stewart Menzies for a financial reward he claimed Dansey had promised him for his work in Holland. It is probable that Best used to his advantage hints he would spill the beans by publishing his memoirs and thus disclosing the blundering failure of the British Secret Service, for he claimed he had repeatedly warned London that the supposed emissaries he and Stevens were meeting were phoney and almost certainly Nazi agents.

In more recent times one researcher and popular author has alleged the whole affair was a scandal the government and SIS were more than keen to keep under wraps. It is said that both the SIS and the government of Neville Chamberlain (which included the avid support of Lord Halifax) were desperate to preserve Britain and its Empire from war, enough to secretly carry on negotiations with Hitler's SD agents. This is extremely unlikely. Chamberlain had by then awakened to Hitler's true nature and had publicly disavowed any hope of ever negotiating with the man again. But it is well known that the British believed in conservative and military opposition to Hitler in Germany, and that this was a hope well entrenched in 1939. The Chamberlain government was willing, and in fact did negotiate with such a believed faction.

Eventually, Stewart Menzies assumed he had bought off Best by handing over £4,000 from SIS funds, but the ex-agent had other ideas and went ahead with his story, which was published as *The Venlo Incident* in 1948. It contained only the bare bones of the tale, with no accusations of double-dealing by Chamberlain, but it is surprising that Best's book was ever permitted to appear because he presented known facts and added conjecture to reach unlikely conclusions.

First, the SD chief Reinhard Heydrich really met his end by assassination at the hands of two Czech agents in Prague in 1942 at the behest of the SIS who, true to long traditions of dirty work, sought revenge for the Venlo affair. The most likely reason for Heydrich's killing is certainly the long-published one, that he had succeeded in quelling much of the opposition to German rule by doubling the rations of those working in the war factories churning out equipment for the *Wehrmacht*.

Next, Best seemed to support the alleged utterances of Walter Schellenberg that he had been poisoned by the British Secret Service. The SD agent seemed prone to bouts of sickness when things became tense, but he died naturally enough in Turin in 1952. He had been rewarded (as were the others involved) for the Venlo operation, presented with the Iron Cross by Hitler and promoted to *Brigadeführer*, in due course becoming chief of SD Counter-Intelligence. He was then sent to Lisbon in June 1940 to try to 'get at' the Duke of Windsor, to suborn or, if need be, kidnap him, for as is now known the Duke was quite pro-German and thought war against them insane, and had deserted his military job in France. In this task Schellenberg failed: he returned to Germany empty-handed as the Duke was with some difficulty removed to the Bahamas by the British.

As for the notorious Alfred Naujocks, he fell from Hitler's favour and therefore Heydrich's, and despite all his valuable work was demoted and sent to the front. After his release as a POW in 1945 he tried to make use of his past by claiming to be the man who had 'started the war' for Hitler, which in a sense was true. Seeing himself as a kind of prototype 'James Bond', Naujocks died in obscurity in Hamburg.

Stevens died of cancer in Sussex in 1968, the same year that saw the passing of Menzies, whose morale never recovered from the Burgess–Maclean–Philby betrayal. Best was seventy-nine when he died eleven years later.

White Bombs

During the early months of the war, the British Air Staff believed in and were determined to carry out strategic air warfare against the enemy. This concept, basically that proposed by the Italian General Douhet, was the conviction that such warfare, if properly conducted, would result inevitably in the enemy's collapse. Specifically, it entailed bombardment from the air to degrade the enemy's war-making capability: the destruction of his war factories and similar installations, perhaps his whole behind-the-lines economy. This had been the thinking of the Union General Sheridan in the American Civil War, when raiding columns were sent behind the Confederate lines to wreak havoc. Inevitably civilian lives were lost, but the same people thinking along these lines could and did reason that the workers who ran the factories and depots that supplied the fighting men were not only the real backbone of a war-making machine, but legitimate targets.

Since the Nazi No. 2 General Goering had been widely quoted as stating that guns were more important than butter, the Allied media soon followed the theme that as a result of such a dictum the German nation were suffering all kinds of shortages. And once the supposed British blockade was set up by the Royal Navy in September 1939 the propaganda and feature writers (including sundry experts) followed up with constant suggestions of a German collapse as a result. The facts were otherwise: Hitler was receiving pretty much all he needed from continental sources; only in a few areas was Germany still to some extent reliant on imports from overseas.

It is doubtful if the gentlemen in the Air Ministry believed the tales published; their whole *raison d'être* was their desire and (they believed) ability to wage strategic air warfare. The problem in September 1939 lay in the Allied governments' reluctance to upset the *Führer* by attacking Germany in any way. That the gloves were off at sea seemed to mean little, and even the RAF's attempts to harm the German fleet at anchor were fruitless. The bomber, however, would win the war. The bomber barons were convinced of this, but wholly constrained by government edicts which prevented them from dropping bombs on Germany itself – which was why the German fleet was bombed in 1939, rather than the war installations on land. The government, however, seemed to have convinced itself of one fact, perhaps a victim of its own wishful thinking, which was that the German nation as a whole were much like the British: decent, hard-working folk who never wanted war thrust on them by the gangster leadership which had imposed itself on that nation. Appealing to the better side of the German people, a nation which had contributed so much to European culture in the past, seemed the proper thing to do in the circumstances; at least, Chamberlain and his advisers, no matter how disillusioned they were with Hitler, decided that at the very least the German people should be informed of the British attitude, of why the friendly chap with the umbrella who had become such a well-known figure to them had decided to declare war. Chamberlain had done this reluctantly, only after suffering the continued perfidy and aggression of

Adolf Hitler, a man who could in no way be trusted to honour agreements made.

All this and more in the way of opinions from Britain would have to be made known to the German folk by way of RAF airmail – leaflets would be delivered, the only sure way to get the British message across, since the SS and *Gestapo* were constantly on watch for any who dared to listen in to Allied broadcasts. Accordingly, the peacetime-trained aircrew of RAF Bomber Command were bemused to see their bombers loaded up with bundles of leaflets, millions of them, measuring about eight by five inches and printed on cheap newsprint. The British airmen went to war over Hitler's *Reich*, and, some would repeat constantly later, at least the resulting prolonged excursions did afford the crews much navigational experience.

The 'white bomb' campaign began on the very first night of the war, when the conflict was not yet twelve hours old. The aircrews were called out to fly further missions over six more nights – a solid week of 'raiding' the German people with British newsprint. 'These preliminary operations were in the nature of an experiment,' ran the Air Ministry account, 'but by 16th September it was decided, in the light of experience gained, that they were a success and that the leaflet campaign should be carried on.' And, after outlining in part the contents of such pamphlets and the great value in reconnaissance and experience gained, 'they were carried out in all weathers; they lasted anything from six to twelve hours. As tests for navigation and endurance they had no equal.'

This latter point was certainly true, but, unknown to both crews and Air Ministry, the bombers often wandered far from their intended targets. Blundering about over a blacked-out *Reich* might be an unfair comment on the efforts of these brave young airmen who often endured much for no result – bar the experience, of course. 'Ice could be heard coming off the airscrews'; 'It was like lightning flashing in daylight all around me'; 'The natives appeared to be hostile'. These were some of the aircrew comments quoted by the Air Ministry. There were many more: about the freezing-up of gun turrets and men, whose bodies began to ice up inside inadequate flying clothing; of aircraft thrown about like toys in violent weather conditions. Indeed, it was the terrible weather the airmen were called upon to fly through, rather than any enemy counter-action, which made these prolonged flights such a problem. Undoubtedly, and inevitably, poor navigation through the most rudimentary aids and the weather resulted in large amounts of paper being scattered across many open acres of German countryside.

The crews flew right across Germany, over the Bavarian Alps, to 'leaflet' Vienna. Then, during the night of 15/16 September they went to Warsaw in Poland to deposit seven million leaflets. During the long return flight one Whitley bomber came down in France, reason

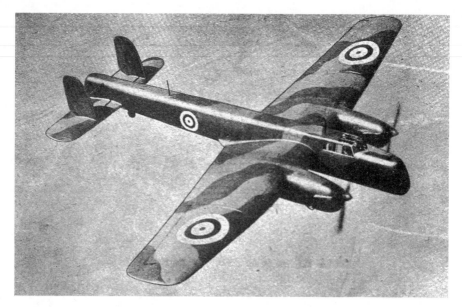

a

b

Mainstay of Bomber Command's long-range
operations 1939–40. The Armstrong Whitley
bomber (a, b), and the crew who landed in
Germany in error (c).

c

unknown. What happened to another was rather along these lines, as the pilot related on 17 March 1940:

> We were flying at about 18,000ft above a cloud formation, and we judged by our wireless instruments and estimated time of arrival that we could not be very far from home. We were very short of petrol.
>
> I saw a hole in the cloud and came down. There were rain clouds covering the hilltops. When I came down to 500ft an anti-aircraft battery fired a warning shell near us. I put on the navigation lights, gave a recognition signal and put down my wheels. There was no more firing.
>
> We landed in a field which sloped up slightly at each end. We unloaded the guns, stopped the engines, and all got out to go and meet the little group of peasants who were running towards us. My companion said to one of the peasants, 'C'est France, n'est-ce pas?' The peasant shook his head uncomprehendingly. 'Luxembourg, alors?' the peasant pointed to another of the group and said, 'Franzosisch [French].' The officer approached the other peasant and asked again, 'C'est France, n'est-ce pas?' The peasant said in French, with a strong German accent, 'No sir, this is Germany; the frontier is about twenty miles away,' and he pointed west.
>
> Like one man we turned and bolted for the machine. Other figures were hurrying towards us from the far end of the field. We started the engines in a flash, and without pausing to thank anybody we got going. The rear gunner reports that the people at the other end of the field opened fire on us as we were taking off.
>
> We did not land again until we were quite sure we were in France. The first certain clue we had was an advertisement for a certain French aperitif. Even when we did land, four of us stayed in the machine with the engines running and the guns still loaded, while we called on our French-speaking expert to make certain. In all we were on German soil for fully fifteen minutes.

This is the only known episode of its kind from the Allied side, but several instances involving *Luftwaffe* aircraft crop up later.

'It's one of ours!'

As all who survived will recall, the winter of 1939–40 was one of the worst on record, sometimes quoted as the worst for forty years. Britain and France were locked into the apathy of the Phoney War, unaware until December that Hitler did not after all intend to sit around for much longer. His long-term plan to drive East required the Western Allies to remain quiescent – or to be immobilised by German action.

While the war at sea had begun in earnest from the beginning and

Britain's RAF and the *Luftwaffe* had been active, on land the chief feature of the news had been a fantasy 'offensive' carried out by French forces alleged to have stormed into German territory. This 'attack' faded from the news as swiftly as it had begun.

Although the expected air-raid terror had failed to materialise over Britain, the German Air Force had pushed small numbers of bombers across the North Sea quite frequently, their crews enduring very long flights from their north German bases, often in inclement weather, their intended targets Royal Navy vessels and merchant shipping around the Firth of Forth, Scapa Flow and down Britain's North Sea coast. Although the RAF quickly instituted fighter patrols to intercept the raiders, it was always the weather which most hampered such sorties. Such conditions, inexperience and the occasional blunder could bring tragedy. The belief among the 'decadent' democracies in overall Teutonic efficiency would die hard; no matter how much the *Wehrmacht* triumphed in those years, the enemy was human and capable of error, fallible, and in certain circumstances as liable to fall down on the job as their enemies.

A good example of this occurred one freezing evening in that harsh winter, 22 February 1940 to be precise. The severe weather had especially affected the German Navy, which, despite its small size compared to the British fleet, had carried out some daringly successful operations, as exemplified by Gunther Prien's penetration of Scapa Flow and sinking of the *Royal Oak.* Its surface vessels had also been active: German destroyers crept across the North Sea to lay deadly mines across the British shipping lanes off Dover and the Thames estuary, some of these being of the new magnetic variety. The magnetic mine was actually a British invention, but it was the enemy who first made extensive use of them, their 'sowings' carried out (or so the British believed) by mine-carrying Heinkel floatplanes which had on occasion been spotted actually alighting on the sea off the east coast. The British never, it seems, suspected that German surface warships had also taken part in such operations.

In that deadly winter the *Kriegsmarine*'s other area of operations, used especially for the training of U-boat crews, was frozen over, large stretches of the Baltic having turned to ice. One of the most pressing needs of the Germans at sea was to keep their own sea lanes free of British mines, or indeed any of their own which had broken away from moorings. The minefields laid after war began were quite extensive, and since they endangered neutral shipping also, their location had to be made public. For both sides the need to send minesweeping vessels to scour the likeliest zones of danger was constant; for the Germans the areas most at risk were the Heligoland Bight, along the Friesian Islands, and off Scandinavia. Whatever the legal requirements of international law, both sides did their best to disrupt their enemy's sea traffic.

The work of the minesweeper crews was arduous and, of course, dangerous; lanes needed to be swept clear of mines, and to remain clear. For both *Kriegsmarine* and Royal Navy the problem was exacerbated by a shortage of minesweeping vessels. The British Admiralty took over civilian fishing trawlers to adapt them for such tasks, but for the Germans the problem continued.

In early 1940 the 2nd Minesweeping Flotilla of the *Kriegsmarine* was docked for repairs and general maintenance. Commander Karl Neitzel of the 1st Flotilla had only three ships plus two torpedo boats available. This tiny fleet was quite inadequate for the job in hand: not only the search for British mines, but the shepherding of what the Germans called their own 'western rampart to the sea', a minefield barrier extending out into the North Sea.

Shortly before 19.00 hrs on 22 February, well after darkness had fallen, a force of six German destroyers set sail and passed through a secret mine-free zone six miles wide. In charge was Commander Fritz Berger of the 1st Destroyer Flotilla, his post in the lead ship, the *Friedrich Eckoldt* (Z16), a craft that had already taken part in five of the eleven minelaying operations mentioned off Britain. Following Z16 at 200-metre intervals were *Richard Beitzen* (Z4), *Erich Koellner* (Z13), *Theodor Riedel* (Z6), *Max Schultz* (Z3) and the *Leberecht Maas* (Z1). These destroyers displaced from 2,200 to 3,100 tons, their main armament consisting of four or five 12.7cm (five-inch) guns, their top speed thirty-eight knots – all very fast, very modern vessels constructed between 1934 and 1936 at Hamburg, Kiel and Bremen. The destroyers were on course 300 degrees, the sea moderate, with a force three wind from the south-west, the air temperature at freezing. Astern a rather swollen full moon had climbed above the eastern horizon, though mist enveloped the sea.

On this night the warships despatched by OKM (*Oberkommando Marine*) were not heading west to lay more mines in the English shipping lanes, their task was a much more unusual one. Over the preceding weeks or even months the British Admiralty in London had, as mentioned, commandeered a number of fishing trawlers from various private companies for manning and use by naval crews engaged in not only minesweeping but also spying; that is, long-range lookout ships sent across the North Sea to watch out for enemy raiders of whatever form. The Royal Navy seamen did their best to appear to be innocent fishermen when patrolling *Luftwaffe* and *Kustenflieger* crews came near. The Germans became suspicious of these 'innocent fishermen', and it became the practice for planes to circle such craft while their crews tried to decide exactly what was afoot, and in due course attacks were made on them, and indeed every British (and often neutral) ship encountered. As a result, a howl of great protest emitted from the British side who declared the enemy airmen 'Nazi air pirates'. In many cases such air attacks were carried out against legitimate fishermen, but it could be argued such seamen were helping to sustain their country's war economy. In any case, once pictures appeared showing such fishing vessels armed with machine-guns, they became legitimate targets for the *Luftwaffe.*

It was this situation that partly, at least, prompted Navy Group West to launch Operation 'Viking 444' (the task was previously called Operation 'Caviar'). Apart from their normal crews of around 300 sailors, each of the six destroyers carried a boarding party under an officer, the captains' orders being to sail beyond the German minefield and intercept British and neutral shipping in the region of the Dogger Bank, an area often swarming with fishing vessels. British trawlers and drifters were to be seized, searched and sunk, while any neutral ships found would be boarded and searched, and contraband destined for Britain taken. Above all, the German Naval Command believed through their bold minelaying operations that they now held the initiative in the North Sea, and they intended to keep it. This can hardly be compared to the much larger-scale attempt by the Kaiser's High Seas Fleet in the earlier war to challenge Britain's Home Fleet, which resulted in the great contest between leviathans known as the Battle of Jutland. Nonetheless, Grand Admiral Raeder had been encouraged enough in these early months of the second war at least to permit a destroyer force to sneak across the North Sea and hopefully wreak havoc among British shipping before returning to their lair at Wilhelmshaven.

German suspicions had been heightened by the sighting of an enemy submarine alongside a trawler; could such 'innocent' vessels in fact be assisting British 'U-boats'? Apart from which, so the German destroyer captains were warned, some of the trawlers were almost certainly disguised and armed, even if their crews were pretending to be fishermen. British vessels captured that could not be brought back to base must be sunk. To assist in the operation, fighter cover had been promised, while suitable bomber units would be placed on standby in case their intervention was needed. The destroyer leader was informed that a bomber group was already alerted and ready to take off at a moment's notice.

What transpired came as a devastating bombshell to all concerned.

Just before 19.15 hrs on that evening of 22 February, the men on watch on the German destroyers heading west heard a droning noise above the roar of the water thrust apart as the throbbing engines drove the ships onward. Aircraft! To hear the hum of aircraft when aboard such a vessel being driven by 70,000 horsepower was an achievement in itself, and suddenly the lookouts spotted a single twin-engined aircraft flying across the moonlit sky at about 2,000ft. The plane circled the warships before flying back alongside the column, then it banked towards them again. Tense and suspicious, the watchers on the ships felt half-sure it must be one of theirs as the black shape continued to manoeuvre over them. Commander Berger ordered speed reduced to seventeen knots. There was good reason for this: ships moving too fast through the sea left a very visible wake which made sure targets for enemy bomb-aimers, especially in moonlight.

The anxious watchmen on the German destroyers breathed more easily and trigger fingers relaxed a little as the aircraft appeared to fly off. Then, at precisely 19.21 hrs, the machine returned, this time flying lower and possibly on an attack course. Now the radio operator in the command ship yelled a warning: *'Achtung! Flugzeug alarm!'*

As the aircraft approached, the gunners manning the 20mm cannon on the second and third destroyers opened fire. Their shells prompted the plane's own nose gunner to reply with his machine-gun, tracers zipping down at the *Beitzen* and *Koellner*. In the circumstances, it seems baffling that no attempt was made by either the ships or the plane to communicate by signal lamp, the most obvious move in such uncertain circumstances. Whatever the reason for this omission, in the next seconds the *Max Schultz* called to all ships: 'It's one of ours!' One of the destroyer's officers claimed to have seen German markings on the swooping plane when its guns flashed, but in view of the aircraft's behaviour the flotilla commander considered this erroneous; the plane had to be British, especially since no *Luftwaffe* bombers had yet been called up. The skipper of *Erich Koellner* agreed; the plane his gunners had fired at was hostile.

These views seemed confirmed after the aircraft flew off but turned back towards them once again. A lookout on the *Leberecht Maas* reported that the plane was 'on the dark side of the moon'. It was almost the last message the *Maas* would transmit. The other German crews saw that the moon was indeed now half-concealed by a small cloud. Then, at 19.44, two bombs struck the sea just astern of *Maas*, and the ships' gunners opened fire. And in that same instant a third bomb struck the ship between funnel and bridge, piercing the deck plating and exploding below. *Maas* signalled it had been hit and required assistance, black smoke billowing up from its bowels. The other ships – barring the leader, *Eckoldt* – turned about to help the stricken *Maas* and were ordered at once by Commander Berger to remain on course; he then ordered his own helmsman to reverse course and draw within hailing distance of *Maas*. But when Berger's own destroyer arrived 500 yards off the bombed ship its crew could see nothing amiss. There was no sign of fire or even smoke, no steam seeping from ruptured boilers.

As the *Eckoldt*'s crewmen readied rescue gear on deck, a great noise erupted as the aircraft zoomed at them again. The guns on *Maas* opened fire in defence. Almost at once flashes were followed by the sound of two heavy explosions; 'a ball of fire rose in the air', reported one witness. Yet on *Eckoldt* no one even saw the attacking plane. The *Maas* was doomed, its narrow hull split wide open by three bomb hits, and a column of fire shot up from the ruptured vessel which now vanished in smoke that rolled across the sea to envelop the command ship. When this fog cleared a little the *Maas* could be seen as two halves which, because of the relative shallowness of the waters in the area, then protruded vertically out of the waves like bizarre markers of doom.

It was two minutes before 20.00 hrs, and in those alarm-filled moments the other four destroyer captains ordered their ships to swing wide in order to present more difficult targets to the bomber, having no idea if they were under attack by a single aircraft or not. On *Eckoldt* everything floatable was being thrown overboard to help the seamen struggling in the oil-stained sea around the lost ship. Some survivors were trying to maintain precarious holds on the upturned halves of the hull. *Beitzen* launched lifeboats, while *Riedel* and *Schultz* took up guard stations some distance away.

Then the unbelievable happened, shattering the Germans' morale even further.

Though the noise of the plane had died away, a fresh and even more spectacular explosion occurred soon after. Another ball of orange-red fire shot up to briefly illuminate sky and sea. Then blackness enveloped the scene again. The amazed sailors had no idea what new catastrophe had occurred. But on *Beitzen* a lookout yelled, 'Bomb attack – direct hit! And machine-gunning!' Obviously, another of the flotilla had been attacked. Aboard *Riedel,* Lt Commander Bohmig ordered his ship swung about to investigate, and then received even more alarming news.

'U-boat!'

The asdic operator aboard the destroyer reported a submarine to starboard, and it began to look as if the German flotilla had ridden into a death trap. *Riedel*'s captain ordered the depth charges made ready and his ship sent in pursuit. At 20.08 the first depth bombs began exploding, but the destroyer captain's carelessness resulted in the charges exploding before his ship was clear; the resulting damage to *Riedel* included broken steerage and the ship began circling, out of control. These events were watched by the command ship's officers and lookouts with amazement as they tried to keep abreast of the succession of disasters.

A quick radio check now revealed *Schultz* was unable to respond. Commander Berger tried to retain some control of a rapidly deteriorating and farcical situation, now convinced they were also menaced by a British submarine. Not only had they heard their sister ship's depth charges, *Koellner* had reported a sighting. For this reason Berger suddenly ordered his ship to speed off at top rate, course 120 degrees, amazing those nearest him who reminded him they were in the process of trying to rescue survivors from *Maas,* some of them still clinging to the lines thrown them. Berger's response was to repeat his order. His first officer left the bridge in disgust.

It is clear from the published accounts that these German destroyer captains lacked the kind of expertise in ship handling common to their British counterparts. This was due to lack of experience and traditions in the British manner, no matter how well crews performed in other directions.

The captains were now verging on panic as yet more asdic reports were made. *Koellner's* skipper gazed about to find the destroyer leader had vanished, so he ordered his crew to continue trying to rescue survivors. Finally, his nerves unable to stand it any longer, the captain ordered his ship to get under way again. Blunder followed blunder, tragedy piled on tragedy, adding to the Germans' misery and confusion. Everything seemed to go wrong. Unrealised by Lt Commander Schultze-Hinrich on *Koellner*, his ship's picket boat, used in the rescue, was still full of survivors. When the captain ordered it cast off he intended to return and collect it later – after, one assumes, helping to hunt down the 'British U-boat'. As his destroyer's engines sprang to life and the propellers churned the sea to raging foam the stern mooring rope attached to the little picket boat was drawn into the revolving screws. The boat was sliced in two, sucking down the survivors and one member of *Koellner's* crew.

At 20.28 *Koellner* was back at the wreck scene, having chased about fruitlessly for the enemy sub. The stern of *Maas* still protruded from the sea, but the watchers on *Koellner* could see no one clinging to the wreck, and wondered if it was the same ship. Yet there were still a few heads trying to stay afloat in the mucky waters. Next, and as if to cap all that had come so far, a lookout reported a submarine in sight and a torpedo track to port. As one German historian wrote, perhaps a little unkindly, 'Gone was the swagger, the fanfares and *Wir Fahren Gegen England!*' Instead came confusion, fear and death.

By an extraordinary fluke, a previous destroyer of the same name had been caught up in a similar situation in World War I. Lieutenant Erich Koellner had commanded an escorting destroyer in the episode, his ship itself sunk in the same minefield. Now, the new *Koellner's* captain had his ship surge away, leaving survivors in the water as the excited lookouts reported more sub sightings and torpedoes coming at them, then a conning tower dead ahead. In true British tradition Hinrich ordered it rammed, but the destroyer's bows sliced through nothing – the 'conning tower' proved to be the still afloat bows of the *Maas*. This fact finally dawned on the German crewmen as they gazed at the forlorn sight in the moonlight; in other words, the wreck they had abandoned just before had to be a second destroyer! Accordingly, *Koellner's* radio operator announced to the surviving boats that two wrecks were in the vicinity, and that they had sighted at least one enemy submarine and torpedo tracks. This was enough for the flotilla commander. Fritz Berger decided he could no longer hazard his remaining ships and ordered an immediate withdrawal from the area. At that moment *Eckoldt, Beitzen* and *Koellner* were once more engaged in picking up survivors.

The tragic proceedings were not yet over.

Crewmen leaning over the rails on *Koellner* now saw a solitary figure clinging to the upturned stern of *Maas*. The man was actually flashing a torch to attract attention. As the rescue ship drew nearer the seaman slid

a

b

c

d

into the sea and managed to reach a float, so the sailors on the destroyer lowered a rope ladder, which became slippery with oil as soon as it hit the water. The hapless survivor was trying desperately to get a grip on this when *Koellner*'s captain ordered his ship to move off again, believing the survivor aboard. The sudden rush of water from the ship's screws washed the man in the sea astern and he vanished from sight. He was the last from *Maas* to be seen, one hour after the *Luftwaffe* Heinkel first appeared. Of the reinforced crew of 330 men on the *Leberecht Maas*, only sixty were rescued, none of the ship's officers among them. From the other destroyer sunk by the same German bomber, the *Max Schultz*, not one man survived and 308 were lost, despite the fact that *Koellner* had passed among the survivors.

Meanwhile, as the terrible drama unfolded at sea, the command staff on duty at Naval Group West, Wilhelmshaven, had been startled to receive a report at 20.30 hrs that the destroyer *Maas* had been sunk. Thirty minutes later they were further shaken on learning the *Max Schultz* was missing, 'probably sunk by an English U-boat'. The chief-of-staff, Rear Admiral Ciliax, suggested the destroyer flotilla commander use his discretion and return to base if need be. The notion of British submarines lurking in the German mine area seemed unlikely, but when records were checked later staff discovered that only a token sweep had been made to check the safety channel by two E-boats three weeks earlier. Was it possible the British had since laid some of their own mines in the Germans' 'safe' channel?

At 23.00 hrs more startling news reached Naval Group West, this time from Xth Air Corps HQ in Hamburg: a *Luftwaffe* bomber had reported attacking and sinking a 'steamer', roughly in the area where the destroyers were lost. Early next morning coastal air units (*Kustenflieger*) were despatched to search for survivors. By midday the shocking news reached Hitler, who at once ordered an immediate, searching inquiry. Not a word had come from the British indicating RAF operations or Royal Navy movements in the area of the disaster.

The resulting inquiry into one of the worst disasters suffered by the German Navy revealed a lamentable lack of liaison and co-ordination, a breakdown in communications that cost 578 lives.

In part, the event came about as a result of Goering's insistence that 'Anything flying belongs to me!'; attempts by the German Navy to muster its own 'Fleet Air Arm' on British lines were thwarted by the vain-glorious *Luftwaffe* chief. Hitler's intervention in the quarrel resulted in compromise, though it was the Navy that really lost its case. By the

Opposite: Just one Heinkel bomber (a) and three small bombs, responsible for the loss of three modern destroyers of the *Kriegsmarine, Lieberecht Maas (b)*, *Max Schultz* (c), and *Richard Beitzen* (d).

outbreak of war all aircraft designated *Kustenflieger* – coastal fliers – were transferred to the *Luftwaffe*, the crews for the main part changing uniforms. The compromise that came was the simple expedient of planes carrying one naval officer aboard, partly as a sop to the Navy but also for the ostensibly practical reason of ship identification. When such aircraft, which usually comprised seaplanes, were forced down by the British, survivors were found to include a crewman in navy blue.

It seems the *Luftwaffe* did its best to co-operate with the system; for the *Kriegsmarine* it was all too new. Slipshod ways and inexperience in air matters led to the breakdown. The operations of Xth Air Corps were quite separate from those conducted by the *Kustenflieger* units, naturally, much as those of RAF Bomber Command had no connection with patrols made by Coastal Command. Indeed, the parallel was there, except that no naval personnel were to be found flying with Coastal Command. It was the *Kustenflieger* units that had been asked to co-operate in Operation 'Viking 444'; the Heinkels of Xth Air Corps (KG26 Lion Group) made the longer flights to Britain, sometimes aided by the new Junkers 88 squadron that attacked the Royal Navy at Scapa as well as shore installations. Xth Air Corps had liaised correctly by informing Naval Group West that some of its bombers would be operating against British targets up to midnight on 21 February; bad weather caused a postponement until the following evening, with the Navy informed. But the teleprint message arrived just after the destroyers had left their base, and the staff commander had no wish to break radio silence by signalling the flotilla leader. The warships were by chance spotted by one of Xth Air Corps' Heinkels as they neared the Dogger Bank. Neither the warship crews nor the airmen in the Heinkel knew anything of the other's presence. No one had told them. Worse, as disclosed during the inquiry, the Heinkel crew admitted they had never before been called upon even to identify ships at sea; whatever they encountered off the British coast were assumed to be enemy and, if possible, attacked. The crew simply never expected to find German warships so far west, and pleaded in defence that though they made several passes over the ships, they only bombed after being fired on by them. Even then, the bombs dropped were only hundred-pounders. The crew believed two hits had been obtained on one 'steamer'.

But what of the *Max Schultz?* The inquiry established that only one bomb actually struck the *Maas*, which later blew up and sank after an internal explosion. In the darkness the Heinkel crew mistook the *Max Schultz* for the same ship, attacked again and hit the *Schultz*, which sank with total loss of life. Tragic though all this was for the Germans, as a combat achievement it was remarkable. That two destroyers could be sunk by two or three small-calibre bombs in darkness seems amazing; ships were notoriously difficult to hit by bombs dropped from 'horizontal' bombers in the best of circumstances. Then, remarkably, the Heinkel crew simply carried on with their prescribed task, flying on to British airspace, still carrying a number of bombs on board, completely unaware of the disaster they had brought about behind them.

If Xth Air Corps had sent its signal sooner the tragedy might not have happened, but then the German Navy had completely ignored the *Luftwaffe* HQ regarding Operation 'Viking', only liaising with the coastal air group – until 18.00 hrs on the 22nd, when it finally warned Xth Air Corps of destroyers heading west. By then the corps Heinkels had already taken off and no message was passed to the bomber crews.

Hitler received Raeder's report in mid-March 1940. The Navy chief had not carried out any severe measures against any concerned in the fiasco, only admitting mildly the failure of Navy Group West to give adequate warning to Xth Air Corps, which 'contributed to the unhappy outcome'.

Fortunately for the Germans, the British did not appear to have learned anything of the embarrassing disaster, but even the shooting down of a British bomber off the German coast could not balance out the day's losses. The day finally ended with more fiasco when one of the Heinkels returning to base was shot down by a storm of naval flak near the island of Borkum.

The *Kriegsmarine* sent minesweepers to ensure a safe lane through its minefields and discovered moored mines sown by the British, concluding that this danger must have existed on 22 February. Not until the war was over was it learned that their former enemy had created a new minefield over a five-mile radius in the area during the night of 9/10 January. It is therefore just possible that the *Max Schultz* actually struck a mine and was not sunk so quickly by one small-calibre German bomb, even though the inquiry concluded that one bomb did hit the destroyer. But was the mine in fact German? No one will ever know.

The lack of effective co-operation which resulted in such heavy loss of life did not of course point to inefficiency on one side only; the British and Americans too suffered such deficiencies. Later in the war, when lapses should have been impossible, human error (again) resulted in Typhoon fighter-bombers attacking a Royal Navy group of small warships across the Channel, using their rockets and cannon to annihilating effect. US submarines are also alleged to have erred in sinking both neutral and their own ships. These are just two examples; there were many more.

The Sinking of the Glorious

In 1929 a German admiral named Wegener published a book entitled *The Sea Strategy of the World War* (i.e. World War I). In this book he put forward the theory that the British sea blockade and stranglehold over the North Sea could and should have been broken by German seizure of the ports in Norway. He had good reason to pen such ideas, for the German nation had indeed suffered through the British naval blockade which had prevented many imports from reaching Kaiser Wilhelm's countrymen. In that war, the German Army had not taken over all its neighbouring territories and, unlike in the second great conflict, Germany did not manage to expropriate or import to anything like the same extent. But Admiral Wegener's book was dismissed by the chief of Germany's small post-war navy, the *Reichsmarine*, though it provoked much interest among lesser officers.

Both Norway and Sweden were of great importance to Germany in both wars, the latter because of its vital supply of iron ore, the first owing to its convenient ports, especially Narvik, for in winter the Baltic sea often froze over, which meant that ore trains had to be routed to the northern port in Norway to be shipped down the coast to Germany. Of the ten million tons of ore exported by Sweden to Germany in 1939, only one million tons travelled directly to the German ports. Narvik remained ice-free from January to April and was the best port of transit.

Another obvious fact was that with ports such as Narvik in German hands, the Navy would stand a much better chance of breaking out into the Atlantic, where its surface warships could wreak havoc with Allied convoys. Which is precisely what happened on several occasions in World War II. Although the 'pocket' battleship *Graf Spee* was eventually lost, it did, with the *Scheer* and *Deutschland* (later renamed *Lutzow*), create some panic at the British Admiralty and sink a worthwhile number of British ships. These were early operations; the Germans had already sent these heavier ships to sea before war came. With Norway occupied, the threat would and did multiply. Risks were taken to interrupt the Germans' ore supplies – mines were laid in Norwegian waters – and when the German prison ship *Altmark* anchored in a fjord the destroyer *Cossack* sailed in to rescue all the British seamen aboard.

British explanations for these breaches were met with strong protests from the Norwegian government and, of course, rage from the German side. This situation enlivened the 'Phoney War' in the early spring of 1940, crisis looming when both the Germans and the British prepared expeditions to occupy at least the port of Narvik. German warships were sighted moving northwards along the Norwegian coast, and the Polish submarine *Orzel* sank the German supply and troopship *Rio de Janeiro* off southern Norway, large numbers of German soldier survivors being rescued by Norwegian fishing boats. The enemy were reported as saying they had been heading for Bergen to help the Norwegians defend themselves against British aggression.

Hitler was sensitive to his northern flank throughout the war; this fear was encouraged by the British, who maintained various fictional threats towards Norway. But the notion that the British and French could seize and hold Narvik in 1940 was a fantasy thought up by the First Lord of the Admiralty, Winston Churchill, the future Prime Minister, fond as he was of dreaming up grand expeditions. On the German side, the *Kriegsmarine*'s Grand Admiral Raeder did all he could to promote the scheme of taking over Norway, for he was a 'big ship man' who still believed in the might of the battleship.

As for the Norwegians themselves, they had been at peace for hundreds of years; not since the days of the Vikings had that nation indulged in war. But the Nazis had been pursuing a relentless campaign of unsubtle propaganda designed to thoroughly undermine Norwegian minds and convert them to the idea of a benevolent, protective *Reich.* As a result, when invasion came the country was quite unprepared. The Nazi theme of 'Nordic brotherhood' had some effect in various quarters. Hitler Youth groups and others made many visits to Norway, bearing gifts and propaganda in an attempt to win over Norwegian opinion to the National Socialist cause. The complete lack of subtlety on the Germans' part was made clear when, during the evening of 9 April 1940, the German minister in Oslo invited many distinguished guests, including members of the host government, to a special film show at the German legation. If the guests had expected a Hollywood western or musical, then their hopes were rudely shattered; the one long feature film shown was the propagandist record of the subjugation of Poland by the *Wehrmacht.* Included in this epic was the bombing of Warsaw, the inhabitants, so the grating commentator assured, having only the Allies to thank for it. The guests filed out in a state of shock and bewilderment; the show had obviously been intimidatory, a warning to Norway, despite all the assertions of Nordic neighbourliness. It was clear the Nazis would mete out similar treatment to any who dared oppose them.

Over the following days the drama escalated as both Britain and Germany despatched military expeditions to Norway. Despite the rushed and in some ways bungled nature of the British–French arrangements, some success was achieved: a foothold was made at Narvik and heavy losses were dealt out to the German Navy during several encounters in the fjords and at sea. But lack of experience at that stage in combined operations, and above all the lack of air cover, brought ever-increasing difficulties for the Allied corps as the enemy succeeded in occupying much of Norway, having already invaded Denmark. During these hard weeks, following Prime Minister Chamberlain's ill-judged assertion that '*Herr* Hitler' had 'missed the bus', and no matter how much supremacy the Royal Navy maintained at sea, fuddled thinking and lack of swift decision-making in London enabled the enemy to gradually squeeze the Allied forces into an impossible position. At least so it seemed to the Allies, the British bearing much of the burden since neither the French Navy nor *Armée de l'Air* did anything to assist. Some success was achieved at the two major Norwegian ports of Trondheim and Narvik, but in the air a handful of obsolete Gladiator biplanes were soon lost, while in the north some Hurricanes ferried over with pilots and ground crews prepared for evacuation from Narvik. In fact, as the Heinkels swept over unopposed to bomb and strafe the Allied troops the decision was made to evacuate all forces from Norway. This, at a time when the German General Dietl had himself decided his troops were unable to succeed at Narvik, surprised the enemy.

The Allied expeditionary corps had landed at Narvik on 15 April 1940 and had fought valiantly for weeks, well past 10 May, when the *Wehrmacht* attacked in the west. On 10 June the last Allied troops left Norway. The Royal Navy and Fleet Air Arm had inflicted very heavy losses on the *Kriegsmarine* – the destruction of ten German destroyers practically crippled the enemy's destroyer fleet – but on 8 June the Royal Navy suffered its own grievous loss.

Unknown to the Admiralty, the German Navy's *B-dienst* radio listening service had been reading most of the Royal Navy's signals. The larger German warships carried such personnel aboard, and all British wireless traffic was monitored so that captains could be kept abreast of enemy ship movements. By breaking British naval codes the Germans learnt that on 5 June the battleships *Renown* and *Repulse* were being sent north with destroyers and cruisers to intercept two German raiders believed to be trying to break into the Atlantic via the Faroes Passage south of Iceland. The *Kriegsmarine* also learnt that the carriers *Ark Royal* and *Glorious* were at sea off Norway. In view of General Dietl's belief that he was losing the battle for Narvik, two of the heaviest German Navy units, the battle-cruisers *Gneisenau* and *Scharnhorst*, plus the cruiser *Hipper* and four destroyers, were despatched to support Dietl's men by bombarding the Allied troops battling around Narvik. Dietl would soon be hailed in Germany as the 'hero' of that battle, which the Germans actually won because of the unexpected Allied withdrawal (a German victory would in all probability have come later had the troops opposing them not been evacuated).

However, the German naval task force was diverted en route to attack British shipping. A tanker and the empty liner *Oriana* were sunk, 274 of the latter's crew being rescued; the hospital ship *Atlantis* was allowed to sail on unharmed. The German fleet commander, Admiral Marschall, then received news from his *B-dienst* officer that more enemy ships were positioned to the north, these believed to be the cruiser *Southampton* with the two carriers mentioned. The temptation to intercept the latter prizes was great. Forgetting his primary task for the moment, Admiral Marschall ordered full speed ahead, his intention to sink the two British carriers before going on to support the Germans ashore. But the warships were no longer needed around Narvik, for the Allied forces were busily embarking for home. The only way General Dietl could notify the Navy of this event was by using a Norwegian telephone via Sweden back to Trondheim where 'Admiral Norway' – Captain Theodor Krancke – had installed himself in the Britannia Hotel. Dietl's report never reached Admiral Marschall, whose small fleet sailed on northwards.

At 16.45 a midshipman in the crow's nest of *Scharnhorst* reported ships off the starboard bow. At first he saw only smoke, but gradually, through his powerful rangefinder, he made out a masthead, the range forty-six kilometres. The German crews were already on alert; they were now brought to action stations, everyone aboard the ships aware that if a more powerful British force appeared they would have to turn tail.

Not until 17.10 was the first enemy vessel seen to be an aircraft carrier, wrongly identified as the *Ark Royal,* a ship Nazi propaganda had claimed was destroyed the previous year. Then came news that the carrier was escorted by only two destroyers. In fact, the carrier was the older-type *Glorious,* which according to the official line, much disputed since, had been allowed to head straight for home owing to a fuel shortage, 200 miles ahead of the main convoy leaving Narvik. Even Winston Churchill, close as he was to the staff at the Admiralty, found this hard to believe, and obfuscation continues to this day. The Admiralty archivist insists that a signal sent by *Glorious* to the cruiser *Devonshire* reporting heavy German units was not received, a vital point flatly contradicted by a surviving telegraphist from the cruiser who swears he delivered such a signal to the bridge staff. This is important, since *Devonshire* had aboard King Haakon of Norway, and most likely his entourage, probably important archives and perhaps even state funds. At all costs, the British government and Admiralty were anxious this party should reach Britain safely – not that this is meant to imply they used *Glorious* and its meagre escort as bait or sacrifice. In fact, no reports of German warships moving north had been received by the Admiralty, whose intelligence at this time seems to have been inadequate.

Meanwhile, the heavy British units despatched to intercept 'two raiders' heading for the Atlantic drew a blank. Both *Devonshire* and *Glorious* were virtually helpless against the far mightier *Gneisenau* and *Scharnhorst,* which carried eleven-inch guns. Even though the cruiser *Hipper* and the destroyers had turned back, the two German battlecruisers would have had little trouble destroying the British cruiser, but fortunately for this ship and its royal cargo they were beyond danger. Not so *Glorious,* which came under fire from the enemy as soon as the range closed. Despite the great bulk of the carrier, the first eleven-inch shells fired by *Scharnhorst* at 17.21 from twenty-six kilometres failed to hit, but by 17.38 both German ships were on target. *Gneisenau* had also been shooting at the destroyer *Ardent,* which was soon set ablaze.

Admiral Marschall and his staff, watching the *Glorious* through their binoculars, believed the British were trying to get their torpedo planes readied on deck, but shellfire soon put paid to this attempt. The German

B-dienst team were listening carefully for any distress calls from *Glorious*, and at 17.52 hrs picked up a rather mangled, oscillating signal which was unreadable. A further, much clearer, message was intercepted at 18.19 hrs and immediately jammed by the German signallers.

German shells wrecked all the Hurricanes and naval aircraft ranged on the carrier's deck, and fires took hold below among the aviation fuel and other stores. The German battlecruisers had first opened fire at maximum range – 27,000 yards, or fifteen miles – their eleven-inch guns fully elevated, the range closing steadily as the enemy drew closer until a rain of heavy missiles reduced the British carrier to a blazing wreck. By 18.30 *Glorious* was listing so badly the remains of its aircraft were sliding off the flat top into the sea. One can imagine the chaos and carnage below. Yet the ship struggled to remain afloat for a further half an hour before finally slipping beneath the waves.

The destroyer *Ardent* was also sunk, but the captain of the other escorting destroyer, *Acasta*, drove his little ship hard at *Scharnhorst*, whose lookouts reported three or four torpedoes fired at the battleship from bows-on. *Scharnhorst*'s Captain Hoffmann altered course drastically while the warship's great guns blazed away at the impudent attacker. On *Acasta*, the captain, Commander C.E. Glasford, had broadcast to his crew before turning towards the enemy: 'You may think we are running away from the enemy – we are not! Our chummy ship [*Ardent*] has sunk, the *Glorious* is sinking, the least we can do is make a show. Good luck to you all!' Leading Seaman Carter would be the sole survivor from this unequal and suicidal attack; David would not prevail against Goliath. It was Carter who fired two of the torpedoes, commenting later that he thought the enemy very surprised at the audacity of it all, *Acasta* emerging very suddenly from its own smoke screen. 'They never fired a shot at us!' Carter recalled. This soon changed as the enemy crew recovered their poise and began shooting at the destroyer with all the weapons that could be brought to bear. According to Carter, *Acasta* got in close before its missiles were launched, yet according to a German account nine minutes elapsed before one torpedo struck *Scharnhorst*. Meanwhile, German shells were peppering the destroyer and a big explosion seemed to lift *Acasta* out of the water. When last seen, the surgeon lieutenant was trying to tend his captain; both men went down with the ship. Some 1,474 Britishers were lost on the carrier and two destroyers (1,515 according to one source). Captain D'Oyly-Hughes of *Glorious* also went down with his ship, and only thirty-nine men were saved by the Germans; another thirty-six were picked up by a Norwegian ship later and returned to Britain.

The torpedo struck the German battleship's starboard quarter, tearing a 36 × 12ft hole in its bow. Again, according to German sources the time elapsed (nine minutes) seemed to indicate quite clearly that the British torpedoes had missed, which was why Captain Hoffman had his ship

The 22,500-ton aircraft carrier *Glorious*, originally built as an unarmoured cruiser, unescorted and sunk in June 1940 (above). The *Courageous*, another disastrous, early war loss (below).

resume its original course – with disastrous results. Forty-eight German sailors lost their lives as sea water and oil from a ruptured fuel tank gushed into the forward compartments of *Scharnhorst.*

Despite Hitler's continued doubts, Grand Admiral Raeder sent *Gneisenau* and *Hipper* to sea again on 20 June. Close in to the Norwegian cliffs lay the British submarine *Clyde* (Lt Commander D.C. Ingram), which put one of its torpedoes into the German battlecruiser, the explosion blowing a hole as big as a house in the warship's bow. The only remaining German battleship serviceable, *Gneisenau* was put out of action for months. In fact, at the close of the Norwegian campaign the greater part of the *Kriegsmarine*'s surface fleet was out of action: apart from those sunk, twenty-four ships were in dock for refurbishment, a further fifteen were being serviced, and seven more had had their crews paid off while refitting was carried out, these including the pocket battleship *Lutzow* (ex-*Deutschland*). The Germans had suffered greatly at sea, their small fleet virtually incapacitated, yet in propaganda terms the victory seemed the enemy's: Norway was lost to Hitler, the Allied corps had withdrawn. The recriminations were muted, overborne perhaps by the far greater disaster in France and Belgium. Hitler secured his ore supplies from Sweden and threw the British off the continent.

All the airmen aboard *Glorious* were lost. None had been sent aloft to watch out for enemy vessels. Such lessons were hard learned; as was proved against *Bismarck*, even antiquated biplanes could deliver deadly torpedo attacks. Aircraft carriers should never have been sent across the North Sea without battleship escort.

Luftwaffe *over Freiburg*

In the dawn hours of 10 May 1940, the bulk of Hitler's armies and supporting *Luftwaffe* units struck across the borders of Holland, Belgium, Luxembourg and France. Long delayed, this offensive was designed to immobilise the Allies into quiescence so that the *Führer* could turn his full attention to the Soviets who were making demands in eastern Europe. The attack should, by Hitler's reckoning, have taken place much sooner; two factors contributed to the hold-up.

While anxious to bring about the collapse of the corrupted French and drive the British off the continent, Hitler was not totally satisfied with the plan of the offensive. The so-called 'Schlieffen plan' was merely a resurrection of that employed in the earlier conflict, when the German divisions of the Kaiser had pushed into Belgium, thus forcing the British Expeditionary Corps to react in support, whereupon more German divisions had struck at the French in the south. This right hook followed by a left punch was a ploy already well known to the Allies; there was nothing they could do about it but react in the predicted fashion when it came, for the British, and even less the French, had no intention of provoking Hitler any further. They hoped to sit out the war behind fortifications (manned by the French on the Maginot Line) until Hitler was forced to sue for peace by sheer economic necessity. This was a pipe dream. The terrible winter also delayed the attack.

The loss of a light plane with two *Luftwaffe* officers carrying the German plan for the offensive soon enabled Hitler to have a fresh scheme put forward, and on 10 May the Manstein plan went into action. An essential part of this was the use of heavy tactical air support along the lines first suggested by General von Seekt in the 1920s; such ideas had been well developed by his successors. Hundreds of attack planes of the *Luftwaffe* would support the ground troops, among them squadrons of Heinkel 111s, then classed as heavy bombers. The use of such aircraft in the tactical rather than strategic role was new and had no equal in the Allied air forces. Each Heinkel carried 4,000lb of bombs, the main loads stowed vertically in a bay behind the pilot.

Among the Heinkel groups taking off in successive raids that day were those of the 51st based at Landsberg, south of Augsburg in southern Germany. Forty-five Heinkels under the command of Colonel Kammhuber took off in the afternoon on their second sortie of the day, their target the French air base at Dijon-Longvic. (Kammhuber was to become better known later in the war when he was installed as chief of German night fighter defence and created the so-called 'Kammhuber Line'. When this failed to stop RAF night attacks he was removed from office.) The heavily laden bombers lumbered off the ground, a long round trip ahead of them, and as they circled their field, climbing to best operating height, they began encountering the lowering cloud levels forecast. The crews had already been warned that if the weather had closed in over the primary target they should switch to the secondary objective, a fighter field at Dole-Tavaux. It was the kind of operational flight the crews had long trained for, and indeed carried out very successfully in Poland the previous September. Kammhuber often flew with them on such missions, and would in fact be aboard one bomber shot down by a French fighter soon afterwards, to be taken prisoner but released after the armistice.

Although the captain-observers of the group had already worked out and noted down their course to the target, they needed to make visual checks en route; there were as yet no pathfinder crews in operation utilising radio beams, and certainly no radar aids as developed for the RAF later. The heaviest responsibility lay with the formation leader, but as the Heinkel pilots struggled to join up in roughly vee-shaped flights behind him they encountered increasing interference from clouds that were rolling in from the west. And as the formation neared the stream that was the Rhine, that too vanished in white-grey mist. The rear dorsal gunner atop the lead aircraft had counted off the forty-four bombers after take-off and reported to his captain, but now he called that many of them were vanishing in cloud. Indeed, turbulence and the fear of collision now prodded the sweating German pilots to open out their formation, some of them becoming quite disorientated. Their experience of bad-weather flying was minimal. Such problems did not exist for the formation leader, and his wingmen were not especially perturbed, but for the rest of the pilots the situation grew worse as the weather closed in completely below and around them. The outcome of this near fatal confusion in the clouds came when one group eventually emerged from the mists to bomb the secondary target – but for one flight a very different course had been taken.

Unrealised by the flight leader, *Leutnant* Seidel, he had led his two fellow pilots in a circle, completely foxed by the dense cloud; even the plane captain-observers had failed to follow their compasses correctly. At 15.59 hrs the three Heinkels emerged from the overcast at 5,000ft, the lead observer at once spotting what he took to be a French target dead ahead. With no time to circle the area he triggered his bomb release, the other observers following suit. Some 12,000lb of high explosive bombs fell to earth, the yellow, grey and black smoke billowing up as the bombers curved away from the target. The three crews were greatly relieved. Their trip had been nerve-racking and now they looked forward to a meal and relaxation back at base before more action the following day.

Then, startling the pilots and observers, their headphones crackled to life as an urgent, almost frenzied call reached them from base: '*Achtung! Bruno–Anton–Achtung! Bruno–Anton. Sie haben einen deutsche stadt gebombt!*' Unable to believe the message, Seidel called for a repeat, only to receive the same frantic call. White-, then red-faced, the pilots and observers hurriedly tried to check their position, forced at length to call for radio directions in order to get on to the course that would take them home again.

On landing, every Heinkel crew was locked in the briefing hall, and at length Seidel and his three comrades stood before their CO, Colonel Kammhuber, who began his interrogation, pending the arrival of the Chief of Air Fleet 5 who was hurrying over from his HQ by light plane.

Seidel's flight of three Heinkels had bombed the German town of Freiburg-im-Breisgau, some distance from the French border, and very far indeed from the intended targets near Dijon. The Nazi Minister of Propaganda, Dr Goebbels, had interrupted his work of preparing bulletin after bulletin announcing German gains in the great offensive to lambast the Allies for commencing terror raids against civilians, for he believed that to be the truth. In the moments the Heinkels overflew Freiburg no one on the ground had identified the machines as German, so when bombs fell the planes were naturally assumed to be Allied – probably French. As a result Nazi propaganda turned its full blast against the Allies, producing leaflets in English with photographs, claiming the American Red Cross representative in Europe had just happened to arrive in Freiburg as the bombers were leaving. This neutral's comments were duly printed in the *New York Times*. Freiburg, he is alleged to have stated, was an 'open town', and the Swiss consul reported that the dead

When Heinkels bombed the German town of Freiburg, Joseph Goebbels blamed the Allies.

...he chief American Red Cross delegate in Europe, Mr Taylor, ...rived in Freiburg at the very moment when the Allied ...irmen were flying back, after having dropped about 50 bombs ...n the town. Speaking to the "New York Times" (see issue ...f May 13, 1940), Mr Taylor declared that although Freiburg ...must undoubtedly be considered an open town, it had been ...bombed by French aeroplanes. The Swiss Consul estimated ...the number of victims to be at least 40 killed and 150 injured, ...all civilians.

Freiburg was the beginning!

Since then Allied airmen have been bombing open German towns of no military importance night after night, and have claimed more and more victims amongst the civil population.

This is not war!
It is murder!

Funeral of the 8-year-old Ruth Jäger and the 6-year-old Manfred Jäger

numbered fifty, with a further 150 injured, twenty-two of the dead said to be children. 'This is murder!' screamed the Germans.

No word of this appeared in the British media, while in the *Reich* the people always believed this early war crime was perpetrated by the Allies. Unfortunately, Winston Churchill's proddings that the gloves now be removed following Hitler's perfidy in invading neutral nations was soon followed by the first RAF bomber raids on Germany, pinpricks which had not the slightest effect on the German war effort and in fact were counter-productive, such as the attack on Munchen-Gladbach where an English woman was among the dead.

The German bombing of Freiburg remained a state secret and is not mentioned in post-war semi-official histories, any more than some Allied blunders in their own versions of that conflict. However, in 1961, the communist East German government, as part of its campaign to 'expose' ex-Nazis serving in the West German administration, published one of several books, *From Ribbentrop to Adenauer*, in which the following appears: 'Dr Trutzschler von Falkenstein . . . worked on the White Book on the alleged French air raid on the German town of Freiburg. In reality this air raid was staged by German bombers under the command of the present chief of the West German *Luftwaffe* General Kammhuber, in order to obtain a propaganda excuse for the barbarous air raids of the Nazi *Luftwaffe* on French and British towns.'

Foraging

Of the armies involved in the western campaign of May–June 1940, only that of the British was fully mechanised. No matter how advanced its tactics, the modern German Army still relied heavily on horse power for its supply columns, the wagons filled with all the essential foodstuffs, ammunition and sundry other oddments needed to maintain the advance of its fighting units. In turn, the horses themselves needed to be supplied – with fodder – and this animal food too had at first been transported in wagons pulled by horses. But as the German troops pushed on deeper into France the supplies of horse fodder brought from Germany ran out, which meant transport troops had to rely more and more on whatever could be foraged from French territory.

As this problem grew, so the soldiers, like those of the past, began to live off the land, at least in so far as its horse echelons were concerned. The Germans went into the French farmers' fields to take whatever they needed, and trouble often resulted. It was sometimes necessary to resort to gunpoint when farmers grew more than angry.

On one such occasion, a French farmer watched with tears of helpless rage as a foraging party of German soldiers loaded up hay and other produce from his fields onto a wagon. The Frenchman cursed them volubly. A raging Frenchman can at times induce more mirth than terror, and the soldiers laughed at him, even though they were not happy to be acting as robbers and knew that whatever compensation the farmer received would be derisory. Eventually, wagon filled, the Germans left, the farmer marching back into his house where his daughter had been hiding in fear of her safety. She watched as her father took a shotgun and some cartridges from his room and ran out of the house. The girl then ran outside, but could see no sign of him.

Half an hour later she heard a commotion in the yard. Running to the window she saw a German staff car followed by a truckload of soldiers. An officer emerged from the car and gave orders to his men, who then began removing a body from the back of the car. The girl gaped in horror: it was her father. Screaming, she ran from the house, crying hysterically, and had to be restrained as the Germans carried the bloody corpse across the yard and into the house. So distraught did she become that the officer was obliged to have her taken outside, and the girl thought she was about to be shot too. Instead, the officer led her gently by the arm and, speaking in French, pointed into the truck, where lay the bodies of two German soldiers shot by her father.

The Germans then left, leaving the girl on her knees, weeping bitterly.

Mail from the Wehrmacht

Owing to some obfuscation on the part of the British government in the early summer of 1940, the Channel Islands were not declared de-militarised until the population had been subjected to *Luftwaffe* bombing. The Churchill government seemed to want it both ways, but defence of the islands was impossible owing to their close proximity to the French coast, and the British Army was in a parlous state following its defeat and evacuation from France. By the end of June the small British force in the islands and a good deal of the population had been evacuated, yet the government in London made no announcement calculated to spare the remaining islanders from German attack. Obviously, as the islands were British territory there was a definite psychological reluctance to admit their abandonment; the very idea of sovereign territory being occupied by the enemy was anathema.

For the Germans' part, it seemed the British must defend their own land, even if it did lie far off in the Channel. Consequently, a *Luftwaffe* reconnaissance plane was despatched to determine the true situation, flying backwards and forwards across the islands, especially Guernsey. The Germans seemed unsure as to the state of the islands' defences, and to discourage any resistance a force of bombers took off on the afternoon of Friday, 26 June. After crossing the comparatively small stretch of sea the Heinkels arrived over the islands.

As head of the newly appointed Controlling Committee, Major Sherwill spoke to a gathering of a few hundred people in the main street of St Peter Port in Guernsey, explaining the realities of the rather gloomy situation, for further evacuations were now out of the question. At the harbour however, life was continuing as usual: a line of lorries laden with tomatoes was lined up on the quay, the produce about to be loaded onto small ships, with the regular mail boat, the *Isle of Sark*, also present. One ship had just loaded cattle and other livestock when the proceedings were shatteringly interrupted by the sound of low-flying aircraft. German planes roared over the harbour, dropping bombs and machine-gunning everything in sight.

A terrible scene ensued as bombs and bullets struck the docks and everything in them, and trucks burst into flames, trapping and burning to death some of the drivers who had taken shelter beneath their vehi-cles. Animals stampeded in panic, slipping about among the smashed crates of tomatoes, the juice mingling with the blood of the victims on the quayside. The German planes machine-gunned at random in what was obviously a pure terror raid designed to cow any resistance. Haymakers and other civilians were hit, as was an ambulance and the Guernsey lifeboat, the coxswain's son killed. More bombers attacked Jersey; bombs fell across the harbour and townsfolk were machine-gunned as they fled for cover. In view of the nature of the air raid, it is surprising that only twenty-nine were killed on Guernsey, a further nine on Jersey. This savagery contrasted oddly with the polite and correct behaviour of the Germans when they arrived.

The *Luftwaffe* aircrew reported they had bombed and strafed military vehicles and personnel on the islands. The air attack was still in progress when Major Sherwill sent an urgent telegram to the Home Office in London, following this up with a telephone call and holding the receiver to his open window so that the official in Whitehall could actually hear the noise of the German aircraft at work. Not until that evening did the BBC broadcast an announcement to the effect that the Channel Islands were undefended. It was alleged that there were a few light AA guns on Sark, the smallest of the islands, but why they should have been placed there is unknown. The Germans failed to hear the broadcast and only learned the truth following a Foreign Office note passed through the American Embassy in London. It was what the British government had foolishly hoped to avoid: an open invitation to the enemy to march in and occupy the islands. In a speech in the House of Lords the octogenarian Jerseyman Lord Portsea rounded on the government for its 'sheer, stark poltroonery', accusing it of behaving worse than Marshal Pétain, the chief French architect of the surrender in his country.

On Sunday, 30 June, the chief of the islands' police force, Inspector Sculpher, was awaiting the arrival of the first German troops, already furnished with a letter addressed to the enemy commander assuring him the islands were demilitarised. Then, to the inspector's surprise – and, it seems, that of the German Navy – a *Luftwaffe* aircraft landed at Guernsey airport, the pilot marching alone into the control building with pistol drawn. At that moment three British aircraft flew over, causing the German to drop his pistol and rush outside, jump into his plane and fly off. Then, some time between six and seven p.m., four *Luftwaffe* transport planes arrived, flying low over the field to scare off some cows before touching down. Presently, the first German occupiers – *Luftwaffe* officers – were shaking hands with island officials, one of the Germans calling on Major Sherwill at seven. The occupation of British territory had begun.

Once detachments of German troops began arriving, measures were taken to maintain their morale. The soldiers were provided with their own newspapers, the *Deutsche Inselzeitung* and the *Deutsche Guernsey Zeitung*, plus popular periodicals such as *Signal*. There were, of course, instructions on how to behave before the islanders, some of whom were

Germans on British
territory: an amicable
meeting and occupation
following savage
bombing of the
Channel Islands.

of French origin. Importantly for the troops, brothels were organised, houses being requisitioned on both Guernsey and Jersey; a number of willing French prostitutes were ferried across to do their duty, for which some at least are said to have earned up to £100 per month, a sizeable sum in those days. Problems arose at once. The islanders were not used to such shocking establishments, easily identified by the queues of German personnel outside. Local doctors were ordered to inspect the women twice weekly, and refused; they were compelled, so they drew lots. A worse problem came when the prostitutes tried to pay in their takings at the nearest bank, for the Germans paid in occupation currency. Once a week the Barclays manager was faced with thirty or forty ladies of the night all paying into their accounts at the same time, which he found most inconvenient. At St Helier the bank manager tried to persuade the brothel manager to collect the cash and pay it in himself. The chief problem lay in the money itself, which the bank viewed as worthless. The scheme apparently was for occupation marks to be exchanged for credits in France, the prostitutes alleging they were only saving up to get married. Indeed, a number of relationships sprang up between occupiers and occupied, lasting marriages resulting in some cases. Sometimes, though, the male of the partnership was posted away to a fighting front and never seen again.

As the Germans tightened their grip on the islands they built massive fortifications, later using prisoners, usually Russians after the summer of 1941. With the ill treatment meted out by Organisation Todt and SS supervisors, many workers perished. Conditions gradually worsened on the islands with German reverses, and the civilians' situation deteriorated through food shortages. That of the German soldiers was worse, but their discipline held. Firm measures were taken against troops accused of theft or worse.

But in the summer of 1940 a somewhat idyllic life began for the occupiers. Duties were light and the islands held much to interest them. And like all service personnel away on duty, they relied on mail to and from their homes, often flown off the islands into a French base for sorting and forwarding. Naturally, the novelty and indeed importance of writing home and (at first) sending presents from British soil was important to the men on the islands.

On 28 August, only a few weeks after the occupation began, a Gotha 145 biplane took off from Cherbourg-Ouest in chilly but fine weather, at the controls a German pilot named Leonard Buckle. The Battle of Britain was reaching its climax. That day about 100 German aircraft assembled over Cap Gris Nez, mostly fighters escorting groups of Dorniers intent on attacking RAF airfields. The Gotha pilot had no intention, of course, of becoming embroiled in the battles that were ongoing through the day; he was (so it was said) routed to Strasbourg in eastern France, right on the German border in fact.

The Gotha biplane mail carrier which landed by mistake in Britain, thereby
delivering much interesting post to the British.

What happened after Buckle took off and headed out over the sea for
France is unclear; one report stated he was 'diverted', but it is not
known by what. If he encountered thick cloud and his compass was
faulty, subsequent events seem more simple. Whatever the cause, the
Gotha flew not east to reach the nearest French coast, but north-east.
Around two hundred miles after take-off we must assume Buckle saw
land beneath him, but unable to recognise landmarks and perhaps
encountering cloud and possibly short of fuel, he saw a suitable spot on
which to land and enquire after his whereabouts. It was a good stretch of
green grass, bounded on either side by white fencing, and the little plane
needed little space for a touchdown. Rolling along, the Gotha soon
came to a halt, so Buckle switched off his engine, looked around at his
immediate surroundings and, after unfastening his straps, climbed out of
the open cockpit.

He had barely begun to stretch his legs when he heard the thud of men
approaching in a hurry and the sound of vehicles. When he glanced
round he was astounded to see several figures clad in khaki and carrying
rifles. In seconds, before he could even consider a fast take-off, he was
seized by British Home Guards, an army truck then arriving to complete
his capture.

He had landed on Lewes racecourse in East Sussex.

In the rear cockpit of the Gotha, well secured, was a full sack of mail,
including important *Wehrmacht* documents, as well as many letters from
soldiers in the Channel Islands, all of which made a rich haul for British
Intelligence.

The hapless German pilot's Gotha was flown off by the RAF, given British markings and used for communication duties throughout the war.

Scrap

Britain's position in the summer of 1940 was perilous. The threat facing the motherland was greater than at any time in its long and far from peaceful history. Across the Channel stood the most powerful army the world had ever seen. Hundreds of thousands of Hitler's soldiers waited on French soil for the order to set sail for England, regaled daily with Nazi propaganda: the German Eagle lay astride the British Lion; England lay helpless. What did it matter if her leader breathed defiance? His countrymen were beaten, the island nation defeated and broken. Almost every day the German soldiers on the French clifftops gazed awestruck at the *Luftwaffe* air fleets flying over them to England,while the bloated chief of that force chortled with glee and covered his ears as the thunderous roar of hundreds of his warplanes sent thrills and anticipation of total victory through the newly created *Reichsmarschall* and his officers. To Goering the music of a thousand racing engines in those black–green–blue machines spelt glory for him and his airmen, the final crack of doom for the decadent Englanders.

Across the sea the island government introduced even more draconian measures to ensure order and stiffen the nation's backbone against the blows now falling. Above the patchwork landscape of old England the fighter pilots of the Royal Air Force hurled their machines against the enemy air fleets, whose missiles were scattered far and wide as many sought to escape death in flames or imprisonment by the enemy. On the ground, civilians and servicemen alike were urged time and time again to carry their gas masks at all times. They would never be needed; neither would most of the great number of cheap coffins stored ready to accommodate the expected victims of Hitler's wrath. Hardly a day passed without some new government edict being made known, and as the summer of blue skies reached its mid-point one of these sparked thousands of not only patriotic citizens but schoolboys into action.

The nation needed scrap, specifically aluminium, old pots and pans, spare saucepans, kettles, anything that could be recycled and used again to make warplanes. How many saucepans were needed to make a Spitfire? The relevant minister of the government had been advised by his experts that there must surely be millions of old aluminium pots about the land that could be useful in the war production drive. Melted down, these precious ingots could be rolled again into gleaming sheet-metal skin for our warplanes – principally fighters. Fighters, fighters and yet more fighters were needed to ward off the aerial hordes of the Hun. Cyrolite, the essential mineral used in the production of aluminium, could only be imported from Greenland, through seas made dangerous by Hitler's U-boats. It was possible to use the substitute fluospar, but this too could only be bought overseas. Obviously, the British had to make the very best use of supplies already to hand, so anything already shaped into household and other goods no longer required was needed. It may have occurred to the astute reader of such newspaper talk that the enemy, too, needed aluminium, as much or more than we did; how did Hitler get his hands on this precious commodity if it could only be imported from Greenland? Through seas allegedly barred to his shipping by the Royal Navy?

Winston Churchill made the Canadian newspaper tycoon and whizz-kid Lord Beaverbrook his Minister of Supply. His appeal for scrap is now regarded as a propaganda stunt; significantly, the most relevant file has vanished from the Public Record Office. As a result, thousands of well-meaning folk throughout Britain scoured their larders and garden sheds for old pots and pans, their imaginations rife as they saw these bits of metal somehow transformed into brand new Spitfires and Hurricanes that would scrap the *Luftwaffe*. Some patriotic citizens did, however, take the scrap drive to questionable lengths. One elderly grandmother sacrificed one of her two precious velvet-covered family bibles, declaring to her bemused granddaughter: 'One is all we need. Those boys over Germany will make good use of the other if it helps to make their planes.' The Germans, in due course, organised their own scrap drives. One photograph in an illustrated paper was seized upon to make propaganda in Britain. It depicted a street stall laden with metal ornaments, with no less a personage than Hermann Goering making an inspection. The pieces included a bust of Hitler.

But it soon became clear that the scheme was yet another piece of ill-thought-out blundering. The consequences, however, would not become known to the public at large.

In the event, while some householders did take the trouble to check their utensil stock, many simply could not be bothered. But some effort was made, albeit hardly on an overwhelming scale, to put the desired items outside front doors, on garden paths and in yards, ready for collection 'by the government'. In fact, the Materials and Salvage Department in Whitehall had made no provision for this at all; collections were left to voluntary effort, women's organisations, and youngsters like this author who, aware of national need, put themselves out to take action.

Always a delicate child, spending hours each day sitting in a chill, damp school air raid shelter, my mother decided to keep me at home. The weather was grand, so with another lad who owned a little home-made cart we toured the houses in our street begging for old pots and pans. When the cart was full we hauled it in triumph to the nearest ARP warden's post. I well recall the look on the warden's face; he hadn't a clue what to do with the scrap and told us to dump it on the pavement outside.

The public responded well following the government's appeal for scrap metal in 1940. Did all these collections end up in private hands, or dumped in the sea?

Our enthusiasm was a trifle dampened as a result, as was that of others who leapt to assist the national war effort. Some idea of the difficulties encountered can be gathered from letters published in the *Daily Telegraph* on 15 July 1940, one of which followed comments already made by 'Sir Albion B.':

> Immediately after Lady Reading's appeal I started, along with two neighbours, members of the WVS, to visit every home in our own and a nearby road. We told the householders exactly when the collections would be made and asked them to put ready on the doorstep all the aluminium they could spare. The result, from three comparatively short roads, was three car loads, or about ten sacks full. But for this house-to-house canvassing and prompt collecting by responsible people practically none of that aluminium would have been delivered up. The complaint from most people was that appeals were made, the things were looked up and put ready, and then nobody bothered to collect them.

'Miss Burgoyne' also pointed out that further quantities of metals awaited collection, that it was useless for local branches of the WVS to sit back and wait for the material to be brought to them, just as it was equally useless to expect boys to canvass or collect. Other letters from the Adelphi Club and a Conservative Club suggested a national collection day: why not make 21 July 'Aluminium Sunday'? 'In this way we can assumedly find the means for our gallant airmen to continue their successful work.'

Following the first flush of enthusiasm on the part of some citizens, particularly among the growing piles of *Luftwaffe* junk around the country, the business of scouring the land for aluminium scrap died from the public view, especially as the Battle of Britain passed its climax and night bombing became routine. Then, as autumn turned to winter a fresh salvage drive began; every piece of metal adorning private and public places was needed for the war effort. Local authorities were urged by the government to remove all park railings and those around houses and public buildings. Hundreds of local workmen were delegated this task, trucks roamed the streets, workmen dismantled and uprooted ironwork everywhere; ton after ton vanished in the name of the 'war effort', some of it quite ornate and decorative. Its disappearance left many a private and public space looking strangely forlorn and empty. Naturally, once again people assumed that plans existed to melt this vast collection of scrap iron down in furnaces, ready to be recast into cannon and other impedimenta of war.

Come 1941 and the drive was still on, freshly denuded areas appearing nationwide, places that would remain changed in that respect for many a long year. Then, with victory in 1945, large numbers of warplanes were left over, ready for scrapping themselves. Vast sums of money had been spent making these machines and much else, just for them to be collected up and parked for disposal. Most were picked up by scrap metal dealers who would make their fortunes – at public expense, for the 'purchase' tax and income tax extracted from the government in the purchase of war materials from commercial companies resulted in huge losses to the public and huge profits for the traders in scrap. Some firms, aircraft factories for example, were churning out warplanes until the last day of the war, the shiny, new models towed from the factory buildings and across the adjacent test airfield to be parked ready for scrapping at knock-down prices. This was commonplace after a war, and one reason why Britain found itself bankrupt in 1945, propped up for many years by American and international bank loans.

But what of the pots and pans collected by the enthusiastic volunteers of 1940? And the thousands of tons of ironwork removed during the halcyon days of scrap collecting for the war effort? It would be very hard indeed to find answers to that conundrum so long after the war; government departments prefer to remain coy in perpetuity in matters threatening even a whiff of embarrassing disclosure. Only by the merest chance may the student of such wars, or perhaps those whose hobby it is to read memoirs, come across a brief reference to the 'Great Scrap Scandal'. One may even discover a letter in the press.

The facts on such national efforts in World War II are indeed obscure, at least in terms of results. In the matter of aluminium, it is occasionally hinted in aviation periodicals that both German and Allied planes shot down could well have ended up transformed through salvage to fight again on the other side. No facts are given, it may be supposition, but it is an intriguing notion. As to the British aluminium scrap drive of 1940, it is believed that the 'experts' who had first dreamed up the scheme were finally faced with the reality as presented to them by the industrialists at the sharp end, which was that it was simply too costly in man hours to begin the time-consuming task of dismantling millions of pots and pans, all too often made of composite metals, or indeed sorting the massive piles of junk into the usable and unusable. There can be little doubt that the pots collected by the schoolboys and WVS and others in 1940 ended up as hard cash in the pockets of scrap metal dealers later on.

Or did they? If we turn to the second puzzle – what happened to the great amount of good old British, much of it Victorian, ironwork confiscated by the authorities during that war – then we might find a better clue to solve the first.

Perhaps once again being forced to bow to the reality presented by those better in the know, the government was finally obliged to admit that the relevant ministry (and specifically Lord Beaverbrook) had got that wrong too. The grand assembly of scrap iron was quietly loaded aboard ships, taken up the Thames and dumped without fuss into the sea off Shoeburyness. At least that is one scenario published by one presumably in the know. The reader may wonder why the railings and other bits of public (and private) metalwork were not returned to their rightful owners. A moment's thought makes clear the impracticability of such an idea. The mind boggles at the notion of a vast pile of such scrap, the government unable to tell what came from where, the owners faced with an impossible task of finding what bits were their property.

The only question that remains is, assuming this metal did end up in the sea, why did the authorities not sell it as scrap, and thereby reimburse either the local councils or indeed the public purse to some small extent?

There was one other area of scrap metal that never became feasible in terms of being recoverable for the war effort, metal that posed a real hazard to anyone unwise enough to go outdoors in a defended area during an air raid. Hot, jagged shell splinters – shrapnel to most – could kill, and did kill those who for whatever reason hung about in the open to watch the fun, or, of course, were caught out quite innocently. Some twelve people were killed by shrapnel in one night raid. Amazingly, this lethal rain did comparatively little damage. Emerging from shelter in the dawn hours one fully expected to find smashed roof tiles and windows, having heard the occasional rattle and tinkle of the steel lumps striking our houses. Yet those who thought about it at the time may have been excused for believing the chances of being struck were less than minimal. But chance is a strange thing, as I can relate from personal experience.

One fine morning, near midday, I stood at the bottom of the rear garden trying to spot a German recce plane that had just passed over at very great height, its passage marked by a few woolly tufts denoting flak bursts. I guessed the plane must have been flying at a height of at least 25,000ft, heading westwards towards central London. Suddenly, as I watched, I heard a brief 'whizz' followed by a plop as a piece of shrapnel struck the ground a few feet away from me, just over the high black railings. Surprised, and an avid collector of such souvenirs, I tried to find it, but the longish grass in the recreation field beyond the fence made it difficult, and of course I had no metal detector. That sliver of metal had hurtled down from nearly five miles high, to miss me by a comparatively tiny margin. Its velocity was easily great enough to have killed me.

As late as the 1970s, at least one dump of wartime scrap metal still lay rusting away in a certain English town.

The Deputy Führer *has Landed*

The flight of Rudolf Hess to Britain in May 1941 is arguably the most sensational event of World War II. It may have been by pure coincidence that it occurred on the same night that Hitler directed his *Luftwaffe* bomber force to deliver one last great raid on London before most of its units were transferred east. The German Air Force would never again have the strength to carry out the kind of attack on England as that of 10/11 May 1941, when its bombers started over 2,000 fires in London, many of them classed as conflagrations, any one of which in peacetime would have made headline front-page news. By dawn on the eleventh, hundreds of fires were still raging out of control, and three nights later, much to the alarm of the authorities, three were still aglow. The worst thing that could have happened in this terrible air raid occurred, a combination of two crucial factors that allowed many of the fires to burn uncontrollably. Large water mains were struck by bombs and thousands of gallons of water were lost to the embattled firemen; unluckily, the raid also coincided with a low tide in the Thames, so the drawing of water from that source proved impossible. It was this disaster that led directly to the arranging of static water tanks.

The main railway arteries were not fully opened for weeks, and many fine old buildings were wrecked or damaged, including the House of Commons, though it was the human cost that weighed most heavily on the mind of Prime Minister Churchill, who continued to receive reports through the following day. Over 3,000 people had been killed or injured. Not that there was anything the PM could do; he had been invited by friends at Ditchley to spend a weekend with them, and by Sunday evening he had settled down with his hosts to watch a Marx Brothers film. But during the film another telephone call came, this time a secretary asking that he speak to a man calling urgently on behalf of the Duke of Hamilton. The Duke was a personal friend of Churchill, and commanded an RAF fighter sector in eastern Scotland. Even so, the PM was hesitant; only when the secretary mentioned the matter was of 'Cabinet importance' did he stir, but he suggested the call be put through to his Minister of Information, Mr Brendan Bracken. A short time afterwards Mr Bracken called to submit that the Duke had indeed arrived in London with the most amazing piece of information: the Deputy *Führer* of Nazi Germany was in Britain. To Churchill this seemed fantastic, though later he was to state he never attached any importance to the event.

To Rudolf Hess the event was certainly the most exciting and adventurous of his not uneventful life; it was also the most dangerous and foolhardy, a gross miscalculation and blunder of the first order that brought enormous embarrassment to his *Führer* and his country. Sometimes referred to as a good-looking, dark-haired young man, Rudolf Hess was born in Egypt where his father was a wealthy merchant. Returning to Germany, the young Rudolf completed his education in time to join the Army for the Great War, serving and surviving a great blood-letting in the List Regiment, the very unit Adolf Hitler had fought with against the British, when the future *Führer* of Germany had written to a friend in effusive terms of his baptism into war, making it abundantly clear he had not only found a true home at last in the Army, but loved war. Not until the autumn of 1918 did Lieutenant Hess gain his pilot's badge, just as the armistice came, thwarting his ambition to become an air ace.

Like many other soldiers who went home to an impoverished, starving Germany rent by dissension and red revolution, Hess fell in with one of the many groups, societies and militias that abounded – the Thule Society, a small group of fanatics won over by the masterly piece of forgery known as The Protocols of the Wise Men of Zion. Fabricated by the Russian secret police as a piece of anti-Semitic propaganda, the so-called 'Protocols' took off across Europe and the world, circulated and publicised here, there and everywhere, and convincing many intelligent people that the 'secrets' in the pamphlet were true, that there really was a worldwide conspiracy among Jews of devilish cunning to take over the world by the back door, by manipulating the banking systems. To those already of anti-Semitic bent it was the right stuff, exactly what they wished to hear, while to others of no particular hatred, the papers had been crafted shrewdly enough to sound convincing. They became a great talking point in the West, were translated into various languages, and even occasioned comment in *The Times.* Hatred of the Jews was the result among the Thule group and others of like mind who fell into plotting various acts of violence, unable to prevent an actual Bolshevik takeover in Munich which was bloodily reversed by soldiers and others loyal to the old regime. Reds were summarily put against the wall and shot, the various battles resulting in a leg wound for the twenty-one-year-old Lieutenant Hess, who was hospitalised.

The ex-corporal, Adolf Hitler, employed as a spy by the Army district command, had played his part in these disturbances, but not until he emerged as leader of the German Workers Party was he noticed by the young Hess. Like most who heard Hitler speak, Hess became hypnotised into joining him, quite unaware he had already met the man in 1914 after the List Regiment had, through incompetent leadership, incurred 'staggering losses' that cost Bavaria the flower of its youth. When Hess had paraded before the new commander he found an adjutant present, beside him at attention a moustachioed Private First Class – Adolf Hitler. Hess gave him only a perfunctory glance. Ten years later, the man who devoted most loyalty and proved most slavish in his adoration of Hitler was busily engaged as a stenographer in Lansberg jail, noting down the utterances of his imprisoned leader which later appeared as the book *Mein Kampf* (My Struggle). Hitler's somewhat absurd role in the bungled '*putsch*' of 1923 in Munich had done nothing to drive away the man who would never relinquish his admiration and love for the *Führer* whom he always saw as 'Germany': '*Hitler ist Deutschland, Deutschland ist Hitler. Sieg heil! Sieg heil!*'

That was the Hess the world came to know, the rather strange but striking head above the brownshirt outfit – the beetling brow, sunken eyes and protruding front teeth were a gift to satirical newspaper cartoonists already well served by the rest of the Nazi clique, especially the increasingly rotund and clownish figure of Hermann Goering – and the right arm that shot up in salute to his leader whenever occasion allowed. The man who was ever at his master's heels, the anti-Semite who, however, for all his devotion, gradually fell away into the background. For whatever reason, Hitler entrusted the more important organising to other henchmen: Goering, Himmler, Ley and others. Following the taking of power in 1933, although named as Hitler's deputy, Hess fell more and more into the background of political life. He continued to appear in public, occasionally in the black outfit of the SS of which he was an honorary member, and at the notorious Nuremberg rallies he was one of the leading speakers, though his utterances were of the banal kind and, as always, devoted to his love for the *Führer*. Whatever his real worth, to Hitler's followers and the public he was Party secretary, to all intents and purposes taking some of the burden off his leader's shoulders, in reality spending more and more time flying and with his family. (There is no doubt Hess became an accomplished pilot, establishing himself as a very competent navigator.)

It must certainly have been perfectly clear to Hess – who, despite some indications to the contrary, was no fool – that Hitler had always intended his adopted land should strike out eastwards. Germans had long emigrated in that direction; various countries had incorporated minorities in sizeable numbers over decades in central Europe, right up to and into the Baltic states, many of the latter forced to flee from the revolution of 1917. Hess, though not present during Hitler's early wartime planning conferences, must certainly have been aware of the coming attack on Soviet Russia; practically the whole *Wehrmacht* and much of the populace had heard rumours of this since late 1940. He must, too, have been as aware as everyone that a two-front war was the worst undertaking imaginable, virtually certain to mean a widening of the conflict and quite possibly suicide for Nazi Germany. Every German general dreaded such a prospect, unconvinced that Stalin's Soviet colossus was really the clay model that would crumble within weeks, as Hitler asserted it would.

Whatever doubts the generals and others around Hitler had, no one had the temerity or guts to tell him he was mad. Not that it would have done any good. The notion of striking east and conquering vast new territories for German expansion was far too deeply engrained for Hitler to contemplate for one second changing his mind. For his generals the problem took on a different light: how to exercise their life's work and training to best effect. For Hess, an obsession began to take hold – but not any feeling of his own that he, as an old comrade, should try to dissuade his former corporal comrade to change his mind, not a bit of it. The problem for Hess was only how to avoid the two-front war that now loomed. True, western Europe had largely been occupied by Germany. This left England unbeaten, though the sturdy, largely Nordic types were, because of their despotic and short-sighted leader, unable to see the reality of their situation. If only the English could be persuaded that their best course lay in reaching an accommodation with Nazi Germany! Hess bent his mind to this problem, and despite his exclusion from the leadership conferences, he was still able to gain Hitler's ear, and this he did. Hess made clear his fears over the two-front war now imminent, surpassing Hitler's own inner doubts over the continued role of England, and making clear too his firm conviction that this enemy across the sea must somehow be approached and made to see reason before it was too late.

Hess had, like other leading Nazis, met a few Britishers before the war, in the heady days after Hitler's 'accession' when the world, but especially western Europeans, were constantly agog as the new dynamo emerged to dominate proceedings. Among the string of personalities and 'names' who had hurried to visit the new *Reich* was the Duke of Hamilton, a pilot well able to meet and chat with a fellow aviator on cordial terms, rather as Hitler did when he met British ex-servicemen – the difference, of course, being that in Hitler's case he had thoroughly enjoyed the mad and exciting terrors and carnage. It came to Hess that through the Duke, a man with connections, he might well be able to reach some politicians of influence in Britain, men he was convinced were sympathetic to Germany and not averse to trying to reach some accommodation with Hitler. This was no wild imagining. There were indeed such politicians and others who would have been perfectly willing to watch from safety while Germany tore the heart out of Stalin's despotic communist state, which they viewed as far more reprehensible than that of Nazi Germany. There had been a time not long before when whiffs of at least an idea, a tentative movement on behalf of some politicians, seemed to be in the wind. But the feelers were so fragile, and in any case scotched by Churchill, that nothing could come of them. Hitler had been kept fully informed, but did nothing, his mind completely doubtful that any understanding with Britain was now possible. No matter how they viewed the Stalin dictatorship with all its tyranny, under Churchill the British government seemed united in their view that Hitler's defeat was the first priority. The prospect of Hitler turning east was, in the circumstances, a godsend.

To Hitler, Hess's ideas grew more implausible, for his old comrade now put forward the crazy notion that he, Hess, should make the attempt to bring England to its senses. The *Führer* had no doubt at all that such an attempt would fail, and he did for good reason forbid it, though feeling inwardly that his friend seemed so determined that anything might happen. Hitler ordered those adjutants around Hess to ensure he was not given access to aircraft and to be kept informed should it appear Hess was about to make any attempt to reach England. He had already made it clear to Hess that the idea was absurd, and that if he did such a thing he, as *Führer*, would be forced to absolve himself and the state from any responsibility and declare Hess insane, or at the very least suffering from illness and delusions.

Soon after 17.00 hrs on 10 May the *Luftwaffe* began testing its *Knickebein* (Crooked Leg) radio beam system, the station at Cherbourg on the north-west coast of France (codename Anton) being the westernmost beam of the scheme, its signal directed on London. Two more stations followed suit. The three beams would intersect to guide the bombers to West Ham in the eastern part of London, an area (with East Ham and Bow) already damaged by previous *Luftwaffe* raids. The Hams and Woolwich were the site of the docks so vital to Britain's survival as a merchant shipping nation and were the focal point of all *Luftwaffe* raids on London. By 17.20 hrs the British knew through No. 80 Wing RAF that the beams were on London. It was this unit's job not only to monitor but interfere with such German navigational aids. The news soon reached the Prime Minister, defence commands, police, fire and ARP services. By 19.30 the German aircrews had been briefed and every available aircraft – some 500 bombers – had been ordered to deliver a savage reprisal attack in response to the latest RAF pinprick raid on Berlin (this motive, of course, added to the desire to bluff the British into believing the *Luftwaffe* remained in force in the West). Even as *Luftmarschall* Hugo Sperrle, commanding Air Fleet III, went over the plans he knew the chief of Air Fleet II, *Luftmarschall* Kesselring ('Smiling Albert'), had already moved his HQ to Warsaw.

At 22.45 hrs, as the British defences waited, *Oberleutnant* Aschen-brenner's Heinkel 111 of Pathfinder Group 100 crossed the Dorset coast. Strung out around and behind him were nineteen more bombers carrying the coloured marker flares the German crews hoped to deposit on or near a certain factory in West Ham dubbed by the renegade broadcaster Lord Haw-Haw as a 'packet of Woodbines' – the McDougalls flour factory. At 23.02 hrs the first German incendiary bombs released by KG100 struck West Ham; these were soon followed by hundreds more fire bombs that littered the eight to nine miles up to Tower Bridge. The raid was under way, London's worst ordeal had begun.

Far to the north, in Scotland, men manning an Observer Corps watch-post not far from Edinburgh heard an aircraft approaching from the sea, and despite the poor light identified it as a twin-engined Messerschmitt 110 fighter. Their report to Fighter Command HQ was discounted; such a type of plane would not have the range to fly so far north and return to its base on the continent. Not long afterwards, a ploughman named David McLean was preparing for bed when he heard a plane roaring overhead:

> Everyone else was in bed, for it was late. As I ran to the back of the farm I heard a crash and saw the plane burst into flames in a field about 200 yards

away. I was amazed and a bit frightened when I saw a parachute dropping slowly through the dark. Peering upwards I could see a man swinging from the harness. I thought it must be a German airman baling out, and raced back to the house for help. But they were all asleep. I looked round for a weapon, but all I could find was a hayfork. Fearing I might lose the airman, I hurried round by myself to the back of the house. There in the field I saw the man lying on the ground, with his parachute nearby.

He smiled. As I assisted him to his feet he thanked me in perfect English. But I could see he had injured his foot in some way. I helped him into the house. By this time my old mother and my sister had got out of bed and made tea. The stranger declined tea and smiled when we told him we were very fond of it in this country. Then he said, 'I never drink tea as late as this. I'll only have a glass of water.'

We sent word to the military authorities. In the meantime our visitor chatted freely to us and showed us pictures of his little boy, of whom he spoke very proudly. He told us he had left Germany about four hours earlier, and had landed because nightfall was approaching. I could see from the way he spoke that he was a man of culture. His English, though he had a foreign accent, was very clear, and he understood every word we said. He was a striking-looking man, more than six feet tall, and he wore a very magnificent flying suit. His watch and identity bracelet were both gold. He didn't discuss his journey, and indeed appeared to treat what seemed to us a most hazardous flight as a pleasure flip. He seemed quite confident that he'd be well treated, and repeatedly said how lucky he'd been in landing without mishap. He was most gentlemanly in his attitude to my old mother and my sister. He bowed stiffly to them when he came in, and before he left he thanked us profusely for what we had done for him.

He was anxious about only one thing – his parachute. He said to me: 'I should like to keep that, I think I owe my life to it.'

The McLean family assumed the 'striking visitor' from Germany was simply another enemy airman. Hess had not revealed his true identity to them, and they were too polite to enquire. When 'officials' arrived to capture him, Hess smiled, assuring them he was unarmed, and holding up his arms to be searched before he was taken away. The sixty-four-year-old mother, Mrs McLean, had asked the man if he was German when he first arrived, admitting she did not feel too friendly when he admitted this was so.

But he was so pale and tired, and his ankle was so swollen that I had to do what I could for him. He spoke like a gentleman and had fine manners. He didn't want us to do anything for him except get in touch with the authorities. We felt he was someone of importance because of his gold wristlet watch and identity disc. His boots were magnificent. They were as fine as a pair of gloves. Although he looked between forty and fifty years old I felt

I had to mother him – especially after he showed us his little boy's picture. He wouldn't tell us why he had left Germany, but he seemed to be glad to be sitting in my cottage beside a good fire.

It was the local Home Guard who turned out in force to take over, the men, up to twenty in all, rushing from their homes to the farm, clutching their rifles, to stand around gawking at the forty-seven-year-old prisoner who one or two remarked 'looked a bit like Hess'. Then their CO, a Home Guard captain, arrived and took charge, the police also having been informed. Inspector Thomas Hyslop of the Gyffnock Constabulary had received word of a German plane down near Eaglesham, Renfrewshire, at 23.15 hrs. By the time he arrived the crowd had grown to around 200, including a special constable. Sentries were posted and the prisoner at last removed to the Home Guard's 3rd Battalion HQ – a girl guide hut where (as one recent write-up put it) a 'Captain Mainwaring' type (actually a lieutenant-colonel) had taken charge. The police inspector noted down the various items the German had brought with him, apart from maps, several bottles and a syringe. The prisoner was then taken for treatment to a Glasgow hospital, where he identified himself as 'Lieutenant Horn' – then claiming he was Rudolf Hess and producing photographs to prove it. A call to London resulted in a Foreign Office official who had known Hess hurrying to establish that the 'German officer' who had landed by parachute in Scotland was indeed who he claimed to be.

Rudolf Hess had, with some luck, got over the first big hurdle in his mission to try to remove the British threat from Hitler's rear when he attacked the Soviet Union. This was not at first obvious in Britain, where the leading question was: what was Hitler's deputy doing here? Did his one-way flight indicate he had deserted the Nazi camp? If so, he must be privy to many secrets. His arrival caused a worldwide sensation. An announcement from Downing Street late on Monday, 12 May stated: 'Rudolf Hess, Deputy *Führer* of Germany and leader of the National Socialist Party, has landed in Scotland in the following circumstances', the statement going on to describe how he had arrived. His identity was proved and confirmed the next day beyond all doubt, this news following closely a brief announcement by Berlin radio that Hess had disappeared after taking off by plane from Augsburg, near Munich, that he had been suffering from an illness of some years' standing, and that contrary to instructions

he once again came into possession of a plane. On Saturday, 10 May, at about 6 p.m., Rudolf Hess set off on a flight from Augsburg, from which he has not so far returned. A letter he left behind unfortunately shows by its distractedness traces of mental disorder and it is feared he was the victim of hallucinations. The *Führer* at once ordered the arrest of the adjutants of

The *Führer*'s deputy Rudolf Hess with his wife (above) – and the remains of his Messerschmitt 110 after he parachuted into Scotland (below).

party member Hess who alone had any cognisance of these flights and did not, contrary to the *Führer*'s orders, of which they were fully aware, either report or prevent the flights. In these circumstances it must be considered that party member Hess either jumped out of his plane or has met with an accident.

At the time of this bulletin nothing was known in Germany of Hess's fate. The British claims, backed by photographs in the newspapers of

the wrecked Me 110, forced Hitler's hand into issuing the kind of statement he knew would have to come if Hess went ahead with his
scheme. Even so, Hitler was understandably furious that his old friend
should have provided the enemy with such a fantastic propaganda tool.
One can imagine the ecstatic glee that kind of event would have caused
in Berlin, and above all to Dr Goebbels, if someone of similar stature
from London had parachuted into Germany. Goebbels would have
been beside himself on being presented with such a gift, and would
have played it for all it was worth for weeks on end. As things turned out,
as Goebbels and the rest of the Nazi government braced themselves
for the expected broadsides of trumpeting propaganda from London,
they were flabbergasted by a sudden silence, as baffling as the exit of
Rudolf Hess. The very fact that Hitler had declared his one-time deputy
mad was bad enough – this alone handed the British a grand opportunity
to poke fun at the Nazi government. Whatever writings Goebbels
hastily prepared in his offices in the Wilhelmstrasse to counter the
offensive of words expected from London, he was now struck dumb by
a complete paucity of further bulletins that to a man of his ilk seemed
incomprehensible.

In the meantime, MI5 had belatedly come into the picture, its officers
without doubt more than irked that all kinds of people had got to Hess
long before the department knew of his arrival. Among them was an
apparently innocuous clerk from the Polish consulate in Glasgow.
Roman Battaglia spent a solid two hours interrogating Rudolf Hess in
hospital, simply because he spoke German and was apparently allowed
access by the local authorities. This unauthorised visit was viewed as
outrageous bungling by one high-ranking MI5 officer, who commented
in a memo: 'How on earth he got to know of Hess's arrival and, furthermore, went out and interrogated him for over two hours, I simply cannot
conceive.' This officer told the Glasgow police to make 'very discreet
enquiries' as to how the Pole had become involved, how he had 'come
to blunder on the scene. At any rate, there has been a good old mess-up
regarding this business.' Battaglia himself observed that fifteen to twenty
Home Guards stood around as the prisoner repeated his story: he had
arrived with a message for the Duke of Hamilton, whom he had met
before the war. The Pole was evidently acting as interpreter, and reported
that the onlookers hurled questions at him, some of which were too offensive to be translated.

One British newspaper commentator, after running through a potted
version of Hess's career, stated: 'It is impossible to exaggerate the significance of his flight from Germany.' Strangely, at the time this did not seem
to be the case in Britain, for following the initial headlined sensation, the
Hess case vanished from the newspapers. Little or nothing more would
be heard of him until 1946, when he was arraigned in Nuremberg for the
war crimes tribunal. Despite occasional, indeed more frequent, reports

of German troop concentrations in the East, the fact of an imminent assault on the USSR was not widely known; for this reason no speculation concerning the reason for the Hess flight took place in that direction, though this soon became apparent, for British Intelligence were well aware of what was to come in the East.

Oddly, despite his paranoiac mistrust of everybody, Stalin continued to believe Hitler would honour the pact between them signed in 1939 that had come as such a bombshell to the Allies, even though the Soviets viewed Nazi Germany as just another capitalist state ripe for conversion sooner or later. But the British he viewed with real distrust and suspicion, even after his alliance with them following the invasion of his country in June 1941. The arrival of Hess in Britain aroused the greatest scepticism and doubts in the Soviets, so that when, later, Stalin met Churchill he made a special point of asking to know the truth about the affair. Despite Churchill's assurance there was no more to tell, Stalin could not bring himself to believe it, preferring to think the British had contemplated making some deal with Hitler.

The German people could only believe what their news services told them; 'We really thought Hess must be mad!' is one German's comment today. 'We had no idea what he was up to. But an uncle said to me: "I believe otherwise. Hess is a clever man. Do you really believe he would fly all that way to Scotland without good reason? I think there is much more to all this than we are told." Well, we did not know what to believe and the great mystery was not solved until after the war.'

And a great mystery it was too for the British people, who learned nothing further themselves until much later. The Prime Minister stated in his memoirs in the 1950s that the affair was of no great importance, by which he meant the arrival of Hess had no effect on the course of the war. But in 1941, during the days following his arrival, Hess made every effort to put across his argument to any official who saw him in his room in the Tower of London, giving long statements from notes, all of which was reported to Churchill.

Hess began by providing a one-sided account of Anglo-German relations in the period from 1900 onwards, then assuring listeners the *Führer* had never had any bad intentions towards England; all he wished for was an understanding that would give him a free hand in Asia. But here Hess pretended that all Hitler had in mind was some concessions from Stalin, denying knowledge of any coming attack on the USSR. Former German colonies would need to be negotiated over, while Germany had to support the rebel Rashid Ali in Iraq. The *Führer* had only reluctantly ordered offensive operations by U-boats and the *Luftwaffe* against Britain, and it pained (indeed horrified) Hess himself to think of the women and children suffering in British cities under bombing – in this connection he thought of his own family in such circumstances. Hess tried to impress on his listeners the hopelessness of Britain's position, of the need to reach a settlement, which was why he himself had flown to Britain to contact the Duke of Hamilton and the 'large peace faction' he believed existed among the British. The *Führer* knew he could no longer deal with the existing British government, but Hess naïvely believed the Duke of Hamilton would conduct him to the King, who would listen and see common sense. If, on the other hand, England did not accede to this offer, sooner or later it would be made to.

Churchill, after receiving such reports, which included the results of a visit by Lord Simon, came to the conclusion that Hess, though far from insane, was such a passionate believer in the mind of Adolf Hitler that he really did identify with all his arguments and theories: 'He was a neurotic, with a split soul . . . but more than a medical case.'

For Rudolf Hess, sadly, it began to dawn on him that his captors were quite unamenable to his case, that he never would meet the King, that he stood no chance of getting through to the 'large peace faction' (if it existed), that his gaolers were simply treating him as a privileged prisoner of war. Once this depressing fact became clear, that he had in truth committed a great blunder, his demeanour changed. Hess began behaving strangely, questioning his food, making demands and generally giving the impression of a man whose nerve had cracked. Despite his being afforded many privileges in isolation, his campaign to try to convince the British he was insane continued. Doctors were unconvinced the prisoner had really gone beyond the bounds of rationality, despite possible attempts at suicide, but he needed watching, and was never permitted to join other high-ranking German prisoners.

Once the invasion of Russia got under way the news headlines about that and events in the African theatre soon brought to a halt any more conjecture on the Hess case. And when the end of the war came he was taken back to Germany to stand trial, a gaunt, haggard, aged figure rather different from that so familiar in pre-war days. To his fellow Nazis in the dock he paid little attention, giving every appearance of oddity and isolation, perhaps having fallen completely into the role he set himself in 1941 following the failure of his mission to Britain. In fact, it is possible the Western Allies would have released him from his life sentence but for Soviet intransigence. In Churchill's view, Hess had atoned for any moral guilt and 'lunatic benevolence' towards Hitler. He was, so the former wartime leader stated, a medical, not a criminal, case.

But in Spandau jail Hess remained for year after year, his case periodically coming up in the press, until he was the only Nazi left in the prison, which remained heavily guarded by military police of the USA, Britain and the USSR. Many visits by his family, including his son Wolf, were permitted, but the Soviets refused any sign of clemency. Rudolf Hess was found dead by his own hand in 1987. Even then he remained in the news, a British major and medic asserting that the man found dead was not Hess; then came the fantasy that he had been murdered by the Allies. These absurdities were believed by Wolf Hess until proved to be nonsense.

His Majesty's U-boat

There is no doubt that the war against the German U-boats in the north Atlantic was the greatest and most crucial factor in Britain's survival during World War II. Despite the harsh lessons already learned during the war of 1914–18, little or nothing was done to protect the nation's life-lines during the first weeks and months of the war. Indeed, apart from hastily inaugurating the convoy system once U-boat warfare started, there was not a great deal the Admiralty could do owing to the neglect shown in providing adequate convoy escort able to detect and drive off, if not destroy, the undersea raiders, the grey sea wolves so fanatically commanded by the ex-submariner Admiral Doenitz. With far too few warships to shepherd the merchantmen and tankers across the ocean and hardly any long-range aircraft, the naval staff in London looked to Intelligence to provide clues that would help them in the battle.

Unfortunately for the British, the enemy were already reading Admiralty signals sent to ships at sea. Admiral Doenitz became aware of the 'hostilities' call from London as soon as it was transmitted on that fine Sunday morning of 3 September 1939. The experts were already grappling with the Germans' Enigma code, but even the setting up of the world's first computer – a gigantic electrical contraption christened 'Bombe' – did not signal the start of successes in the intelligence code war. The real breakthroughs in beating the U-boats came via blunders committed by the enemy at sea.

On 27 August 1941 the four-man crew of an RAF Coastal Command Hudson of 269 Squadron, led by Squadron Leader J.H. Thompson, were on anti-U-boat patrol in the north-east Atlantic. The weather was foul, with high winds and rain, the crew's hopes of spotting anything of the enemy practically nil. In fact, of the many crews who flew out over the Atlantic during the war, most would spend thousands of hours staring out of their planes at the grey-green ocean with no result; hundreds of aircraft with their crews would go down with nothing to show for their sacrifice.

But on this day the crew of *U-570* commanded by *Kapitanleutnant* Rahmlow ran out of luck – or rather their lookouts were caught napping on the surface, perhaps due to the bad weather. The submarine was probably recharging its batteries; in any event, the bridge lookouts seem to have neglected their much-practised drill and failed to close all the boat's vents and hatches in the panic to submerge. As a result, sea water flooded in, the batteries at once producing deadly chlorine gas which forced

Rahmlow to reverse orders and get the boat on the surface again. The Hudson pilot and his crew were amazed to see the U-boat emerging in the heavy sea and crewmen bursting up from below; not unnaturally the fliers assumed the submarine must have been damaged by the plane's rather lightweight depth bombs. It looked as if the U-boat's planes were damaged and the boat could not submerge. The Hudson's turret gunner opened fire and the German seamen tried to scuttle to safety down the conning tower hatch, just as the rest of the forty-four-man complement were trying to escape the poisonous atmosphere below. The result was the utmost confusion, a shambles witnessed by the RAF fliers who now circled low overhead, guns trained and aware the enemy were not in fact returning fire with their machine-guns.

The aircrew were even more surprised to see something white fluttering from the U-boat, some sort of white flag indicating surrender. A signal had already been sent to their base in Iceland; now another was despatched calling for a relief plane and surface craft to take possession of the prize. Meanwhile, the Hudson continued to circle the sub, aware of the whole German crew who seemed to be jam-packed into the small space of the conning tower bridge and anti-aircraft platform. Later, the Hudson captain in his report commented that the Germans appeared to be the glummest-looking bunch he had ever seen. Understandably, it was something like three hours before a Catalina arrived to relieve the Hudson, which was very low on fuel. It was even longer before the nearest Royal Navy ships appeared to take the Germans off *U-570*, which was then towed back to a British base, its war flag presented to 269 Squadron as a memento. Once repaired, the German sub was put into commission by the Royal Navy as HMS *Graph* and sent to the Mediterranean. While being towed up the North Sea on 20 March 1944 it broke away from its tugs and was grounded and wrecked off the east coast of Scotland. The wreck finally broke up in 1961. It was a sad end for 'His Majesty's U-boat'.

The Germans in the POW camp to which the crew of *U-570* was sent soon learned the circumstances of the U-boat's capture. The first officer, Bernhardt Berndt, was held responsible and branded a coward. As a result he attempted to escape, allegedly to try to reach his boat, which was being held at that time in Barrow-in-Furness shipyard, his crazy hope to scuttle it and regain his honour. He did not get far: he was shot dead by Home Guards on 19 October 1941. After the war, *Kapitanleutnant* Rahmlow was refused membership of the German U-boat old comrades association.

This triumph enabled the British to inspect and probe an example of the enemy's prime weapon in the Battle of the Atlantic: the Type VIIc U-boat. They were very impressed with its modern construction and especially its robustness. Important though it was, however, the capture of *U-570* had already been preceded by even greater successes when

Bombed by a Coastal
Command Hudson
(below) and disabled, a
U-boat is captured; like
others, it revealed vital
Enigma secrets.

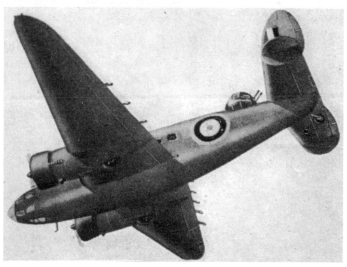

elements contributing to the final breaking of the *Kriegsmarine*'s Enigma code 'Hydra' were captured, again through enemy blunders.

On 2 February 1940 Royal Navy warships caught *U-33* engaged in minelaying off the Firth of Forth, and before the sub sank a boarding crew was able to retrieve three rotor arms for the Enigma encoding machine. The British already possessed one of these machines, smuggled to the West by the Poles in 1939, but that had been insufficient to solve the different codes used by the various Nazi services. Next, on 7 May 1941 the Navy intercepted the German weather reporting ship *München* and took the Enigma code settings current for the following three months. And in another blunder committed by the enemy only two days later, the Navy caught none other than the notorious German U-boat skipper Fritz-Julius Lemp, 'hero' of the *Athenia* disaster, who had just despatched a salvo of torpedoes at a convoy. Coming up to periscope depth to observe results, Lemp was surprised by warships, his boat disabled and forced to the surface. In the engagement Lemp was lost, but just as the captain of HMS *Bulldog* was about to have his ship ram the U-boat he recalled his orders and instead sent an armed boarding party to try to capture the submarine and its documents. While the corvette *Aubretia* circled the scene, the two destroyers *Bulldog* and *Broadway* closed in with guns trained on the German crew lining the U-boat's deck.

Amazingly, when the officer in command of the British boarding party went below on the submarine he not only found it entirely devoid of crewmen, but in searching for documents discovered a sealed envelope in Lemp's own little desk. This and other papers he took back to his commander. The envelope contained Enigma code key instructions and enabled the codebreakers at Bletchley Park to finally complete the defeat of Admiral Doenitz's U-boat code system. Doenitz himself had become over-confident and had sent too many messages to his men in the Atlantic on all topics relevant to them, not merely operational instructions. Doenitz cosseted his submariners, doing his best to reassure them on home matters, such as the fate of their families under air attack. All were read in Britain.

The Enigma encoder aboard *U-110* survived to tell (in recent times) how he was twice, with his comrades, ordered by Lemp to forget everything below and get on deck. Yet there was one item this German seaman refused to leave without and he went below once more to retrieve an illustrated book of love poems he had spent many hours preparing for his lady friend. He totally ignored the vital secret code papers.

The lieutenant commanding *Bulldog*'s boarding party received the DSO at Buckingham Palace. The King commented that his deed had been 'one of the most important of the war at sea'.

Breaking the Enigma U-boat code enabled the British to pinpoint the position of every German submarine at sea, including the large 'milch cow' supply boats, all of which were tracked down and sunk. The blunders by the Germans at sea which allowed these codes to fall into enemy hands resulted in forty U-boats being sunk in May 1943, a most fantastic loss which signalled defeat for Germany in the vital Atlantic battle.

A Reward of 100,000 Reichsmarks

When Hitler's troops completed the occupation of Czechoslovakia in March 1939 they interrupted the training of the latest intake of that country's fighter pilots. These young men had completed their ground training and passed their elementary flying lessons and were due to go forward into fighter plane school. Instead, as the Germans marched in, the colonel in command of the flying base presented every man who had passed with his wings and a certificate and sent them home. Not un-naturally, the young pilots were in a state of bemused shock, but most recovered swiftly and began making plans to escape the Nazi net, their intention to fight the enemy from foreign bases. For some, the best course seemed to head for Russia, for had not the West betrayed them at Munich, selling out their country to Hitler? In fact, Soviet propaganda had already influenced and permeated the ranks of the Czechs, irrevo-cably in some cases.

Whatever they thought of the sell-out by Britain and France, many preferred to slip over the border into Poland with the help of that country's intelligence agents, who so smoothed the way that they were able to pass on into France, where they were welcomed and taken under the wing of the *Armée de l'Air*. There followed mixed fortunes, with many of the Czechs sent to the south and enrolled in the air component of the Foreign Legion, actually travelling across the Mediterranean clad in French uniforms and finally allowed near antiquated biplanes. Things further deteriorated when the unit was reorganised and returned to France, where further reshuffling and a complete lack of proper organ-isation led to month after month being wasted until at last, on 10 May 1940, the Czechs again found themselves under threat as the *Wehrmacht* launched its great offensive in the West.

What followed was the final eye-opener for these pilots, as they witnessed the most incredible scenes of chaos and dereliction among the supposed French forces around them. 'Most of the French personnel were openly defeatist', one Czech said later; most of their allies seemed only concerned with the fate of Paris – and, of course, their bellies. The Czechs had been well fed by the French, all meals naturally including copious amounts of wine, without which it seemed the native soldiers were unable to function. Would Paris be declared an open city? That was the chief question on all the French airmen's lips. They even agitated against fighting for their country at all. 'Let the Germans come! What is the point of getting killed? Why fight against the German workers? Hitler is the German Napoleon! Once the Germans see we don't want to fight them they will simply go home!' There was enough of this sentiment among the French forces at all levels to ensure the collapse; only here and there did units put up a fight, sometimes to the death. The Czechs were aghast, baffled and completely disillusioned. They found the French females much tougher in their attitudes to the invaders; at least they seemed to have the will that so many of their menfolk lacked. Which might explain why so many are alleged to have 'queued up' to get themselves a stalwart German warrior when Paris was occupied, out of disgust with the performance of their own menfolk; and why (again, it is alleged) one German divisional commander had all his troops removed from the French capital because he feared the women and other delights would corrupt them. 'A disorder of immeasurable magnitude struck France,' was how one Czech pilot described this catastrophe, 'but their servicemen couldn't see it. They seemed overjoyed when it was all finished!' In other words, and thinking of their own skins without regard for the shame and suffering to come, they accepted the German occupation.

Incidents happened in this final period that shamed the name of France, hitherto seen as one of the leading warrior nations, now fallen low. Rather than allow others of stouter heart to fight, saboteurs wrecked warplanes, some of these wretches communists who, following Hitler's alliance with Stalin in 1939, toed the party line until Moscow decreed in June 1941 that the West was its ally. In June 1940 the majority of the French air force crews simply gave up. When the *Luftwaffe* attacked the air base at Tours the French anti-aircraft gunners were absent, taking a meal off base; some had actually taken the day off, and of course there were no officers around to maintain discipline or ensure inspections. One Czech airman rushed to a deserted French flak post, manned a machine-gun and succeeded in setting a low-flying Heinkel ablaze so that it force-landed.

The Czechs were forced to flee by the advancing Germans, eventually boarding one of the last ships to leave Bordeaux under fire from enemy artillery. On reaching Falmouth in Cornwall they were very pleasantly surprised to be met by efficient organisation that worked calmly and smoothly. RAF personnel met them and took them to waiting trains where they were given tea by WVS volunteers. The refugees were further impressed to be absorbed into the RAF in short order, and provided with British uniforms and ranks. The junior officers and NCOs found themselves lumped together as aircraftmen second class, given RAF service numbers and sent to an aircrew assessment centre. Whatever their slight grumbles, they soon realised that though they were obliged to start their flying training from scratch again, it was the best way to assess their worth and absorb them into whichever role best suited them. How vastly different it all was to the endless inactivity and time-wasting in France. In due course, most of the Czechs passed out on the most modern aircraft and were posted to Czech fighter units flying Hurricanes and Spitfires.

All this took time, many months, for the British were most thorough in dealing with foreigners whose temperament did at times go beyond what passed for the norm in RAF circles. By this time the Battle of Britain had been fought and won, and some Czechs had fought and died. The main battles were yet to come as the RAF began invading enemy skies, and the Czechs were formed into a complete wing.

But all was not totally smooth among these Czech pilots, and no matter how well they had been received and trained by their hosts, it is sad to note there were a dissident few who most certainly had slipped into Britain without being screened by Intelligence. With the great influx of refugees from Nazi Germany which began in the 1930s, MI5 and others were hard put to maintain vigilance and prevent the intrusion of German spies and sympathisers into Britain. When this exodus became a flood in 1940, delays occurred as thousands queued at the ports to enter Britain, the British staffs obviously finding it very hard to check the bona fides of everyone. However, the Czech airmen had come by a different route and by all accounts had not faced interrogations or searching enquiries; the fact that they were a unit of servicemen made all the difference. Yet among them were a few of not quite the same mettle as their tougher comrades.

'I listened to some foolish talk during those early days at RAF Cosford, when a chap argued about the superiority of *Luftwaffe* aircraft above all others, about the inevitability of defeat', one Czech airman-historian has recorded. The man in question further tried to lower morale among his fellow pilots by criticising the Czech government-in-exile, and the alleged incompetence of their own officers. This kind of talk would have resulted in such a man in the RAF ranks being charged; worse were the small core of 'Sovietised' airmen who took every opportunity to spread propaganda of the communist kind. Again, such activities would never have been tolerated in the British forces. 'These people', the same Czech patriot observed, 'were dangerous to our morale with their insidious, subversive political preaching.' This caucus of communist influence was obviously doing all it could to follow the line ordered by the Comintern (Communist International), which until June 1941 stipulated by secret directive to all fellow-travellers around the world that Moscow was always right, which in 1940 meant subverting any who fought Hitler outside their own league.

But the incident which forms the climax of this tale may have had other causes; there is a lack of evidence surrounding it, and it is one more 'secret' the British would rather keep. That there were cowards and those only interested in the Soviet view among these Czechs is true, that they were a very small minority is also true, but whether their hosts were aware of them is doubtful. They were certainly not aware of one Czech pilot who is alleged to have been a *Gestapo* agent.

For on some date unspecified, but almost certainly in 1941, this pilot, named as Sergeant Augustin Preucil, stole a Hawker Hurricane Mk II fighter, flew across the North Sea and landed at the nearest available *Luftwaffe* base in Belgium, where his amazed captors soon greeted him effusively after learning to their satisfaction he was a genuine defector. Whether it was as simple as that remains unknown; one source speaks of Sergeant Preucil 'causing mayhem' in Belgium. In any event, the Germans are said to have rewarded him with a gift of 100,000 *Reichsmarks*. Obviously, both Czech Intelligence, who were very good, and the British should have got wind of the traitor. But their blunder was in their view avenged when, after the war, Preucil was caught, tried and hanged in Prague.

A Heavy and Far-reaching Defeat

There is no doubt that a time came in the 1940s when some in the Allied camp wished heartily that British and American missions had stayed clear of Japan in the previous century. The Japanese, following a period of conquest in China, withdrew back to their own country, which then entered into a long phase of isolation.

Europeans had learned of the island race on the far side of the world towards the end of the thirteenth century through the great explorer Marco Polo, and it was not too long afterwards that well-meaning Christian missionaries set off to try to convert the people they thought of as heathen, even though the Japanese already had their own religion, a form of Buddhism. Over some three hundred years around a quarter of a million Japanese citizens were made Christians. Nevertheless, in 1592 the warlord Hideyoshi left Japan to make war in Korea. But by 1638 these same feudal rulers decided to cleanse their land of devilish, foreign influence and all the Christians were slaughtered. The Japanese nation withdrew into isolation once more.

The new, tentative approach by Westerners in the nineteenth century met with more interest. Quick to learn and good organisers, the Japanese shot into the twentieth century with astonishing ease. Entrepreneurs and soldiers gazed out beyond their own islands, wondering what the outside world could offer them. It was not long before brand-new domestic industry had built a navy competent enough to defeat the Russian Czar's fleet, and when World War I came the 'new' Japan allied itself with its benefactors. From such a tiny homeland sprang a giant with all-embracing intentions, a modern industrialised economy fuelled by a new, dominating breed of warlords who seduced their youth with pseudo-religious mania of the bloodthirsty kind, moulding an army poised for fresh wars of conquest overseas. First Korea, then China were invaded (again), the aggressors clashing with the Soviets in Manchuria.

Ten years of war-making that involved the most ghastly atrocities in China fed increased tensions in the Far East, and above all warned the Western colonial powers and America of Japanese intentions. American economic embargoes designed to force Japan to cease its aggression led to negotiations in Washington, which came to nothing, suiting the warring faction in Japanese ruling circles who had long cast greedy, envious eyes on the rich colonies owned by some Western powers, most notably Great Britain. In these designs the Nazis lent a hand, for it was greatly to Hitler's advantage for Britain to weaken itself even further by sending more troops and materials to bolster its eastern Empire. In March 1941 the Japanese Foreign Minister, Matsuoka, was in Berlin to be lectured by Joachim von Ribbentrop on increasing pressure on Britain and attacking its possessions if necessary. Such action the Nazi government felt sure would draw off more British strength from the homeland and leave that nation too weak to carry out aggressive action against Germany, thus leaving Hitler's rear more secure when he attacked the Soviet Union. The Japanese needed little prodding. The great British base of Singapore would be of immense value once Japan launched a war of conquest across south-east Asia and the Pacific. Just as important, the economic prize of Malaya beckoned, most especially to the new Japan whose industry relied heavily on imports. Under British control and management, Malaya produced 38% of the world's rubber and 58% of its tin. Depriving the British Empire of such raw materials would harm it greatly.

There was another less obvious advantage whose implications went unrealised by many in Britain: the provision of a great object lesson in defeating the white masters in their eastern colonial empire. The coloured races would, through Japanese initiative, throw off the yoke and reap the rewards. The Japanese would invite these underdogs to join them in creating a grand 'Co-Prosperity Sphere' that would engulf south-east Asia and much of the scattered territories of the Pacific. The fact that the conquerors intended to exploit these lands even more ruthlessly than the existing colonialists was not, of course, mentioned. The Dutch in Java with its oilfields tried to carry on as usual, while the Vichy French administration in Indo-China also did its best to ignore belligerent noises emanating from Tokyo. Then, under pressure, the French permitted the Japanese to enter its territory in Indo-China to set up bases for the campaigns to come.

In London, MI6 kept a careful listening watch on the Japanese diplomats, though Prime Minister Churchill allowed his perceptions to be clouded when he wrote to his ally President Roosevelt, telling him he did not expect the Japanese to be unwise enough to attack both Britain and the United States, and especially the base at Singapore. But when the PM memoed the Chief of the Imperial General Staff, General Ismay, he commented on the folly of reinforcing Hong Kong island; he felt the whole British position in that area would become untenable in the event of an all-out Japanese attack. Indeed, Churchill took the realistic view that the Hong Kong garrison should be reduced to a symbolic strength. Later on, he was persuaded otherwise, allowing two Canadian battalions to be despatched, which resulted in their loss and much bitterness against the British later.

The flurry of Japanese diplomatic activity in London in February 1941 subsided, though the war of nerves continued as Japanese naval units manoeuvred around the seas of Siam and Indo-China. When the Japanese ambassador next called on Churchill the latter remarked that he trusted Japan had no intention of attacking Singapore. Churchill was somewhat won over by the Japanese diplomats' great charm, politeness and apparent reassurances, while in Japan itself the military were busy furthering their plans for assault.

In order to advance their plans for the conquest of Malaya the Japanese High Command set up a committee to study the problem of jungle warfare, and while this got to work a certain Major Terundo Kunitake was seconded to the ambassador in Singapore as a spy and proceeded to tour the whole Malayan peninsula, mapping and noting everything of use to an invading army. Among other things, Kunitake found that 250 bridges existed along the main highway from Singapore island to the border with Thailand, and since it seemed obvious the British would blow them up when an attack came he recommended the provision of an entire engineer regiment for every infantry division employed. Once adopted, his plan was put into effect by the training of such engineers on Formosa. Then, with French agreement, the Japanese Navy, Army and air groups set up an attack base in Saigon (later the South Vietnamese capital). Conferences between the Navy and Army were fogged by the former's objection that their warships would be at too much risk. Their own Admiral Ozawa, as Combined Force Commander, insisted that the landings in Malaya take place without any prior naval bombardment.

Meanwhile, a general to lead the attack was found, a man who would be tried for war crimes after Japan's defeat. Lt General Yamashita was appointed rather late in the day, on 5 November, perhaps because of opposition from his enemies, including the military politician the Americans came to hate most, a man who seemed to epitomise every-thing treacherous and barbaric in the Japanese character: Hideki Tojo, who had taken over after the fall of the less aggressive Konoye Cabinet. Tojo had good reason to distrust the man some Japanese generals saw as the most able; Yamashita belonged to the extremist 'Emperor Group' which had tried to seize power in 1932. On finally accepting Yamashita, Tojo insisted he be kept away from Tokyo.

Churchill became convinced through his talks with Japanese diplomats in London that they were sincere in their desire for peace with the British and Americans, and, as is now known, there were those conservative representatives among the Japanese of the same leanings. These men were, unfortunately, at the mercy of the aggressive military clique in Tokyo, though to some extent Churchill did not seem to realise this following his polite chats with Ambassador Shigemitsu, even following the signing of the Tripartite Pact in Berlin which the ambassador was forced to concede could bring his country into conflict with Britain and USA in certain circumstances.

The occasional talks in London were matched by foreign Minister Matsuoka's briefings and diatribes from Hitler and Ribbentrop in Berlin who recounted Nazi Germany's triumphs and impregnable position, and the rebuff delivered to Stalin when he demanded territorial concessions from Finland, Romania and the Baltic states. Hitler reminded Matsuoka that despite all Stalin's assurances his agents of the Comintern were still carrying on subversive propaganda across the world. In fact, the Soviets went ahead and occupied Latvia, Estonia and Lithuania, their secret police removing and liquidating the intelligentsia in the usual Soviet pattern. The three-power pact between Germany, Italy and Japan was designed to further unnerve Britain and America.

Matsuoka continued his tour by travelling to Moscow where, to the Germans' surprise, he signed another pact, a treaty of friendship with Stalin, while informing the Germans it would make no difference to the pact just signed in Berlin. Back in Tokyo, Matsuoka himself was surprised to find that despite the dominance of Tojo, Konoye and his conservatives were still determined to pursue a policy of conciliation towards America, which had offered to mediate in the Japan–China war providing the former withdrew its armies first. All these manoeuvrings were futile. The Japanese military were aghast at any further delays and their plans for attack went ahead.

Meanwhile, the British in Singapore, aware of the possibility of a Japanese attack since 1932, following the invasion of China, had made provisions only for defending the seaward side, preparing 'impregnable' fortifications including heavy guns that could conceivably ward off any seaborne attack force. Only much later did it dawn on the defending staff in Singapore, perhaps in the light of events, that such an assault might possibly come from the north. As the Japanese advanced into southern China this chance seemed increasingly likely. Further notions previously thought outlandish began to rear up again. What if the Japs attacked in the monsoon season, between November and March? Could they penetrate the 'impenetrable' jungles of Malaya? In his post-war memoirs Winston Churchill remarked how three coldly calculating empires made blunders disastrous to their ambitions and safety. Stalin chose to ignore warnings of the Nazi axe about to fall on him, while the Japanese missed their best chance of realising their dreams. Exactly what he meant by this is not clear, and one can only assume the 'third empire' referred to was Britain's. What is known about these crucial days is that Allied blunders, specifically Britain's, led to the resulting disaster in Malaya and the death and terrible suffering of many thousands of Allied servicemen and civilians.

Actually, Matsuoka had been far from convinced by the Nazi arguments, but found himself at odds with his government who, under the bullying of Tojo, decided to go ahead with its occupation of Indo-China, though allowing the French administration to remain. However, in trying to face both ways Japan put herself in a difficult position, on the one hand promising the Nazis she would 'fight Bolshevism in Asia' and on the other holding out the hand of friendship to the arch proponent of that creed. And Matsuoka was not the only objector in high office to Tojo's plans. Admiral Yamamoto also saw only disaster ahead if the attacks proceeded, but like Matsuoka he was overruled and, in the event, agreed to follow orders, becoming the architect of the attack on Pearl Harbor. Matsuoka resigned and vanished into obscurity.

Long before, in 1937, the British government had set up a committee headed by Major-General Dolbie to study the problem of defending Singapore, because the political decision to ignore the Japanese occupation of Thailand would allow them to push on into northern Malaya before suitable counter-measures could be taken. Obviously, the previous stance of looking on the defence of Singapore as a purely naval problem had been overturned; it was now seen as possible that the Japanese would invade from the north. The British response was half-hearted and amounted to political indecision and conflicting views among the military staffs, some officers viewing the Malayan peninsula as quite undefendable. A series of blundering compromises were made which sealed the fate of Fortress Singapore and the thousands of people in it. In truth, it was a familiar story, repeated since, of a government clinging to empire but unwilling to devote sufficient forces to defend it. Just one battalion and £60,000 were allocated to the problem, while propaganda was put about boasting of the impregnability of Britain's greatest Far Eastern bastion.

The Japanese, in the meantime, had done their homework well and were far better informed about Singapore's defences than the British public: the defences facing seaward were strong, but those facing inland toward Johore were weak. The RAF was equipped with no really modern warplanes, while the army that would face the Jap invaders consisted of five to six divisions, at best perhaps up to 80,000 men, of whom fewer than half were white soldiers. It would have been logical for the Japanese to have assembled a force of overwhelming strength; this would have been the military logic, allowing for up to one third losses. The XXVth Army comprised about 60,000 men, with divisional artillery, two regiments of heavy guns and the 3rd Tank Brigade equipped with light and medium tanks, many of them obsolete. Support for this force would be provided by 459 planes of an Army air group, a further 159 aircraft supplied by the Navy. At sea, Admiral Ozawa's Southern Squadron comprised one battlecruiser, ten destroyers and five submarines. When the invasion of Malaya finally took place the British public were told of hordes of little yellow men, many of them bespectacled, who were able to overwhelm the normally superior white soldiers with hugely greater numbers.

By 1941 the British had concluded the key to defence lay in air power; any attempt to land by sea would be shattered by the RAF, and the Navy and Army would simply mop up the remnants. To foster this illusion an Air Staff study recommended a force of 200 planes, to be built up to a strength of 566, or thirty-one squadrons. However, the air commander, Air Marshal Sir Robert Brooke-Popham, stated that the air defences should be made strong for all-round defence so that the Japanese would recognise the folly of such an adventure. As usual, compromise was the result. The chiefs of staff permitted a build-up of only 336 aircraft, and even that strength would not be reached until the end of 1941. Another infantry division would be sent from India, but even these paltry measures met with Churchill's disapproval, his estimation being that the situation in the Far East did not justify such reinforcements. In view of the Prime Minister's certain intelligence of Hitler's imminent invasion of Russia and the virtual impossibility therefore of any German landing in Britain, his attitude signalled a gross misunderstanding of reality. Despite the intervention of Rommel in Africa, there were troops to spare for the Far East. Reading Japanese diplomatic codes did nothing to alert the Prime Minister to the real situation in the Far East – until it was too late.

Despite Churchill's objections, an Indian division was sent to reinforce the 8th Australian Division in Singapore, not that this satisfied the commander of the 'fortress', who warned the War Office that a minimum of six divisions plus corps and ancillary units was needed. The Japanese had in fact overestimated the troops already available. But the British politicians continued to delude themselves with false hopes. When the Minister of Information, Mr Duff Cooper, arrived in Singapore in September he believed Japan was preparing for war with Russia, re-stating the old dream that with the monsoon season due in a few weeks no Japanese attack could be expected that winter. Throughout that autumn and into November the Allied garrison in Malaya remained too weak to repel a determined invasion, in fact by its commander's estimate short of two infantry divisions. Unhappily, this was not all. The troops' morale had never been high, undermined by the white plantation owners' refusal to allow the military to exercise across their fields and through the rubber tree groves. For years, the formations had carried out few or no manoeuvres, remaining in a static role, usually tied down to airfield and highway defence. The soldiers had no jungle training and never expected the Japs to advance overland. The life and attitudes of the dominant white class in Singapore and Malaya was wholly tuned to commercial interests and a very nice lifestyle. They had no time for the military, preferring to bury their heads in the sand when talk of Japanese attack erupted.

The seaborne segment of the Japanese invasion set sail on the morning of 4 December 1941. 'The moon like a tray was sinking in the western sea and the deep red sun showed its face to the east.' So wrote a Japanese colonel on one of the twenty ships of the invasion fleet bound for the east coast of Malaya. The die was cast and it seemed an inevitable fate awaited many on the peninsula as Japan entered its most despicable time of infamy, its soldiers about to commit yet more crimes of bestiality and slaughter. Not that the invaders' timetable went entirely like clockwork. Trouble was experienced in launching the troops' landing craft in rough seas, some commanders were hesitant, rivalries and even hatred existed at the top. Yet despite occasional rebuffs and difficulties of terrain, the invaders gradually outmanoeuvred and drove back the defenders. Amateurishness, incompetence and a breakdown of discipline in some units followed, and the troops began to lose all confidence in their officers, which was fatal. Adding to the commander's difficulties were the million civilians crowding onto Singapore island.

As Commander-in-Chief Far East, General Wavell noted with alarm during a visit to the battle zone on 20 January that the commander, General Percival, though having a plan to withdraw from the mainland onto Singapore island, had done nothing to implement it. The C-in-C signalled Churchill that once the mainland was lost Singapore itself would become untenable.

The battle went on. By 13 February the Allied troops were pinned into a twenty-eight-mile perimeter, with conditions deteriorating by the hour, chiefly through disorganisation and the increasing number of deserters who had gone into hiding in the city, emerging after dark to start looting for food and drink. One of the worst chapters in British military history was reaching its climax. Air raids had destroyed food supplies and cut the water mains, but General Percival viewed the situation as by no means hopeless; despite the great numbers of troops and civilians squeezing into the beleaguered city he urged resistance to continue, though signalling Wavell that holding out beyond a couple of days seemed doubtful. By return, Wavell ordered him to continue inflicting the maximum penalty on the enemy, by house-to-house fighting if necessary. This was impossible owing to the crowds of civilians in the streets.

Unrealised by the defenders, the Japanese were also in trouble. Casualties had been heavy and supplies were running out, the troops becoming exhausted. General Yamashita faced a deadline, estimating his army would become immobilised in three days owing to the breakdown of his supply system. But Yamashita was tough and forced his men to continue attacking, even down to the last bullet, in an attempt to bluff his opponents.

It worked. On the morning of 15 February a Japanese outpost on the 28 Division front saw a white flag among the trees before them; another flew from the city radio building. An officer of the 25 Army Staff met a British staff car and surrender terms were discussed. 'I prepared myself against being deceived', General Yamashita said later, ordering General Percival to meet him in person. When the British commander came, accompanied by two more officers and Major Wild to act as interpreter, Yamashita presented him with a surrender document, insisting it be agreed and signed without argument. General Percival read half of it before requesting twenty-four hours' grace to consider the situation. These proceedings were filmed by the Japanese, General Yamashita showing irritation as he informed Percival that if the document was not signed at once his troops would recommence fighting.

'Do you surrender unconditionally or not?'

Major Wild had not taken part in the proceedings. A Japanese interpreter conveyed the exchanges as both generals sought to gain the advantage, Yamashita thumping the table with impatience until the British commander meekly answered 'Yes', whereupon his Japanese opposite told him hostilities would cease at 10 p.m. their time. General Percival then requested time in which to pass on the news to all those in Singapore, Yamashita giving him until the following morning, in addition 'guaranteeing' the lives of the Australian troops and the many civilians, saying: 'Yes, you may be sure about that, I can guarantee them absolutely.' General Percival signed the surrender document at 6.10 p.m. It would soon become apparent just how much the Japanese general's 'guarantee' was worth.

So ended one of the most badly fought and disastrous campaigns in British history. The seventy-three-day battle had cost the Commonwealth forces 9,000 soldiers killed and wounded; their attackers suffered 9,824 (3,000 killed). Among those Allied troops ordered to lay down their arms were many who, had they known what lay in store at the hands of the enemy, would have chosen to go down fighting. Most of the men were amazed when the terrible news reached them. Whatever the shortages, their ammunition had not run out and they were in a position to hold off the Japanese, who, as related, were in dire straits themselves. As to the actual number of combatants who fell into Japanese hands, the figure seems to vary from source to source. It has long been common to quote 80,000 Allied soldiers being taken prisoner, otherwise 60,000 or 130,000 all told (including Chinese). Certainly it was the biggest British surrender ever.

Much of the blame for this disaster was heaped on General Percival, perhaps rightly – he was simply not up to such a task. But at that time it

The British group goes to parley with the Japanese (a); within twenty-four hours scenes like these depicted the catastrophe for British arms in the Far East (b)

a

b

would have been hard to find a British general ruthless enough to tackle the job. The politicians in Whitehall, dominated by Winston Churchill, were equally if not more to blame. It was their vacillation and parsimony which led to the enormous suffering meted out to the prisoners taken by the Japanese in Singapore. The enemy soldiers were soon at work killing the wounded in hospital and raping nurses and other females; thousands would die through neglect and ill treatment. General Percival himself survived three years of Japanese captivity, his captor General Yamashita going on to the Phillipine islands, to be taken prisoner in 1945 by the Americans and tried as a war criminal in February 1946. Just before his execution he wrote: 'I believe I have done my duty to the best of my ability throughout the whole war. Now, at the time of my death and before God, I have nothing to be ashamed of.'

In Britain this disaster, coming as it did after a year of terrible news, seemed to signal even further incompetence as part of our lot in war. The newspapers had announced the Japanese invasion of Malaya on 8 December, the enemy advance leading to the blowing-up of the Johore causeway, the siege of Singapore starting on 31 January. By 11 February the enemy were fighting in the city suburbs, the 'outnumbered' defenders 'fighting magnificently' and 'counter-attacking successfully'. As late as 14 February the Allies still held the two reservoirs, though later accounts blamed the rupture of water mains as the reason for the surrender the next day.

The fall of Singapore was serious in another respect: its docks were the only ones capable of taking a battleship between Durban in South Africa and Pearl Harbor in the Pacific. Some Allied commentators asserted that the enemy could never make real use of the base owing to Allied control of the seas around it and Java, assertions soon proved wrong. In announcing the loss of the £30 million base (a vast sum in those days), Winston Churchill referred to it as 'a heavy and far-reaching military defeat'.

And no historian can ignore mention of the other dire consequence which resulted from the British government's bungled approach to the defence of its Far Eastern empire: the sinking of the battleships *Repulse* and *Prince of Wales*. These two capital ships had been despatched to the Far East in perhaps the vague hope of deterring the Japanese from going through with their aggressive plans. Though old, the *Repulse* still packed a very powerful punch and could have made mincemeat of any Japanese troop transports encountered. The *Prince of Wales* was Britain's latest battleship to enter service and had already been in abortive action against the mighty German *Bismarck*. When the battlecruiser transported Winston Churchill to meet President Roosevelt it still bore scars from that encounter.

Having arrived in Singapore early in December 1941, the two warships

 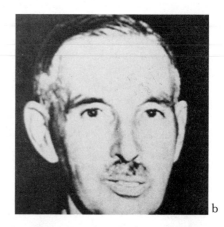

General Yamashita, conqueror of Singapore (a); General Percival (b) surrendered
'through lack of water'. Admiral Tom Phillips (c) and Captain Tennant (d)
lost their capital ships to Japanese air power.

were quickly sent to try to intercept Japanese troop convoys off the east
coast of Malaya and Siam, Admiral Phillips and Captain Tennant well
aware of the risk they were running by sailing without air cover, which
was not possible since the Admiralty had failed to provide an aircraft
carrier for the zone. Once the puny RAF force lost its three bases in
northern Malaya and many of its planes, it could not help. It seems the
lessons learned off Crete in the Mediterranean earlier in the year did not
deter the naval staff from taking this gamble.

Hopes that the two battleships and their three destroyers acting as
escort had escaped Japanese air reconnaissance seemed justified as the
small fleet encountered low cloud and rain squalls during 9 December.
No Japanese surface ships were encountered, but when the weather

a

b

A last picture of *Prince of Wales* after arrival in Singapore harbour (a).
An aerial view of the battlecruiser *Repulse* (b).

cleared the next day the British ships were at once located by enemy spy planes as the fleet turned back for Singapore. Both high-level and torpedo bombers arrived to begin a series of attacks, the bombs coming close but doing no damage; the torpedo bombers, however, scored several hits and both ships suffered serious damage. The *Repulse* sank before 12.30 p.m., while the *Prince of Wales* wallowed around, its rudders gone and three of its four screws out of action. Soon after it was struck again, capsized and sank, the destroyer *Express* backing off hurriedly, its decks packed with survivors. The other two destroyers, *Electra* and *Vampire*, were busy

105

picking up men from *Repulse*. In all, some 2,000 men were rescued of the 3,000 aboard both ships; Admiral Phillips was not among them. Perhaps surprisingly, the enemy did nothing to hamper the rescue work. Indeed, one report alleges a Japanese plane dropped a wreath over the ships' grave.

As an aside, and to illustrate what kind of people many of the British colonials were in Singapore, the experience of one of the survivors from *Prince of Wales* is of interest. Though suffering from bomb shock and really unfit, Sub-Lieutenant Alan Franklin was sent off with more survivors to try to effect the evacuation of civilians from the island of Penang off north-west Malaya. The small steamers used as ferries were now without their native crews, who had fled before the advancing Japanese forces. The British sailors took charge, but at Penang found white women waiting with mountains of baggage. One woman protested volubly when told to get aboard without much of her luggage – otherwise (Franklin told her) the steamer would leave without her.

'What right have you to talk to me like that?' the woman yelled. 'Who are you, any way, and what are you really doing? You are just one of those army and navy men who have let us people out here down! I want your name! I shall report you when I get to Singapore!'

Franklin's mild response was to tell her that if she didn't get a move on she would find herself reporting to a Japanese general, adding that it would be inadvisable to address *him* as 'boy'.

Another of the evacuees said, 'Boy! Take my luggage! What are you standing there for? I'm not accustomed to carrying my own luggage!'

When the group finally arrived back in the doomed city of Singapore it was not long before Sub-Lieutenant Franklin collapsed – in the CO's office. After stays at various hospitals he served on the destroyer *Jupiter* just before it was lost. He finally arrived back in Britain on May Day 1942.

A Practically Virgin Copy

Of the many warplanes that flew in World War II, the Supermarine Spitfire proved the most enduring, capable of development through twenty-four marks and still in service not only in Britain but overseas well after the war. No British aircraft became more popular with its pilots – those who were transferred to non-Spitfire units bemoaned their fate. From its first introduction to front-line squadrons in 1939 it showed itself capable of meeting and very often beating the best the enemy could throw at it, the proviso for success, of course, depending too on the quality of its pilot. This entailed experience, and this had to be bought at cost, the hard way.

By early 1941 the technicians had mastered armament problems that would enable the fighter to deliver a greater weight of fire, for it had been found that this was the key to success in air combat. Too many German planes had escaped in the Battle of Britain riddled with .303in bullet holes, none having struck vital parts. It was different with explosive cannon shells, just one of which could cripple a warplane. In the swift free-for-all of air combat a very few seconds were often all a fighter pilot had in which to line up and fire his guns; the weight of shellfire delivered in that brief encounter could spell the difference between success and failure, even life or death. The *Luftwaffe* had already armed its fighters with shell guns; the RAF were slower to adopt the 20mm cannon, and though a few Spitfires were so fitted during the Battle, teething troubles ensured their failure.

But when spring turned to summer in 1941 and the battle was won, RAF Fighter Command took to 'sweeping' the Channel and making incursions into enemy-held airspace, the intention to finally wrest the in-itiative from the enemy and enable bombers to strike in daylight at the many targets along the continental coast. Naturally, these aerial parades were also designed to draw the enemy fighter units into combat, and if possible wear them down. It became common for Spitfire squadrons to range along the French coast and encounter no enemy at all, for the *Luftwaffe* commanders were well aware of RAF strategy and only sent their own units into action when it suited them. The air battles that resulted were usually of the briefest kind; 'dogfights' on the lines of the earlier war rarely occurred. Sometimes the enemy managed to gain the all-important height advantage and bounced the RAF formations. The Germans' tactics never varied: one fast pass with guns blazing and the combat was over. The Messerschmitts dived hard for lower levels and usually vanished from sight, sometimes leaving smoke or flame trails behind them as RAF machines went down; if lucky, the pilots were left suspended in their parachute harness to fall in the sea or on land, often becoming POWs. Others simply vanished into the sea. The German pilots never saw themselves as inferior in any way, but knew that to stay alive they had to be quicker than quick off the mark, or the Spits would catch them. For the RAF boys the problem always was to catch the enemy, to fasten on his tail just long enough to get in one good squirt of fire before he vanished from view. These were not the days of 'ace-making'; victories were slow in coming. Despite this, with much of the *Luftwaffe* transferred East, the British commanders were able to gain a kind of ascendancy over their opponent.

But in the late summer of 1941 the position changed completely. During July and August RAF pilots began reporting brief appearances of a new kind of enemy fighter, quite different and easily distinguishable from the well-known Messerschmitt 109, now in its F mark. The new plane had a radial engine and a blunt nose, and appeared to be very fast, manoeuvrable and well armed. These early sightings were put down by some intelligence officers as French-bought, American-built Curtiss Hawk 75s. In any case, the type had not appeared in any numbers, and events continued much as before until more reports came from Polish pilots and in such a manner that it soon became clear the new enemy fighter, far from being inferior old Curtisses, were in fact a radical new type of *Luftwaffe* interceptor that outclassed the Spitfire Vs then in general use by the invading RAF squadrons. Before long, interrogation of RAF pilots enabled commanders and indeed the staffs in London to ascertain more about the German plane. It was appreciably faster than the Spit, able to break off combat at will, and once it did this there was no way the Spitfire could catch it. It was indeed for combat purposes as man-oeuvrable as the Spitfire, which had always been able to out-turn the Messerschmitt; worse, it carried an armament of cannon and machine-guns. At last the Spitfire had been outmatched, and in the hands of the various *Experten* still resident with the *Luftwaffe Jagdgeschwadern* in the West the new fighter soon turned the tables on the RAF.

As a result, and inevitably, the morale of not only the British but other Allied fighter pilots crossing the Channel suffered as they learned of the superior enemy equipment facing them. The RAF commanders were forced to try to formulate new tactics that would enable their pilots to survive, for there was no question of giving up the cross-Channel offensive – the 'circuses' and 'rhubarbs' would go on. For the RAF fighters, and the light bomber and fighter-bomber crews, it would entail an increasing toll, from German fighters and the deadly flak. For the escort fighters – the Spitfire Vs – the dominance of the enemy would continue for well nigh a whole year.

The Focke-Wulf 190, designed by Kurt Tank, had suffered teething problems such as were common to most warplane designs, in this case engine fires and inadequate armament. The first examples were evaluated at Le Bourgot in northern France. The first *Luftwaffe* unit chosen to convert from their Messerschmitts was the 6th *Staffel* of JG26 at Marsiele in Belgium in July 1941, though the first combat against the RAF was not recorded until 1 September when four 190 A1s of 6/II *Gruppe* of JG26 encountered a number of Spitfire Vs over Dunkirk, bouncing them and destroying three without loss. Since the RAF aircraft had been caught in an ambush they put it down to ill luck that enabled the inferior 'Curtiss Hawks' to catch them napping. Not that the Focke-Wulf's superiority would enable it to escape scot-free every time. On 18 September Group Commander Walther Adolf (twenty-nine victories) was lost while attacking Blenheims off Ostend. Even so, the Spitfire's ascendancy over the Messerschmitt had been reversed by the appearance of the Focke-Wulf (though some pilots discovered the Spitfire V equal to the Focke-Wulf at low level, when both types clocked only 322 mph).

Urgent conferences took place between the RAF fighter chiefs and the Rolls-Royce company, both realising that drastic action through engine modification was needed if the Spitfire was to carry on the fight against the *Luftwaffe* on anything like equal terms. It would suit the British very nicely if they could inspect one of the enemy's new machines; to fly it and assess its real capabilities and secrets would enable appropriate counter-measures to be set in train. A notion that one might be stolen by commandos or other raiders proved a pipedream, and as the type began appearing in increasing numbers the British had to swallow the fact of *Luftwaffe* fighter supremacy over the Channel.

Kurt Tank's design was in fact ingenious. The aircraft's powerful, growling BMW radial engine was extremely closely cowled, the cockpit set well down into the fuselage with all-round vision provided by a one-piece hood. Its well-spaced undercart gave it excellent ground-handling qualities, something especially important on rough satellite airfields when ground manoeuvring became more difficult. By 1942 its armament was set at four 20mm cannon and two fast-firing MG151 machine-guns, a combination providing a very heavy punch. The Focke-Wulf fighter proved much more amenable to development than the Messerschmitt 109 in the fighter-bomber mode, while its later 2,000hp engine with supercharger provided short bursts of power enabling it to escape Spitfires at will at high and medium levels. One aviation historian has referred to the type as a 'fighter pilot's dream'. Designed from the outset for large-scale production, the FW 190 was soon being contracted out to other German aircraft firms.

But on 23 June 1942, a perfect, almost virgin copy of this 'dream fighter' fell into the hands of the British. Returning from a bomber escort mission, a Czech squadron of Spitfire Vs was ambushed by Focke-Wulfs of JG2 over Torbay, the Czech wing leader being killed at once when his plane collided with one of the enemy fighters. The *Luftwaffe* had cunningly sent its premier fighters to catch the Spits as they returned home short of fuel. Wing Commander Vasatko's Spitfire cut into the German plane's tail which pitched forward, its propeller slicing into the Czech airman's cockpit. The German pilot escaped by parachute but Vasatko never got out. A confused combat took place as more Spits of 19 Squadron arrived on the scene; they shot down another FW, but lost one of their own. More Czechs of 310 Squadron scrambled to help as one more of their comrades ran out of fuel to make a rough landing at Bolt Head satellite field.

One of the Czech pilots of 310 Squadron was Franta Trejtnar. He took up orbit over Exeter, as did others to protect the landing ground there from attack. Hardly had he received an order to land than he spotted 'the yellow belly of a FW 190' directly above him. In combat with this German pilot the Czech gradually forced his enemy further north-west, but was then struck; his Spitfire caught alight and he baled out with a broken arm. The victorious German pilot was now in trouble, seriously short of fuel and cut off by the many Spitfires milling about in the sky above.

'A practically virgin copy': Arnim Faber's FW190 fighter on the ground
at RAF Pembrey, Wales.

What happened next has been the subject of passing reference, sometimes mistaken, in many an aviation journal since. In one case an eminent
writer simply referred to the German pilot as a deserter, which was hardly
the case, though some may see it that way. The facts, plus details not
apparently published in the kind of magazine mentioned, were even
more unusual.

It seems to be true that *Oberleutnant* Arnim Faber did perform a couple
of 'victory rolls', but then swooped down to make a perfect touchdown
at RAF Pembrey, just inside the Welsh border. As his fighter rolled across
the grass he must have been aware he was not back in France; stories that
Faber was disorientated are not borne out by what is alleged to have
occurred next. He taxied his machine towards a petrol bowser parked
near the control tower where, despite the then close proximity of what
was clearly a German fighter complete with red nose, rudder and a
fighting cock on its cowling – not forgetting the usual black–white crosses
and swastika markings – Faber was 'offered' refuelling facilities by what
must have been a half-asleep ground crew. The RAF lads were said to
have remarked, 'Funny-looking kite you've got! And what kind of oil do
you Norwegians use in the engine?' To which the German pilot is said to
have replied, in perfect English, 'Good evening. I think we'd better leave
the refuelling until later. By the way, I'm not Norwegian.' The duty officer
in the control tower was a little more alert and, astounded as he was,
grabbed a pistol and ran outside to arrest the *Oberleutnant.*

Is it conceivable that Arnim Faber's blunder, if it can be termed that way, might even had led to an even greater one by the RAF ground crew? Fortunate it was that the ATC officer had the presence of mind to act swiftly, for his action enabled the British to capture a very valuable prize which was soon rushed off to Farnborough for test evaluation before being featured in aviation periodicals then and ever since. The Focke-Wulf 190 proved superior in all respects from 1,000 to 25,000ft, with the exception of the turning circle and at the lowest levels, where the 190 did seem at times to fail to pull away from the British fighter of the day. The Air Ministry could only make certain recommendations to its fighter pilots facing the Focke-Wulf until such time as better equipment arrived to strike a balance.

Already under continuous development, the Spitfire was boosted greatly by the arrival of the Rolls-Royce Merlin 61 as fitted into the Mk 9 model, which did indeed bring the two opposing fighters into near perfect equality (as in other spheres of combat, much always depended on the user of the equipment).

It would be nice to record that this particular Focke-Wulf was preserved and is available for inspection in one of the museums in Britain, where at last much effort has gone into refurbishing and presenting such historic machines. However, Arnim Faber's fighter plane made its last flight as RAF aircraft No. MP499 on 29 January 1943, piloted by Flight Lieutenant Robertson of the AFDU (Air Fighting Development Unit), Duxford, Cambridgeshire, now home to many fine war exhibits. By 18 September it was no longer on charge; its airframe was used for firing trials and the BMW engine for bench tests.

During 1943, the *Luftwaffe* attempted to augment its 'tip-and-run' reprisal raids using fast *Schnellkampfflugzeuge*, i.e. Focke-Wulf 190 fighter-bombers, in night attacks. But the pilots were not well trained in night navigation, and errors costly to them occurred.

During the night of 16/17 April, reports of enemy activity resulted in RAF night fighters taking off on patrol; one of these was a Beaufighter of 29 Squadron based at West Malling. Later, the men manning a search-light battery in Kent heard an aircraft, assumed it was the returning Beau, and directed one of their beams vertically into the sky as a beacon. Then, in the usual manner, as the plane circled, the beam was dropped to point the way to the base at West Malling, the plane flying off in that direction.

As soon as the duty officer at the airfield heard the single-engined aircraft arrive he thought it must be a Defiant night fighter in trouble, even though the type was by then out of use. He had the airfield beacon and runway lights switched on. The aircraft touched down and taxied to the watch office at the control tower. Men on duty in a fire tender then saw the pilot climb out, but when one of the Britishers went forward he realised the airman was calling in German and rushed back to get a rifle. An astonished *Feldwebel* Otto Bechtold was taken prisoner.

Minutes later, a second aircraft was directed to West Malling by the same searchlight beacon, this too landing on the grass runway to be met by a thoroughly alert crew of a Beaverette gun platform vehicle. But the pilot of this plane, another FW 190, realised his mistake and attempted to take off again. The British gunner opened fire and the German fighter burst into flames, the pilot leaping out to struggle with the British, who tried to catch him. Breaking free, the German rushed off, only to cannon into the RAF station commander, who happened to be Wing Commander Peter Townsend. *Leutnant* Fritz Setzler surrendered.

The eventful night was far from over. A third aircraft appeared overhead, and, with the airfield defenders of RAF Regiment and Army personnel now alerted that no friendly planes were about, they opened fire. Despite this, the Focke-Wulf attempted to land at West Malling, the pilot undershooting the field to crash on a farm. *Oberfeldwebel* Otto Schultz escaped with cuts and bruises and was given tea by a local. The same navigational problems also beset *Oberleutnant* Kurt Klahn, who abandoned his FW at low level, his parachute failing to open in time to prevent his death at Staplehurst.

And the *Luftwaffe* failed to learn from this disastrous night, continuing to use single-engined fighters on fruitless night attacks. During the night of 19/20 May, *Unteroffizier* Ehrhardt was taken POW after landing in error at Manston.

The intact Focke-Wulfs were eventually taken over by the RAF's Enemy Aircraft Flight.

Junkers Galore

Both sides were able to acquire examples of each other's aircraft types in World War II, and in a number of cases these were either in flyable condition or made so. While the RAF was able to build its Enemy Aircraft Flight, the *Luftwaffe* too made up a collection of Allied planes which, as in England by the RAF, were used for various purposes. It has to be admitted that the enemy were (as far as is known) more audacious, since before the war ended the *Luftwaffe* had used captured types to fly over England in Allied markings to reconnoitre and photograph air bases.

For the RAF, the capture of Junkers 88s in almost pristine condition proved valuable as the type was the best all-round aircraft produced by the Germans. As early as 28 July 1940 a Junkers 88 crew lost their way due to the failure of the plane's direction-finding equipment, the bomber coming down in a clover field at Buckholt Farm, just north of Bexhill-on-Sea in Sussex. By 31 August the almost intact aircraft had been taken

to Farnborough for a thorough evaluation. The Junkers suffered an ig-
nominious end by being taken apart for spares at RAF Duxford in 1942.

On 19 September, a Junkers 88A1 was captured after landing intact at
RAF Oakington in Cambridgeshire. This was no blunder. The crew chief
Leutnant Knab, as captain, must have reckoned their chances of survival
slim, his two sergeants and corporal perhaps in agreement with him.
They had taken off from Caen airfield in France at 14.00 hrs and were
ordered to carry out a reconnaissance photo mission, but having done
the job the Junkers's port engine developed trouble and RAF fighters
appeared in the vicinity. Instead of zooming down to low level and
heading out to sea, the pilot put down on the nearest RAF field, which
happened to be the bomber base at Oakington. For some reason the
wheels were not lowered, so the bomber suffered some damage as it
touched down on its belly. The crew were taken prisoner and despatched
for interrogation at the 'London Cage', Cockfosters. Only eleven days
later yet another Junkers 88 crash-landed at Gatwick racecourse in
Sussex, one of its sergeant crew killed in the process.

After later models of the same type had entered service, an A5 model
took off from Lanveoc in France at 23.30 hrs to bomb Birkenhead. The
crew flew via the Scilly Isles and up the Irish Sea to the target, and after
bombing the pilot turned south to return by the same route. But at some
stage he misread an RAF beacon for a German one, became disorientated and, believing he was over France, landed at an incomplete RAF
field at Broadfield Down, near Bristol. The bomber was subsequently
used in tactical trials until one day it was involved in mock combat with
a Beaufighter. The British plane stalled at low level and crashed into deep
mud; neither plane nor crew were recovered. The Junkers ended its days
in storage.

Two more Junkers 88s were captured, one following crew bungling.
On 16 November a Junkers crew had been out hunting British shipping
over the north Atlantic. Failing to spot anything, they touched down at
RAF Chivenor before realising their mistake and trying to take off again.
A burst of tommy-gun fire around the cockpit dissuaded them, one
crewman being wounded. This was the 88 that appeared in the famous
Noel Coward film *In Which We Serve*. Another Junkers 88 had appeared
in an earlier war epic.

These captures, valuable though they were, pale into insignificance
when compared to the Junkers 88s taken over in 1943 and 1944, the
second a blunder of the greatest magnitude by its pilot, Sergeant Maeckle
of the 7th *Staffel* of Night Fighter Group 2 based at Volkel in Holland.

By that time (July 1944), the 'radio war' between the *Luftwaffe* and RAF
had been in progress for years, with first one side then the other gaining
technical advantage. In the winter of 1940–41 the German bomber force
in north-west Europe held the ace card with its *Knickebein* radio beam
system. Such a system had already been in use by some American

airlines. The *Luftwaffe* Pathfinder Group 100 perfected it sufficiently to use it to great effect in the blitz on British towns and cities. Despite some success in 'bending' the beams with radio interference, by and large the *Luftwaffe* was able to carry out heavy raids on every target chosen. Not until 1942 did RAF Bomber Command begin receiving electronic equipment of its own which enabled it at last to begin much more effective raids on Germany. German counter-measures included fitting their night fighters with successively more effective radar detection devices. It was a constant battle of attack and defence, the pendulum of advantage swinging first this way and then that. By the spring of 1943 the initiative in night fighter defence had been wrested by the German scientist-engineers who had designed equipment able to latch on to the British bombers' own radar transmissions.

During the afternoon of 9 May 1943 one of the very latest *Luftwaffe* night fighters flew over the North Sea on a test patrol, a Junkers 88R1 coded D5+EV of the 10th *Staffel Nachtjagdgruppe 3*. But instead of curving back at the limit of its patrol area and returning to its base at Kristiansund in Norway, the Junkers flew on westwards, finally making landfall north of Aberdeen, by which time it had been met by Spitfires. The German pilot took no evasive action whatsoever and not one attack pass was made by the Spitfires as the German aircraft descended to make a perfect landing at RAF Dyce, a small airfield fifteen miles north-west of Aberdeen. Within twenty-four hours the Junkers had been flown off for secret testing of its latest enemy radar interception capabilities, using a Halifax bomber in mock combat. The results shocked the British (its FuG 202 Lichtenstein radar was found to be superior to its British equivalent), and immediate counter-measures by way of modification and fresh instruction went out to all Bomber Command bases. In other words, the pendulum swung back again in favour of the attackers.

Naturally, this gift of a German night fighter remained a secret, but the arrival of the Junkers 88R1 restored British fortunes in the night air war over Germany. The plane was eventually handed over to the Enemy Aircraft Flight and, unlike many other captured machines, survived intact into peacetime. Indeed, the aircraft, shorn of its long nose radar antennae (which now resembled stub-nosed cannon or machine-guns), was one of those exhibited annually on Battle of Britain Day during the Horse Guards parade in London. The aircraft is now on display in the Battle of Britain Museum at Hendon.

Many years later, in 1974, the popular West German periodical *Bild am Sonntag* published an amazing account purporting to be the truth concerning the loss of this Junkers to the RAF. It was a tale almost surpassing fiction, of the British Secret Service subverting the German aircrew into defecting with their secret night fighter to Britain, the feature quoting the aircraft's manufacturing number as 360043. The pilot was *Oberleutnant* Heinrich Schmitt, son of the one-time secretary to the

The German crew of this still extant Ju88 are said to have defected. The two views show it complete with radar probes and insignia of the *Luftwaffe*'s night fighter arm, then later in RAF charge.

earlier German Minister for Foreign Affairs in pre-Hitler days, Gustav Stresemann. Schmitt Jr was said to have been working for the British since 1940, regularly supplying them with secrets which were sent from his family home in Thuringen via relay contacts in Switzerland and Portugal. Furthermore, the magazine reported, Schmitt and his crew (Sergeants Paul Rosenberger and Erich Kantwill) had actually flown to England in a Dornier 217 during the night of 20/21 May 1941, landing by prior arrangement at an RAF field in Lincolnshire. The Dornier was taxied only briefly across the airfield. A British officer was thrown a package by the German crew, who took off again at once to fly back to their base on the continent.

Then, so the magazine alleged, the same crew under Schmitt defected quite cunningly in their night fighter. At 16.40 hrs on Saturday, 9 May 1943 the radar and radio control staff of 100 Night Fighter Group at Grove in Denmark picked up a distress call from a Junkers 88C6/R1 (D5+EV) of the 3rd Night Fighter Wing which had taken off from Aalborg, also in Denmark, on a special mission to intercept one of the Mosquito courier flights en route to Sweden. The German crew reported an engine fire; this signal was followed by news they were abandoning their machine. The crew then released their rubber dinghies into the sea, but flew on towards England. The German controller at 100 Group, Lt Colonel von der Pongartz, alerted the rescue services, which soon set off across the North Sea, heading for Quadrant 88/41. When a search plane arrived at the spot it found three empty dinghies and called for a small rescue craft to search the area.

Just after 18.00 hrs two Spitfires of 165 (Ceylon) Squadron were on patrol between Peterhead and Aberdeen when they sighted a German plane, which had already been reported by ground radar posts. Flt Lt Roscoe with Sergeant Scaman gave chase; some five miles off the Scottish coast the Junkers changed course, heading south. The German aircraft was one mile inland when the Spits went in to attack, the two British pilots amazed to see the Germans lower their undercart in surrender and begin shooting off red flares from their cabin. Roscoe then ordered Scaman to take up position behind the Junkers, while he flew alongside to signal the German pilot to follow him in to land at RAF Dyce.

The success of this defection was apparently signalled to listening Germans via the British secret transmitter operating under the call-sign Gustav Siegfried Eins, the key phrase 'May has come' meaning all had gone well. (The British ran several radio stations for German benefit, one addressed to U-boat crews (*Atlantik*), another especially for the *Luftwaffe* over *Soldatensender* Calais.) It is also alleged that none of the RAF staff at Dyce had any idea that the German aircrew of this plane had defected by arrangement with MI6. If the Spitfire pilot's account is true, Schmitt and his two friends came within an ace of being shot down.

If the Junkers 88 crew really defected they certainly proved a worthy

116

investment, allegedly going so far as helping the RAF in the night counter-measures radio war, broadcasting fake messages over the *Luftwaffe* ground controllers' wavelength to confuse their former comrades in the air. But the capture of another Junkers night fighter came by the German crews' blunder, rather than by arrangement.

The radio location contest had again swung in the Germans' favour when, at about 04.30 hrs, the duty crews at RAF Woodbridge in Suffolk heard the sound of aero engines coming from the North Sea coast, some ten miles away. It was misty, and though the personnel on the ground could hear the aircraft as it circled the field they had trouble identifying it and no radio calls were received. Wing Commander Raymond assumed it was a Mosquito trying to land after a night over Germany, so he fired off a green flare, which was the signal permitting the pilot to land. This the plane did, coming in at once and rolling along through the banks of mist. 'Then I heard the engines stop as they were switched off,' Raymond related later, 'so I drove towards the machine in the big vehicle we used to fetch crews.' All the RAF officer could see was a dark silhouette in the fog, but was then perplexed by the sight of three crewmen emerging out of the mist – if the plane was a Mosquito, there should only have been two. 'I drove nearer, and there were three German airmen standing before me, no less surprised than I was. I drew my pistol and they surrendered without resistance.'

Raymond had the Germans walk to the control tower while he cruised along behind in his truck. The Junkers proved to be a G model carrying the very latest night interception equipment; the FuG 220 SN-2 and 227 Flensburg radar sets were operating successfully against RAF night bombers. Two days later it was flown off by Wing Commander Roly Falk to RAF Hatfield for testing, where it was found that the German equipment could home in on the RAF's Monica tail warning system. Bomber Harris cancelled all further use of this device until further notice, some RAF crews ignoring the order. The Junkers crew had only just completed 100 hours' training and had flown the wrong compass course.

'Are you afraid?'

Well before the Normandy invasion in June 1944, the Hawker Typhoon had been rescued from near failure to become the most potent ground attack aircraft in use anywhere. For once, at least, the propaganda claim that its salvo of rockets was equivalent to a cruiser's broadside was the truth.

Originally conceived as a fighter to replace the obsolete Hurricane which had served so splendidly in the Battle of Britain, the Hawker design team had again provided a machine fitted with very strong wings, massive in fact, to carry a heavy armament of four 20mm cannon. It can be assumed these extra-thick wings helped considerably to limit its high-level performance; this poor showing fell so short of expectations that both manufacturers and the Air Ministry saw little or no future for the type. The RAF would be forced to rely on the Spitfire as its chief and probably only fighter weapon. Another serious snag had emerged, however, and this was the problems encountered with the new Napier Sabre engine, a massive twenty-four-cylinder job that invariably exasperated ground crews with its reluctance to ignite. Use of a Coffman starter cartridge system all too often failed, and this would prove embarrassing in a 'scramble' situation.

Yet faith in the beast and its troubled 2,000hp motor was not entirely lost; test pilots had reported very favourably on its great speed and performance at lower altitudes. One operational pilot, Roland Beamont, felt constrained to prevail on his superiors: give him just one squadron of Typhoons as an experiment and he would prove its worth. And so the type entered limited service, taking part in the disastrous Dieppe raid which provoked a lively *Luftwaffe* reaction. It is said that during the air combats over the Channel some Typhoons fell into the sea, minus their tail structures. This proved to be another, potentially disastrous fault which was never fully cured. Weakness in the rearmost fuselage resulted in the complete tail assembly breaking off under certain high-stress circumstances. The fitting of external strengthening plates partly cured the problem, but not before a number of pilots were killed.

The Typhoon enthusiasts went into action in the low-level assault role, beating up German airfields, shipping and other installations with cannon fire, bombs and then rockets. They proved deadly. And when the *Luftwaffe* 'hit-and-run' raiders made their very brief sorties against south coast towns the Typhoons were on standby, ready and able to scramble and catch the attackers before they could escape across the sea. The Typhoon proved faster than the speedy Focke-Wulf 190.

But it was in the ground attack role that the Hawker machine proved invaluable, so much so that one (Belgian) pilot later claimed the Battle of Normandy would never have been won without them. Typhoons proved the scourge of the *Wehrmacht* in France – and on occasion, through misidentification, the British too. Yet when Hitler sent his forces into a dangerous counter-attack against the American southern front, an SOS called in the Typhoons to intervene. They inflicted such terrible losses on the enemy at Mortain that the *Panzer* attack was halted.

In all this warfare, the cost was high. Too many of the greatly enlarged Typhoon pilot complement were lost to fierce German flak. Then, before the Normandy battle was won, came a disaster, perhaps the worst incident of its kind on the Allied side. Bombs had fallen on Allied troops in the line from their own planes before, and brought heavy casualties and

Slaughter in the Channel: RAF Typhoons attacked a Royal Navy minesweeping flotilla with devastating effect.

disruption, but this was different, an incident which naturally enough the public never learned of, and which has hardly been well publicised since.

On Sunday, 27 August, 1944, four Royal Navy minesweepers of the 1st Flotilla sailed from their base at Arromanches to complete the job of sweeping clear an area off Le Havre known as Cap d'Antifer. The crews had already spent four days in the zone and had been ordered to a fresh assignment, but their chief, Commander T. Chick, declared one more day was needed for him to be satisfied that the first sea lane was clear. At this point a breakdown occurred at lower staff level at naval HQ which cost the little fleet dear. Commander Chick's force, consisting of the minesweepers *Britomart, Hussar* and *Salamander,* were accompanied by two converted trawlers out into the Channel, en route to their previous location (this fact, it seems, was unknown to the operations staff at naval HQ, who believed the ships were en route to their new task). Around 1.15 p.m. lookouts on the ships spotted aircraft approaching, or rather they heard the angry buzz of Sabre engines, and then identified sixteen Typhoons escorted by a dozen Spitfires. Arriving overhead, the formation began circling the ships, the crews naturally becoming apprehensive – and they had every right to be, for despite the Typhoon leader, Wing Commander John Baldwin's radio call to naval HQ that the 'enemy' vessels were in fact British, the officers ashore insisted they could not be and must be attacked immediately. In fact, it would have been impossible for such a German force to be in that area, given the state of play at the time. When the Typhoon leader persisted that he believed the ships to be British, one naval officer ashore in HQ is alleged to have goaded him, saying: 'Are you afraid?'

Eventually, and despite misgivings, Baldwin ordered his 266 Squadron Typhoons into the attack. What followed was later described by a surviving captain: 'The fury and ferocity of concerted attacks by a number of Typhoons armed with rockets and cannon is an ordeal that has to be endured to be fully appreciated.' Commander Chick of HMS *Jason* was lucky; he survived into old age. Seventy-eight seamen died that day, with 149 wounded. HMS *Britomark*, *Hussar* and *Jason* were sunk and *Salamander* was left a smoking wreck; both trawlers were damaged. The trawlers helped to pick up survivors, aided (incongruously) by an RAF rescue launch.

An immediate inquiry led to the court-martial of three senior naval officers; two were acquitted, and the third was found guilty but only lightly punished since the source of blame lay with a junior who had failed to amend the necessary orders.

The RAF pilots had, of course, flown back to the airstrip B3 in Normandy, most believing they had done the job given them well. Only later would they learn the terrible truth.

The ships and crews that ran up huge RN battle ensigns that day would never have suffered such destruction but for the fact that one naval office clerk neglected to send a signal marked 'COPY TO FOBAA' – FLAG OFFICER BRITISH ASSAULT AREA.

Stukas in Fog

The Germans, as shown elsewhere in this study, were also prone to military blunders. On more than one occasion their ground control proved lacking, with the result that planes bombed their own troops. In one such episode the *Luftwaffe* struck at a bridge in Poland just as a German corps was crossing it. But the amazing event now to be told, which must be unique of its kind, was of a rather different nature.

Even today, raking over and retelling events of World War II, the Stuka is referred to as a Nazi air weapon of terror, an instrument of *Blitzkrieg*, all too often seen in the popular press as responsible for strafing civilians during the Western campaign of 1940. General Udet had pushed through the idea of such a dive-bomber, copying the idea from the Americans, the early Stukas serving in Spain between 1936 and 1939. By 1940 a newer version, the Ju 87b with a Junkers engine giving twice the power, had entered service; armed with bombs and carrying machine-guns, the Junkers 87 Stuka (an abbreviation of *Sturz-Kampf-Flugzeug*, or 'Dive-Battle-Aircraft') was intended to act as highly mobile artillery for the German Army. In mid-August 1939, the Germans had massed divisions and *Luftwaffe* units in the eastern *Reich* to attack Poland, among them Stukas of the 76th Dive Bomber Group.

As a final rehearsal, three Stuka squadrons of this *Gruppe* were detailed to carry out a demonstration attack on the army training area at Neuhammer in Silesia. The formation commander was *Hauptmann* Walter Sigel, who was proud of his '*Graz*' squadrons, so-called after the location of their usual base in Austria; they were all volunteers, every pilot and radioman-gunner, and had trained hard and successfully. In command of No. 1 *Staffel* was a certain *Leutnant* Pelz, who would survive years of combat to become a General of Bombers. He organised the 'Little Blitz' on England early in 1944.

Sigel led his Stukas towards the target, flying at 12,000ft. The latest weather reports indicated 8/10ths cloud over the target, and in view of this Sigel ordered his crews to dive through the cloud, dropping their concrete smoke bombs and pulling out no lower than 900ft. On Sigel's right and left flew his adjutant and technical officers, and the moment they saw him wave and thrust the nose of his Stuka downwards they followed suit. The nine planes of the first squadron to attack screamed earthwards in steep dives, the increasing, rough howl of their engines alerting the assembly of staff officers watching below. Among the officers was *Luftwaffe* General Wolfram von Richthofen, commander of the air support units and cousin to the World War I fighter ace Manfred. General Richthofen had opposed the notion of dive-bombers, but had been forced to accept Stuka units into his command. He had changed his tune once he saw them in action.

The Stuka pilots had practised the manoeuvre many times, trying to keep their nerve as they saw the earth hurtling up at them. The early versions of their planes were not fitted with an automatic pull-out device; it was up to the pilots to watch their altimeters and judge the right moment to start hauling back on the control column. The most daring left it until it was almost too late – a plane diving at the ground at over 300 miles an hour takes some seconds to be moved off its death-defying course.

In Sigel's cockpit the noise reached new heights as he saw the whiteness of the cloud bank envelop his plane, and a second or so later was amazed and horrified to see the dark green and brown of the earth and trees rushing towards him. In terror he hauled back on his stick and greyed out for some seconds, at the same time yelling into his throat mike, 'PULL OUT! IT'S FOG! PULL OUT!' The violent pull-out, as usual, led to a black-out. When normal vision returned he knew the 'cloud' they had tried to penetrate was ground fog, which hovered almost down to ground level, tricking the pilots and luring them into death dives. Then Sigel glimpsed a forest right ahead, and only at the last moment saw a cutting or 'ride' among the tall black-green mass of branches, kicking his rudder bar to swerve the Stuka to safety with only a few feet to spare. A

Perhaps the most bizarre aircraft accident of all? A squadron of Stukas dived into the ground.

yell in his earphones from his comrade and gunner behind made him glance momentarily over his shoulder to see his wingmen, Eppernan and Muller, hit the trees. One of the Stukas hung, suspended like a broken bird, the other burst into flames as it impacted into the forest. Sigel was forced to concentrate on flying his own machine away from danger, climbing and curving upwards as greater disaster came to his men behind.

Nine Stukas of 2 Squadron dived headlong into the ground or into the trees of the forest that day; by a miracle, most of the following 3 Squadron planes escaped. *Leutnant* Hans Stepp had just started his dive as leader of the first section of 1 Squadron when he was startled to hear Captain Sigel's urgent shout over the radio. Stepp and those pilots nearby pulled back their control columns and saved their lives.

In all, thirteen Stukas were seen by the amazed and horrified watchers on the ground to crash to earth; twenty-six young German airmen died. When Hitler received the dire news he stood gazing glumly out of a window for some time. There was no one to charge for the awful accident, yet it must have been a blunder for General Richthofen not to have warned his aircrews of the dangerous foggy conditions around the target which, by common sense, made such a dive-bombing attack at the very least inadvisable.

Cain Disabled

As already indicated, the destruction of friendly aircraft by air and ground forces was a practice, however regrettable, that was established early in the war, and an astonishing example occurred in France before the first month of hostilities was over.

The RAF's so-called 'Advanced Air Striking Force', together with its attached Hurricane fighter squadrons, soon began losing planes to French anti-aircraft batteries. In order to correct this situation, our ally requested that silhouettes of (for a start, one assumes) the Hurricane be supplied – surprising as it seems that such information was not already to hand. The RAF obliged by despatching a New Zealand pilot, Flying Officer Derek 'Bill' Cain, who took off for Calais on 29 September 1939. Presumably, Cain intended to give ample demonstration to the French AA troops and probably deposit the customary three-view silhouettes with them.

This the New Zealander was prevented from doing.

Though expected, the French opened fire on Cain's Hurricane and he was forced to land his damaged machine on the beach at Calais. His Hurricane, serial number L1588, was replaced on 73 Squadron by L1826, which was by coincidence taken on by a fellow countryman of the same

'Cobber' Cain (right), the New Zealand Hurricane fighter ace who rolled once too often.

name, Pilot Officer Edgar James Cain, who as 'Cobber' Cain became famous as the first RAF fighter ace of the war. Sadly, 'Cobber' Cain committed an elementary blunder himself after being ordered back to England on 7 June 1940. After taking off in Hurricane L1826 he attempted to perform a roll at low level, overlooking the inevitable speed loss, and went into the ground. He did not survive the accident.

The Petrol Thief

The well-known adage that the law is an ass seems to have been well proved on numerous occasions, especially in more recent times. It is a belief that received confirmation during the war, when millions of civilians inducted into the services tried (in the main) to adjust to military law and discipline. This aspect was not always the reason why some personnel found themselves under charge; there were those who tried to 'get away with it', in various ways.

Following the fall of France, the *Luftwaffe* began raiding RAF bases, the one closest to their newly won territory of course being Manston, situated on the tip of the Kent coast. The Messerschmitts found it good tactics to fly low across the sea to try to catch the defences by surprise, beating up the airfield and vanishing again in lightning attacks that caused considerable damage and disruption. During one such attack a petrol bowser was holed, the precious fuel leaking on to the ground, which prompted the RAF quartermaster in charge to suggest that airmen be detailed to save as much petrol as possible by the use of buckets. The CO refused: no men could be spared as several RAF fighters were about to touch down following an air battle and required immediate servicing. The quartermaster, to whom we shall refer as Warrant Officer Jones, was forced to comply, but could see no sense in letting all this fuel go to waste. He used some of the leaked fluid to top up the tank of his little car, and after duty that day drove off the base, intending to meet some chums in nearby Broadstairs.

By this time, petrol was indeed a precious commodity and strictly rationed, which had led to some illegalities being committed by those few civilian motorists lucky enough to be offered a little extra through contacts in the right places. In addition, there were those crooks who seized on the chance to dabble in yet another line of supply, with the occasional serviceman being suborned to co-operate, for service depots had their own petrol stations. Well aware of the dangers, the War Office, in its wisdom, had taken steps: all military petrol was coloured red. Furthermore, in the prevailing emergency, civilian and military police patrols were empowered to stop any vehicle to check the contents of its tank.

124

Which was how Warrant Officer Jones's small bit of common sense used for his own ends assumed the proportions of a major blunder. His car was stopped at an MP roadblock before he reached Broadstairs, a sample was taken from his fuel tank, and the hapless WO was arrested for misappropriation of WD property. Indeed, so intent were the military authorities on pursuing the case and setting an example that they ordered a court-martial. The siphoning off of a gallon or two of petrol that would otherwise have disappeared into the earth was a grave breach of discipline, one that warranted a barrister being sent by the Judge Advocate General's department to argue the legal nicety that the petrol was WD property as it dripped from the holed bowser; only on disappearing into the ground could it be written off. Warrant Officer Jones, by catching the fuel mid-flight, so to speak, had unlawfully interfered with that process.

Despite long and conscientious service as a regular airman, WO Jones was found guilty and dismissed from the service in disgrace. The RAF and the nation were denied his valuable service, the man doubtless bitterly regretting his rotten luck in being caught out. But how much more sensible it would have been to have his own CO admonish him and possibly 'award' some loss of pay, or even reduce the WO one step in rank.

The Big Three

In 1943 there occurred the first meeting of the 'Big Three', a summit between Prime Minister Churchill, President Roosevelt and Marshal Stalin held in the Persian capital Tehran. Although the propaganda and indeed actual purpose of this get-together was to outline further co-operation in defeating Nazi Germany, for Stalin it meant but one thing: the Soviet demand for a 'second front' in western Europe. Stalin brought his large bodyguard of heavily armed Georgian toughs; Roosevelt was cosseted by a similar posse of FBI and Secret Service agents, both groups reportedly riding roughshod over all in their attempts to ensure complete security, the American heavies allegedly pushing the British PM aside during one of their room searches. Churchill is said to have taken it all in good humour, unaware he would very shortly go down with pneumonia. His own bodyguard, apart from his usual detective, consisted of a single MP corporal who stood unobtrusively out of the way. However, a detachment of the Buffs were on duty to provide both honour guards and night sentries around the British Embassy and its environs. And it was one of these soldiers who pulled a gaffe that most certainly provided him with a grand tale to tell both chums and family later on.

One aspect of the Tehran conference not mentioned in the propaganda

The 'Big Three' meet at Tehran: Marshal Stalin, President Roosevelt and
Prime Minister Churchill.

communiqués and publicity pictures was the abysmal behaviour of Stalin
and his entourage – cold and brusque much of the time and displaying
their usual suspicion, never acknowledging the enormous material
aid that had been and was still being sent them by Britain and America,
thawing only at the day's end when quantities of liquor were imbibed at
the various receptions held at the embassies. And it was following one
such party that Prime Minister Churchill and his aide, Foreign Secretary
Anthony Eden, decided to stroll back to their own quarters in the British
Embassy, doubtless hoping the cool night air would refresh them and
clear their heads.

When the British sentry on duty behind the barred wicker gate of the
embassy heard two apparent revellers approaching, he grinned, perhaps
wishing his boring midnight to two a.m. duty was over. The pair outside
had traversed some mean streets, passing dark alleys, oblivious to any
hazards; German agents could well have been lying in ambush and
pulled off a fantastic coup. As it was, the rather tipsy pair reached the gate
and demanded entry. The soldier inside wasted no time telling them to
'Fuck off!', repeating this injunction a couple more times, convinced as
he was the two were drunken servicemen, Yanks even, especially when
one called out rather thickly and probably in lisping tones that he was
'Winston Churchill'.

'Fuck off!' the sentry called again, now less amused.

Not until the voice outside assumed graver tones did the Tommy finally decide he should make certain. He opened the little peephole in the gate and at once discovered to his absolute horror and mortification how wrong he had been.

No action seems to have been taken against him, but another blunder occurred of almost equal farce during this summit, this time involving the son of President Roosevelt's principal adviser, Harry Hopkins. As Private Hopkins of the US Army, he had been sent to Persia and given permission to stay with the President. But on arrival and reporting to the British guard compound his slovenly appearance led to his immediate arrest as a suspect. The little misunderstanding was eventually straightened out, but Hopkins Jr. found himself in more trouble later when he stepped out on to a balcony to cool off, drink in hand. He was at once seized by an over-zealous American agent lurking in the nearby shrubbery, again unrecognised and believed to be an unauthorised visitor.

Bubbi

By September 1941 the huge armies of Adolf Hitler were deep into Soviet territory, their centre group battling their way towards Moscow where foreign diplomats were preparing evacuation. One of the divisions spearheading this drive to the Soviet capital was the 2nd SS *Reich*, formed over the previous winter by taking two regiments of the old *Verfuegungs* SS *Division-Deutschland* and *Der Führer*, whose home bases were Munich and Vienna. Added to that was the motorcycle regiment *Langemarck*, a unit made up of both German and 'Germanic' personnel, the latter racial Germans from outside the fatherland proper, plus some 'Nordic' volunteers.

Although the invasion had taken the Red Army almost entirely by surprise and had carried the Germans forward in an astonishing drive at vast cost to the defenders, losses among the attackers had steadily increased and had whittled down the strength of the spearhead troops, not least among the SS divisions. And soon, Hitler made one of his classic blunders, his disastrous interventions, diverting units from the central to the southern front and so fatally weakening the push towards Moscow. Despite the tenacity of the German point units, the advance slowed and ran out of steam, this accentuated by the necessity of relieving some units as they became too weak and exhausted to continue effectively. Among those permitted a brief respite was SS *Reich*, and among its men a certain *Haupscharführer*, or company sergeant-major.

This CSM, normally a tough nut and veteran of the armed SS corps, had endeared himself to his men by allowing them to call him 'Bubbi', a somewhat derogatory term, the nearest equivalent in English being 'booby'. The title had stuck, though the CSM permitted its use only in the field, when all were suffering and comradeship was at its highest. However, as time passed Bubbi had mellowed enough not to reprimand the men under him when they used the term off duty, jumping on them only during more formal occasions when officers were present.

It should be mentioned that in combat SS discipline involved an absolute commitment to comradeship through all ranks. This 'palship' was unparalleled in any other army, the intention being to create a great bond of trust that would breed indivisible discipline in battle. It was this practice, an essential bulwark of SS combat training, that contributed so much to the formidable *esprit de corps* of that corps.

Bubbi, however, was one of those very tough men who had his limits. He had seen a great deal of action in all the campaigns his unit had taken part in – Poland, France, and in the East – having been in continuous action since Operation 'Barbarossa' began on 22 June. The strain had begun to tell; he was in fact showing signs of cracking up as his final reserves of nerve and courage were used up. It was not unknown during the war for apparently impregnable NCOs to falter and fall apart in their first combat, while others apparently seemed able to go on for ever. In fact, every soldier has his limits, and whatever their seeming determination to carry on to the bitter end, the time comes when they must take a rest from combat, or collapse. And in some cases, once the nerves had gone, they were not recoverable. In such circumstances, when men are exhausted and somewhat demoralised by bad conditions and losses, they require careful handling by commanders, an application of sympathy without breakdown of discipline. Most front-line COs know about man management, though some find it more difficult to apply. In Bubbi's case his own commander, a major, lacked the gumption to keep a close enough eye on his soldiers after they were removed from combat. His failure to recognise the symptoms led to tragedy for the CSM.

For a start, Bubbi's commander decided that despite his unit's heavy losses and all the terrible discomforts suffered, they had become slack; discipline needed to be tightened again. He sent for Bubbi.

'*Hauptscharführer!* Your men have suffered, I know, but they have become slack, discipline has fallen. Obviously this cannot be allowed to continue. From now on you must act like the senior NCO of the SS that you are. This means that you must from now on be addressed at all times by your own rank, and not as "Bubbi". Do you understand?'

'*Jawohl, Herr Major!*' responded the CSM, his face red with embarrassment.

Despite this acknowledgement, Bubbi made some mild protest, but his commander cut him short, so the admonished CSM returned to his men, his mind now in a curious and potentially unbalanced state. For his condition had become fragile, and it needed but a spark to drive him over the edge. It seemed that even in the 'invincible' SS human frailties could erupt if circumstances allowed.

It was the curt interview and mild dressing-down that provided the spark that drove Bubbi beyond his limits. Not that the commander had any idea of his CSM's true condition; Bubbi had managed to conceal his state very well, and the blunder committed by the officer was unintentional. Had he known the NCO's true state he might have acted differently, even though it was his duty as commander to hold the unit together before its slackness became dangerous. Poor Bubbi had seen so many of his comrades die or leave in maimed condition, too many old and valued faces had gone for ever. His morale had collapsed, his inner sensitivities were breaking through the toughly moulded exterior, though he seemed outwardly to his men to be his usual self. At least he had been – until the embarrassing interview with the CO.

As soon as Bubbi arrived back in the semi-derelict Russian cottages used as unit billets, his men began to notice his odd behaviour. He rambled on about some order just received from his commander in a most amusing fashion, and no one took him seriously. But suddenly, looking round at their faces, he began breaking into wild laughter that soon amounted to hysteria, so that his men were forced to restrain him as he began almost going berserk. And when these efforts appeared to have little effect the doctor was sent for, but only an NCO medic arrived to find Bubbi thrashing about like an imbecile. It took much struggling before a sedative could be administered which finally put him to sleep.

Soon after that the unit was ordered into action again and made ready for combat. But when the commander went to inspect them he found his CSM missing, and then learned of his breakdown. The main pillar of the unit was unavailable for combat. Amazed, the commander demanded to be shown the man, unable to believe the hard-bitten soldier had fallen out. And when he was shown to the man's billet he was even more amazed to find Bubbi flat out with an empty schnapps bottle by his side. The medic assured the commander the liquor had been provided by him.

When Bubbi finally came to later that day, he discovered his men had gone off to war again without him. Grabbing up his weapon and equipment he rushed off to join them in battle. By then it was nightfall, and when Bubbi arrived at the front the combat had been in progress for hours and the commander had been killed. As a temporary measure, and because there was no one suitable left, the CSM was promoted to lieutenant and given command of the company.

That night, following a Russian attack, Bubbi's company put in a counter-attack and he was killed.

Bari's Dark Secret

Although the *Luftwaffe* caused great damage to British towns and cities with its blitz campaign of 1940–41, it never did achieve any great *military* effect. It is a fact that the German air effort produced its best triumphs elsewhere, especially in the Mediterranean, where in December 1943 Allied error contributed greatly to one of the worst and most covered-up disasters of the war.

The Germans did not take too kindly to their Italian ally's defection in September of that year. How much the supposed anti-fascists counted on sparing their country further damage is not known; in the event the Germans made a swift occupation and Italy became a hard-fought-over battleground. Once the Allied armies established a foothold in the country their prime need was for a port at which they could unload the many thousands of tons needed to sustain the troops in the field. One base captured and used thereafter was Bari, an important port on the Adriatic coast east of Naples with a population of 250,000. The *Luftwaffe* had long shown itself to be a potent force in that theatre. If further proof were needed of this and the advanced state of German weapon technology, then it had already come as a nasty surprise to the Allies and the Italians when their fleet was made to comply with the Allies' surrender terms. Italian battleships and other units were ordered to sail to Malta, but were intercepted by *Luftwaffe* bombers carrying radio-controlled glider bombs. At first, the Italian sailors assumed the aircraft approaching were Allied, come to escort them into Malta; they soon discovered differently. The battleship *Roma* was struck by one of the German weapons and blew up in spectacular fashion, taking down its admiral and crew to the bottom of the sea. A cruiser was also crippled but towed to Malta.

The urgent need for supplies by the British 8th and US 5th Armies fighting in Italy led to the military port commander at Bari ordering the harbour area to be fully illuminated so that the unloading of ships could proceed without delay. This was blunder number one, the second being the complacent failure to set up standing night fighter patrols and a proper warning system for the AA defences already in place. Not that the ninety-six German bombers that had taken off from airfields near Milan needed any signals; the *Luftwaffe* commanders were already well aware of the juicy targets available. But when the German crews climbed in their Junkers 88s to 22,000ft they were astonished to see the great beacon of light beckoning them from afar. They would, it seemed, need no pathfinder flares over Bari.

Before the Germans arrived they dropped *Düppel* – tinfoil strips the British called 'Window' – to upset the Allied radar trackers on the ground and night fighter crews already aloft. In fact there was not an Allied interceptor fighter near the port, which remained ablaze with light as if in peacetime. Not until the first bombs began to fall did the lights extinguish and the flak guns open fire, throwing up a wild display of fireworks that did nothing to stop the German airmen going about their deadly work. The most important Allied supply base in their continental toehold seemed very poorly protected. The crews looked around in vain for barrage balloons, and not a solitary searchlight beamed up at the diving Junkers.

And now the Allies paid the price for their folly.

Two ships loaded with ammunition were struck by bombs and blew up with the most tremendous blast that shattered every window within an eight-mile radius. A tanker was ruptured and its load of refined petrol seeped into the harbour water, and on meeting the oil burning from a ruptured pipeline the flames spread across the harbour, igniting every-thing including ships in their path. After twenty minutes the German bombers left the scene, among them the ace bomber pilot Major Hajo Herrmann; they left behind them a complete chaos of sinking, blazing transports, nineteen of which sank, a further seven severely damaged. Over 1,000 guards and seamen were killed and the port was put out of action for many crucial weeks, which affected the Allied campaign on land, including the landing at Anzio, which had yet to come. Of all the air raids in World War II this was one of the most successful, yet the German air crews were in ignorance of what deadlier problems they had caused. No matter how justifiably their news bulletins crowed, there was an additional factor the Allied authorities felt had to be kept a secret for decades.

The freighter *John Harvey* carried 100 tons of mustard gas in 100 bombs. By that stage of the war the Allies felt Hitler might be desperate enough to try anything in order to stave off defeat, though why such a deadly cargo should be placed in a crowded port well within range of enemy attack seems at the very least questionable. The *John Harvey* was sunk with its crew, but it was some time before the medical staff trying to help the many wounded taken from the quays and water itself were told by the Command that mustard gas had been aboard one ship. It was found that 617 men had been poisoned; eighty-three of them died, some a month later. Then, like some ghastly tale of fiction, survivors picked up by the undamaged ship *Bistera* were taken on to Taranto, the crew completely unaware the wretches had been dipped into water poisoned by the gas. By the time the crew of the *Bistera* reached Taranto every one of them was fully or partially blinded, and trouble was experienced in mooring the ship as a result.

The port authorities blundered terribly in failing to notify the strug-gling medical staffs in the jam-packed hospitals of the gas disaster. Men not seriously hurt were allowed off into ordinary billets, everyone unaware their clothes were impregnated with gas which gave off a smell like garlic. It was not so much the incompetent defence of Bari that the Allies saw fit to remain mute over after the war as the fact they had deadly nerve agents practically in the field, in this case ready for offloading should the need arise.

Off Target

Pressed as they were in their many-front war, not even the ten thousand 88mm flak guns deployed by the Germans against Allied air attacks were enough to cover every town and city in the *Reich*, which was how towns like Darmstadt and others were so easily razed by the RAF. And, not for the first or last time, Allied bombers blitzed the wrong place, namely Saarlouis, which was marked by the early pathfinders of Bomber Command and virtually destroyed during the night of 1/2 September 1942, the real target being Saarbrucken which was spared the 120 tons of bombs intended for it. Recovering from this blunder, the RAF sent Mosquitos fitted with Gee radar and markers to light up the next target – Frankfurt-am-Main. This time both markers and bombs landed in the countryside, twelve miles away.

Attack on Oregon

The only 'air raid' carried out against mainland America in World War II must surely rank as one if not the most significant event in the war. That such an event was possible could never have entered the heads of the US authorities, despite the setting up of tentative ARP networks. Which of their two principal enemies had the capability of launching such an attack? Even though the Germans were drawing up plans for a 'New York bomber' of four engines with the range to do it, such ideas were little more than aviation designers' sketches and feasibility studies. And the Japanese had no heavy bombers capable of strategic warfare.

Vague rumours of fires among the forested areas around Oregon in the eastern United States sprang up in September 1942, as well as panicky talk of some kind of Japanese air attack. The American military blundered when it failed to cover its eastern seaboard adequately with radar and patrols by sea and air, much as it had completely failed to provide any defence at all against German U-boats along its Atlantic coast following its declaration of war against Hitler. It was many months before some kind of protection such as a convoy system and warship escorts for the tanker traffic was organised; during that time the U-boat crews

Super-large Japanese submarines captured by the Americans.

enjoyed their 'happy time', cruising up and down the well-lit coastline, sinking ships at will with torpedo and gunfire.

Credit has to be given to the wily Japanese for even contemplating such an enterprise and having the courage and determination to carry it through. Like a couple of other nations, they had developed and used an extra-large submersible, the *I-25* of 2,195 tons, big enough to carry a float-plane. This submarine crossed the Pacific and arrived off the Oregon coast on 9 September 1942. The crew had been frustrated by stormy seas for ten days, but on that morning the young pilot of the aircraft in the small hangar of *I-25* was able to gaze through the periscope and see the lighthouse at Cape Blanco and the mountains wreathed in mist. When he commented on the favourable weather, the sub skipper, Captain Tagami, told him he would make history – the first man to bomb the USA!

In fact, the attack scheme had been the pilot's, one of the youngest in the Japanese Navy called Fujita, who had his plan sent to the famous Admiral Yamamoto, architect and executor of the devastating raid on Pearl Harbor. But the actual originator of such a far-out notion had been the ex-consul at Seattle, who had advised the military that the best way to stir up panic among the Americans was to set fire to the great tracts of forest along the west coast. It was not a new idea; the RAF had such schemes which were allegedly carried out in tentative fashion in 1940–41. Now it was up to one Japanese pilot with his observer, Okuda, to prove it could be done. The airmen made their wills and left these with other personal effects before being catapulted off the submarine to fly over Cape Blanco.

Unfortunately for the Japanese, their plan did not include the obvious tactic: to litter the American woodlands with incendiary devices. As the sun rose the seaplane flew some forty-two miles before its crew dropped a single bomb onto the forest land. Nine miles on they loosed their only other missile before flying back over the sea, dropping down low when Fujita saw two freighters. They found their submarine and were craned inboard safely. Amazingly, and without being detected, the *I-25* continued to cruise around in American waters until 29 September, when Fujita again took off in his seaplane, this time by night, to bomb the same area, fifty miles east of Cape Blanco. Even then, the plucky Japanese only dropped one bomb.

However, that the Americans were not unaware of the intruder seems to have been indicated by broadcasts designed to alleviate public fear, for on Thursday, 10 September (the day after the first raid), Radio San Francisco repeated assurances that only a single plane had dropped 'several incendiary bombs' over Oregon, causing damage in the woods that resulted in several deaths, the intruder presumably having been launched from a submarine. With such inspired guesswork it should not have been difficult for naval and coastguard patrols to locate such a large object. The fact that *I-25* was still lurking about in American coastal waters at the end of the month proves otherwise.

Some indication of what was to come later from Japan in the field of electronic gadgetry can be seen in a further attempt at incendiary attack on America's west coast. In November 1944 the B-29 Superfortresses began their raids on the Japanese homeland; by way of reprisal the enemy launched large balloons of 30ft diameter designed to be carried by the prevailing winds at high altitude (29,000 to 35,000ft) across the Pacific. Charred remains of one balloon bearing Japanese markings were picked up by children in Montana, investigation at the Naval Institute revealing the substance comprised several layers of vellum fastened with animal glue. Later, it was found that these clever devices carried sand-bags which would automatically be offloaded once the balloons dropped below 29,000ft, while a second tripping device would allow gas to escape if the balloon climbed above 34,000ft. The balloons carried up to four incendiary and several shrapnel bombs, but despite this ingenuity the Japs bungled by assuming all the balloons would function well. About ten did not work at all and were found intact.

The assumption that panic would result was also proved wrong, for the

A Canadian naval officer points to the remains of a Japanese incendiary balloon.

American and Canadian authorities placed a blackout on the news, so the enemy never gained the satisfaction of knowing how their incendiary campaign had fared.

The Wailing of the Sirens

To leap back to the first days of the war, the night of 3/4 September 1939 to be precise, nervous bungling on the part of some authorities in Britain resulted in terror for some little ones. For the third night young children evacuated from London were curled up in their clothes on heaps of straw in the classrooms of an empty school at Pakefield near Lowestoft on the east coast. This complement had disembarked late Friday afternoon from a paddle steamer more used to transporting holidaymakers; another batch had landed at Yarmouth by similar means.

At some time in the dead of night, probably around midnight, the whole neighbourhood was aroused by the howling of the air-raid sirens. The racket was particularly horrendous for the children in Pakefield school, for the local siren for that area was, for whatever reason, attached to the outside wall of the top-floor classroom. The half dozen or so kiddies using that room as their makeshift bedroom were therefore especially terrorised to be woken up in such a shattering manner, barely able to hear a word their guardian teacher spoke to them as he tried to guide them by the light of his torch out of the room and down the stairs. All the children were hurriedly assembled in the hall, where they had been having their somewhat scanty meals since arrival. They were then marched in columns of two outside, across the yard, through a back gate and across a field to a shallow, dried-out ditch where they were told to crouch down, as if in a shelter, even though they were completely in the open. And there, chilled and sleepy, by the faint light from a harvest moon low in the southern sky, they stayed for a while, ears strained for the first sound of German raiders. None came, and when at last the 'All Clear' sounded they were taken back to their classroom sleeping quarters.

None of the various alarms of air attack in these first days were justified.

Bomber Disasters

Controversy among historians and others continues to this day concerning the value of the Allied bombing campaign against Hitler's Germany. It is customary for sceptics to point out that despite an enormous tonnage of bombs dropped, German war production rose to its highest level, yet 'Bomber' Harris persisted in his relentless, and some would say vengeful, campaign to eliminate every German town and city. That his critics may be right is perhaps signalled by one particular example (there are more).

In one of the war's last great raids on Cologne, which had suffered enough, RAF bombers deposited the absolute maximum deluge of high explosives possible on this comparatively short-range target; specialists had advised Harris that a mere 20% of the tonnage delivered would have sufficed – at least, that is the assertion. There are those to whom 'Bomber' Harris remains a hero, while others, certainly most older Germans, regard him as a war criminal. But in 1941 Harris was a mere group commander, yet aware that all was far from well with Bomber Command's efforts to damage Germany's war industry. Indeed, that year saw the low point in that Command's fortunes, as it did Britain's as a whole. And things could hardly have been grimmer for the two or three bomber squadrons saddled with the jinxed, luckless Avro Manchester.

The firm of A.V. Roe had perhaps been surprised to win an Air Ministry contract to participate in the great expansion of the heavy bomber programme. Designer Roy Chadwick's Type 679 to meet the official specification P13/36 comprised a large aircraft to be powered by two of the new Rolls-Royce Vulture engines. It was this engine which signalled the death knell of the Manchester, potentially a superior design to the competing Handley-Page Halifax and Short Stirling types. How the renowned firm of Rolls-Royce ever came to produce such an abominable power plant remains a mystery; new, yes, powerful, yes, but plagued by horrendous design faults which produced an unending series of disasters for the young men assigned to fly the Manchester. These proved conclusively that the type was too large for twin-engine power, so that by early 1941 Avro had virtually abandoned the design in favour of a version powered by four tried and trusted Rolls-Royce Merlin engines – soon named the Lancaster. But the young airmen risking their lives in the doomed Manchester knew nothing of this. Every time they took off on tests or on ops their lives were at great risk.

The reps and engineers of both firms spent hundreds of man-hours on site and in their factories, trying to solve the problems. Since it was underpowered, pilots usually had trouble even clearing the airfield boundary hedge – it was not too unusual for radio aerials to be clipped from nearby cottages. And once struggling to remain aloft, Manchester crews frequently found their bombers were unable to climb beyond a few thousand feet. They had to continue at this height to Germany – provided the normal engine failure did not occur – and once over the *Reich* became a grand target even for the enemy's lighter flak weapons. To add to this misery, design problems in the accursed engines assured that on many flights overheating and fires resulted. Not only RAF aircrew but test pilots died in the resulting crashes.

Why did Bomber Command not refuse to operate a bomber so plagued with apparently unsolvable problems? The answer is that as things stood great pressure existed to operate even the small bomber force available; when a mere eighty bombers set off on raids it was considered a heavy attack, a 'maximum effort'. A whole book could be filled with the sorry tale of fantastic mishaps and shattering experiences of the young airmen of the three Manchester squadrons whose persistence and bravery in the face of suicidal odds upheld the finest traditions of the force and country. These lads were not only saddled with an aircraft that was an obvious no-hoper, they encountered the cruellest ill luck – in truth, death through the blunders of others.

On the evening of 21 June 1941, eighteen Manchesters of Nos. 61, 97 and 207 Squadrons were assigned as part of a force to attack installations at Boulogne. The bombers were routed south, to pass west of London towards the Channel. Unfortunately, that night German intruder planes were active, hunting RAF bombers over Lincolnshire, and one of these was tracked by the Observer Corps, its course overlapping that of Manchester EM-Y of 207 Squadron, piloted by F/O Withers. A ground controller homed a Beaufighter on to the German's track, which coincided with Y-Yoke. But the Beaufighter pilot was alert enough to recognise the bomber in his sights as British. The ground controller refused to believe this news, and even after the RAF fighter pilot flew alongside the Manchester and clearly saw its RAF markings, the same officer on the ground continued to insist he was wrong! The Manchester crew had seen the Beaufighter and fired off 'colours of the day' recognition signals. They must have felt relieved when the fighter dropped away out of sight.

They were swiftly and devastatingly disillusioned a moment later when a blast of cannon and machine-gun shells struck their aircraft. Incredibly, the Beaufighter pilot had obeyed the orders given by his ground controller, and the Manchester fell away out of control, blazing, its crew dead or killed seconds later when it struck the ground at Wollaston, Northamptonshire. It was 01.55 hrs. The Manchester's bomb load exploded after impact, ensuring the plane and crew were blown to pieces. Flying Officer Withers and his crew had died after a mere twenty minutes of operational flying.

But the summer night was still young.

The hard-luck squadron's next mishap came when the front gunner in F/O Mike Smith's bomber accidentally tugged his parachute release handle, the silken canopy spilling out over the bomb aimer's position and then carried by the usual draughts up and through the pilot's cabin. With silk and rigging lines threatening to become entangled in the many controls, the pilot opted to return to base.

Flt Lt Sherwood had completed his part in the Boulogne trip and descended to 4,000ft, heading for his base at Coningsby, when suddenly the aircraft was riddled with bullet strikes from below. A Defiant night fighter had discovered them and, having been assured by a ground controller that no friendly planes were in the area, had opened fire. The Manchester survived, to make a hasty touchdown at base with one engine stopped and the other enveloped in steam through damage to its cooling system. The crew counted 300 holes in their kite next morning.

The Defiant pilot was court-martialled, but at his base at Wittering the Manchester crew learned how the offender had come to make this error, and how the ground controller had only just come on duty, a paper warning of RAF planes returning from a raid hidden beneath others on his desk. The Defiant crew had only broken off their attack when the Manchester crew desperately fired off recognition signals. Obviously the fault lay elsewhere, and the pilot was let off with a reprimand. The fate of the ground controllers in these two incidents is not recorded; it is safe to say, however, that being officers they would have escaped heavy penalty.

In the greater context, those who planned RAF bomber raids under Air Chief Marshal Harris also erred, and no worse example can be made than the disastrous attack on Nuremberg on 30/31 March 1944. Bad decisions at the top resulted in Bomber Command's most terrible and fantastic loss. Everything seemed to contribute to disaster that night: the weather was wrong, diversionary raids across the North Sea were cancelled, and clear moonlight en route to the main target led to the bomber stream leaving a trail of condensation which enabled the German night fighters to spot them with ease. One RAF crewman counted *forty* bomber wrecks blazing on the ground on the way to Nuremberg. Every one of these bombers had cost the British taxpayer some £25,000, plus the cost of crew training, ground maintenance, bombs, etc. Then, to confound navigators, spring gales blew the planes off course, dispersing the bomber stream. But conditions proved ideal for the enemy night fighter crews, who reaped a harvest. The enemy planes carried the latest radar detection equipment – not that gadgets were needed; the moonlit roads of smoke drew the Messerschmitts, Junkers, Dorniers and FWs to the bombers like moths to a flame – and the slaughter proceeded. Those multi-engined German planes carrying *Schräge Musik* – a pair of upward-firing cannon – were able to simply cruise below the British bombers and let fly into the vulnerable petrol tanks on each side of the four engines, then escape before the fat bombers blew up in fire. Of the ninety-three Halifaxes despatched on 30/31 March, thirty were destroyed; some 210 men were lost. Lancaster losses were worse.

Those bomber crews that survived the long and terrible run-in under fighter attack were surprised to find Nuremberg unlit – the pathfinder crews arrived forty minutes late. To add to the waiting bomber crews' difficulties, the city itself was cloud-covered, and without accurate marking by the pathfinders their bombing would be mere guesswork. In such circumstances, to wait around under attack by heavy flak and fighters, not forgetting the danger of collisions, irked every crew and, not surprisingly, bomb loads were jettisoned, not simply because crews grew more and more jumpy, but because fuel was getting low. After flying all that way through such danger no crew had any thought of returning to England with a load of highly volatile explosives.

The crews were, in any case, at odds with the planners who had in the face of protest routed the bombers over or near known flak zones and fighter beacons. That night the *Luftwaffe* scored its greatest success against the RAF bombers, shooting down seventy-nine of the four-engined attackers, one Me 110 crew downing seven of the enemy, all Halifaxes. To aid the German airmen over Nuremberg, the flak defences illuminated the cloud from below with 600 searchlights, so that the British bombers were silhouetted as well as lit up from above by the moonlight. Some bombers which had not yet been fitted with H2S air-to-ground radar wandered off and bombed Schweinfurt by mistake; others bombed at random, the unnerved crews just glad to get away, some diving to low level to escape fighters.

It was, of course, to some extent a combination of ill luck and bad planning that brought the terrible end result as announced over the BBC next

139

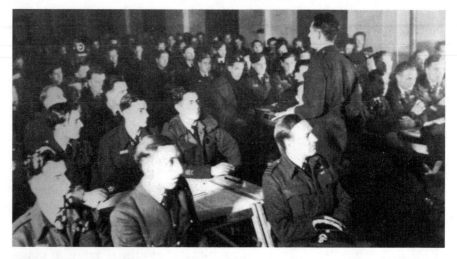

Many of these aircrew at briefing prior to the disastrous
raid on Nuremberg 1944 were doomed to die.

'Christmas Trees': the pathfinder
flares go down.

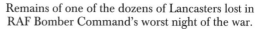

Remains of one of the dozens of Lancasters lost in
RAF Bomber Command's worst night of the war.

day – of the 795 four-engined bombers sent to Nuremberg that night, ninety-five were destroyed over Germany, seventy-one were heavily damaged, and a further twelve made crash landings in England – the bulletin as always stressing that this loss included all operations carried out the previous night. Credit must be given to the home side for making such an admission, which shocked the public and certainly gave heart and extra impetus to Harris's critics, and he had them in high places as well as among certain clerics. Later, he would assert he had only been carrying out orders, a rather familiar plea and heard from the other side later, after the war. Harris also said that some in high places (namely, Churchill) who had backed him later got cold feet and tried to dissociate themselves from the bombing campaign.

The tonnage of bombs dropped on the raid was 2,460, the damage to the target minimal: one war factory was partially destroyed, three slightly damaged. For this result 545 British airmen died and 159 remained seriously wounded in German hands. The *Luftwaffe* lost ten planes, while on the ground sixty civilians and fifteen foreign labourers were killed.

The bottom line has to be that bungling occurred at planning level in England, from the decision to send over such a force in moonlight onwards. No air force could sustain such losses or the subsequent drop in morale among aircrew. No more big raids were made for some time; in fact by April 1944 Harris was forced to abandon the main theme of this assault, having been temporarily ordered to divert heavy bomber forces to the interdiction campaign in western Europe in preparation for the invasion. This, too, would bring (inevitably) death to civilians, sometimes grievous, sometimes, it seems, quite unnecessarily.

Swiss Intrigue

Leutnant Wilhelm Johnen would live to write his memoirs, but during the night of 27/28 April 1944, in the midst of a raid by RAF bombers on Friedrichshafen, it seemed his luck and that of his two crewmates had run out. On that night he carried not only his radio operator-observer, but the NCO inventor of the *Schräge Musik* guns in the rear cockpit of his Me 110G-4. The plane carried the brand new SN-2 radar, and something they should never have taken into the air: a briefcase filled with lists of the month's codes and signal procedures, which were changed frequently.

They had just shot down two Lancasters in quick succession when, after ninety minutes' manoeuvring, they became disorientated and were suddenly blinded by searchlights. Johnen ordered a green flare fired as identification, believing the lights to be German. In fact they were Swiss – they had overflown neutral territory. Then they saw runway lights so

Wilhelm Johnen's Me110 night fighter, impounded in Switzerland and the cause of a Nazi–Swiss wrangle.

brilliant they had to be Swiss, but when Johnen tried to escape the lights caught him again and they decided because of their aircraft's bad fuel state to comply. Switching on his lights he made a good landing on the airfield at Dubendorf and was met by a Swiss officer who took them off to internment.

Once apprised of their fate, the realisation that the still secret night fighter with its precious equipment could somehow fall into the hands of the British sent alarm bells ringing all the way to Berlin. Worse, the Nazi command was suspicious that the three-man German aircrew might actually have defected to the enemy. Hitler, despite Goering's protests that only he had the right to carry out counter-measures, ordered Himmler to send a commando group into Switzerland to snatch or kill the aircrew before the British could get to them. (It has to be remembered that at this time the Germans had gained the advantage once more in the radio war.) Himmler called in Otto Skorzeny, the man who had snatched Mussolini in a daring coup from the mountain prison on Gran Sasso. In the meantime, a desperate Goering offered the Swiss twelve brand-new Me 109 fighters if only they would return plane and crew. The Swiss refused and, canny enough to suspect a threat, removed the fighter's radar gear to a safe place. Goering pleaded, assuring the Swiss he would deliver six Messerschmitts in advance and the rest at once on receiving plane and crew back in the *Reich*.

The negotiations went on, Himmler actively pursuing his own plans with Skorzeny, until, still refusing to release the plane, the Germans asked the Swiss to destroy it. This too failed, even though Goering promised still to turn over twelve fighters. Eventually, with war over the issue looming between the two countries, the Swiss agreed to allow a Captain Eggers to come to their field at Dubendorf with an explosives expert to supervise destruction by the Swiss of the plane. This took place under secrecy and under cover, and the two Germans departed with their aircrew.

The three German airmen were quite unaware of what was going on as they enjoyed Swiss military hospitality, but during this time the airmen's homes had been searched by the *Gestapo* and their families removed for questioning. It was not until the fighter crew had been thoroughly interrogated in Berlin and established as innocent that their kin were released.

The Turkey Shoot

On 19 June 1944 the Japanese and US fleets in the Pacific again squared up for another showdown: Vice-Admiral Ozawa, with nine aircraft carriers and the support of land-based planes, faced the US 58th Fast Carrier Task Force off the Phillipines. The Japs had an advantage at the start since their planes had the longer range, and Vice-Admiral Ozawa became aware of the American fleet's position before his enemy had located his. But in the course of the day's battles, the Japanese commander made a grave blunder that cost him dear.

Before the main clash came, the US submarine *Albacore* had tried to torpedo the carrier *Taiho*, the Japanese commander's flagship, but in a fantastic manoeuvre of self-sacrifice a Japanese pilot, on spotting the torpedo, deliberately crashed his plane into it, thus saving the carrier – for the time being.

By 11.00 hrs Ozawa had sent up 80% of his aircraft to attack the US fleet. The Japanese pilots began an eight-hour assault on the American warships, but most were spotted on radar 155 miles away. As a result the Japanese air fleet en route suffered 218 casualties, while only shooting down twenty-nine Americans. Only about forty of 375 enemy planes managed to penetrate the American fighter screen, and by late afternoon 401 Japanese aircraft had been destroyed before getting nearer than sixty miles to the US fleet. The battleship *South Dakota* was seriously damaged, the sister ship *Indiana* and cruiser *Indianapolis* damaged. The *Taiho* was then torpedoed by the *Albacore* and was eventually abandoned with many of its remaining planes aboard. The carrier *Shokaku* was also torpedoed (by the sub *Cavalla*) and, like the *Taiho*, sank by midnight.

Next day the remaining Japanese warships were caught refuelling from oilers by American strike planes. Ozawa's miscalculation meant that only thirty-five of his fighters were able to defend his fleet against 216 Americans. The carrier *Hiyo* and two oilers were sunk; two more carriers, a battleship and a heavy cruiser were damaged, for the cost of only twenty US planes. Ozawa was then ordered by his commanding admiral to retreat, having now lost 480 planes in what came to be known as the 'Great Marianas Turkey Shoot'. Vice-Admiral Ozawa lost three-quarters of his fleet, the outermost defence ring of the Japanese empire was lost, and the Americans were free to continue their landings in the Mariana islands.

Trail to Poltava

On 20 June 1944, some 2,500 American heavy bombers and long-range fighters attacked German targets, most flying to Berlin, where 2,000 tons of bombs were dropped in a battle lasting thirty minutes which cost the Americans forty-four planes. But 114 Fortresses escorted by seventy Mustangs turned south and bombed a fuel plant in Lower Silesia. The formation then turned east towards the Soviet Union – this being one of the 'shuttle' raids arranged with the Russians. The scheme seemed novel, even brilliant, but the Americans miscalculated, underestimating the enemy reaction. As the Americans flew east they were tailed by a long-range Heinkel 177. The German crew carefully noted how seventy-three of the Fortresses peeled off to land on a base at Poltava, the rest of the Americans going to two other Soviet bases.

That night, at 23.35 hrs, the American CO at Poltava was notified by the Soviets that a force of German bombers was headed in his direction. There was not a thing the Americans could do, and believing they were safe they had neglected the usual, basic precaution of dispersing their Fortresses. When eighty German bombers of the 200 Heinkels and Junkers despatched arrived over Poltava their crews were amazed to see silvery American bombers lined up as if on parade. The Soviet flak proved ineffective, and of forty Russian night fighters only four took off. The German attackers destroyed forty-seven B-17 Fortresses, fourteen Mustangs and one Soviet Yak fighter without loss to themselves. And when a further force of Junkers 88s arrived at 02.00 hrs they strafed the field and destroyed the entire fuel and bomb stocks.

Fourteen more bombers on that day's operations had landed in Sweden, bringing the day's total losses to 199 aircraft, the worst loss suffered by the US 8th Air Force in World War II.

A Flakless Paris

An Allied blunder enabled Hitler to wreak his revenge for total defeat in Normandy with an air raid on Paris. On Friday, 25 August 1944, French and American troops entered the capital, and before long the tall figure of General de Gaulle was seen striding among the crowds, before sniper fire panicked them.

At midnight the air raid sirens sounded. Although there was some vestige of defence in that, no flak artillery or fighters challenged the force of fifty German bombers that now flew over Paris, the last of the once great Air Fleet 3. They had flown from Rheims, encountering no defence, and now proceeded with their wanton attack on the city, cruising backwards and forwards at low level and releasing high-explosive and incendiary bombs that started great conflagrations, killing 213 people and injuring 914. Some 593 buildings were destroyed or badly damaged. Not one flak gun challenged the bombers, which then flew home without hindrance.

Paris was then scheduled by Hitler to receive the first V2 rocket attacks. On the morning of 6 September, Major Weber commanding the 44th Test Battery set in train the long preparations for launching rocket No. 18 583. Just after 10.30 hrs the button was pressed and the V2 began to lift off from its base south of Liège in Belgium, but after hissing on its way a few feet off the ground it fell back and crashed. At 11.40 a second rocket had been prepared (No. 18 593) – with the same disastrous result. Bungled engineering of this fearsome weapon had resulted in premature disengagement of the fuel supply. It took time to discover and rectify this fault, by which time Major Weber's battery had been forced to flee the British Army's advance and set up shop in northern Holland for shooting their weapons at London. Paris was spared.

Stripped of their Pride

The great battle recently concluded in Normandy had cost the Allies dear and put a great strain on British manpower; at least, with other war fronts to supply, the number of trained infantrymen available for the struggle in France seemed to be drying up. As an emergency measure men of the RAF Regiment and Royal Marines were drafted over the Channel, as were surplus RAF aircrew put into ground duties, the latter measure announced in the press. But what actually occurred during this reinforcement never got into the news bulletins and involved a crass blunder for which survivors have still not forgiven the brass hats of the British Army.

In a comb-out, a number of men in various RAF ground trades considered surplus were sent to the RAF Regiment depot at Kidderminster to receive a short course of infantry training lasting only a month or so. These men were already completely demoralised, having been snatched out of what they considered safe jobs for the war, put into khaki battledress and put through a battle course. Then, following an inspection and pep talk parade by the CO, the whole camp was trucked to the south coast and put aboard craft bound for the war across the Channel. Until they actually arrived behind the front the regular RAF Regiment soldiers had been keen to get into action, but what came next brought a near mutiny among the regiment.

Following a welcoming speech by an Army colonel the troops were then amazed to be taken off to a nearby stores tent, told to strip off their RAF Regiment uniforms, and handed complete sets of British Army battledress and equipment. The protests from officers, NCOs and men flew thick and fast, but even representations to the camp CO proved of no avail. The RAF officers tried to placate their men by promising to take it further, but they knew full well that by donning Army uniforms their unit pride and cohesiveness were destroyed. The RAF had built up its own traditions since 1918, and had no great opinion of the Army anyway. If they, as soldiers, were to fight the Germans, then they would go into action bearing RAF insignia. It meant a lot to them.

This never happened.

In no time the regiment, despite further protests and arguments, was trucked to the front line where they fell cursing into foxholes, much to the bemusement of the regular infantrymen already in place. In the following battles against German Army and SS troops at least 50% of the RAF lads became casualties, a ratio one surviving veteran swears would have been more favourable if they had been left as an RAF Regiment unit.

And what of the famous Royal Marines?

Like the RAF men, many of these soldiers, left out of the small marine commando units, had spent a rather dull war ashore, manning guns or performing other duties. When they were paraded at a south-west barracks and told they were going into action at last 'to help Monty', many were keen and relieved that at last it seemed their training would bear fruit. However, like the RAF men their hopes were short-lived – at least in the sense that they too were taken to a camp in Normandy, fed and welcomed before being asked to relinquish all their gear and don battledress without badges. One can imagine the US Marine Corps in such a situation; all hell would have broken loose. Which was very nearly what did happen when the British Marines were asked to give up their unit identity. Their protests were even more enraged than those of the RAF lads – understandably, for the Royal Marines traditions went back hundreds of years. Somehow, their officers just managed to restore order and promised the men that if they did as asked their grievances would be pursued. But, as with the RAF men, nothing came of it. The marines, now utterly disgusted and looking like unitless squaddies, went into the front-line foxholes where jeers from the residing infantry led to fights.

As on the 'RAF front', the Marines suffered more casualties than necessary, for the question of unit pride is directly connected to *esprit de corps* and therefore efficiency in action. If morale is poor, performance suffers. It seems fairly obvious that the Army chiefs did not want the enemy to find out that the British were now being forced almost to scrape the bottom of the barrel, so to speak, for manpower reserves. Yet later on General Montgomery stated he knew nothing of the above events, and denied knowledge that the two regiments involved had been stripped of their identities, alleging he would never have allowed it.

The Bodenplatte *Aftermath*

On New Year's Day 1945, while Allied troops and airmen were to some extent celebrating, over 1,000 German planes struck in Operation '*Bodenplatte*', able to take the Allied air bases on the continent completely by surprise. But, if the Allies blundered by not waking up until too late, the enemy too made an error that proved devastating to the attackers. First, eighteen Polish Spitfires, about twelve other Allied planes and several petrol bowsers went up in flames at St Denis-Westrem in Belgium. At Brussels, eighty-five planes were destroyed on the ground. At Eindhoven in Holland a Canadian unit lost all its Typhoons. The Germans claimed 439 Allied planes destroyed on the ground or in the air, admitting a loss of ninety-three. But on their return flights a further 184 German aircraft fell victim to their own flak gunners, who had not been warned of these planes' routing.

Invasion of Sumatra

When is a bungle in war no more than a miscalculation? The best-laid plans, schemes, plots and military endeavours may have taken weeks or months to hatch, only to vanish in disaster within minutes, even seconds. Among the very carefully and craftily laid Japanese plans to create an empire in the Far East was one rather more clever and in fact 'shameful', as those Allies on the spot saw it at the time.

Vice-Admiral Ozawa's plan to seize Sumatra was based on the need to use the island's airfields and capture the important oilfields, refineries and industrial complexes built by the Dutch colonial power. It was mid-February 1942. The Japanese were about to capture Singapore; the yellow tide of their all-conquering imperialism was spreading fast across south-east Asia and the Pacific. On Saturday, 14 February, units of the Japanese 38th Division were landed near Palembang, aided by carrier-based aircraft and cruisers. At the same time, in an operation unique of its kind, paratroops were dropped inland from American-type planes, Lockheed 14s which were built under licence in Japan and called the *Ro-Shiki*. They were virtually indistinguishable from the civilian Lockheed Electra which, converted, flew with the RAF as the twin-engined Hudson for reconnaissance purposes.

Well aware of the Japanese threat, British and Dutch demolition squads were standing by to destroy vital installations to prevent their use by the invaders. Everyone took shelter when enemy bombers appeared to deposit their eggs from high altitude, troops and civilians emerging once the raid was over. It was then 18.00 hrs, and they next saw a large number of planes approaching Palembang from the north. These flew in at low altitude and were easily identifiable as Lockheeds, painted in similar colours to RAF machines and actually carrying red, white and blue roundels. What happened next dumbfounded the watchers who had been waving to the planes: figures began falling from them, and in seconds multi-coloured parachutes opened – the Allied personnel were under attack from Japanese paras. It was the signal for the AA defences to let fly at the aircraft, some seventy in all, some of which diverted towards the city.

The enemy ruse was a violation of international law. 'Shameful!' one witness called it. Yet despite all the careful planning that had gone into the operation, sixteen of the *Ro-Shikis* were shot down, many full of soldiers, while every Japanese paratrooper who dropped to capture the oil refinery was killed. However, the enemy succeeded in capturing the airfield. When the troops of 38th Division arrived they found only a tangled ruin of an oilfield.

Running Rackets

The machinations of certain individuals at home in Britain during the war led to various scandals, and this situation occasionally resulted in public trials. At a Colchester court-martial in 1942 four officers of the Royal Army Service Corps stood accused of certain irregularities – namely, receiving stolen goods, coal and paraffin, food, drawing servants' accounts, and running a side racket by allowing Army garages and work-shops to be used for the servicing of civilian vehicles, employing both soldier and civilian mechanics for the work. Bungling at some point resulted in exposure, so the soldiers were allowed to leave the Army (i.e. dismissed from the service), an apparently derisory sentence. Civilians would have been sent to prison.

The filching of goods by some military personnel became rife throughout the war; occasional carelessness saw some felons ap-prehended. The worst, virtually habitual, criminals were early in the war posted to a secret detention camp and finally shipped out to fight Rommel in Africa, where many were killed, wounded or captured.

The Home Guard

Ask any male citizen who was a boy in the summer of 1940 and anywhere near the scene of enemy activity if his memories are exciting, and few would deny it. Of course many people were not disturbed by *Luftwaffe* activity at all, usually those living in more remote areas out of earshot even of warning sirens. A few citizens were so blasé they were able to carry on much as usual, sleeping soundly during night raids and inconvenienced perhaps only by disruptions to essential services. Thus the early *Luftwaffe* incursions brought excitement and new experiences to many, no matter what later historians would document as the terrible 'blitz'. Added to the raids was the much exaggerated fear of invaders dropping from the skies – paratroops, spies and saboteurs of whom we had learned alarming tales from the press during the Battle of France. Apparently they could easily drop in on us in all manner of disguises. The rumours and beliefs then prevalent seem absurdly silly these days, but at the time such ideas were taken seriously. They were in part why Anthony Eden made his radio appeal in May 1940 for civilian volunteers to form the Local Defence Volunteers, and later Home Guard, often known at the time as 'parashots' – and not without reason.

Oddly, perhaps, at first these enthusiastic men – young, middle-aged and elderly, many of them veterans of the earlier war – carried out their training and duties in a somewhat 'democratic' fashion. They were not properly disciplined by any means and officers were appointed by reason of social standing or line of work – hence Captain Mainwaring's standing in the famous *Dad's Army* TV series. The men were not under War Office and therefore Army control. As the threat of invasion and para-dropping became acute, these men became more hyped-up (to use a modern term), proceeding in too many cases to take matters into their own hands, committing blunders and generally prompting both citizenry and authorities to wonder what kind of monster had been created. Some fifty civilians were killed by over-zealous Home Guards, with more casualties occurring during the realistic training that came later.

In those tense, exciting and, of course, dangerous days millions of British people in the south witnessed the drama of planes and airmen descending from the sky, yet despite the daily bulletins admitting RAF losses, it seems that for some folk, at least, any man coming down by parachute had to be a German. Again, it seems ludicrous that any one or even a whole German crew of four could pose any threat, yet in some cases such airmen were shot at by those armed and anxious to receive

Britain's Home Guards did a grand job, but proved a little too zealous on occasion.

them on the ground. In most cases this involved Home Guards and regular soldiers.

Drawing again on personal experience, I recall vividly the big daylight raid of 31 August 1940 when our local fighter field at Hornchurch in Essex was bombed. We emerged from our near neighbour's shelter to see two parachutists descending from a great height. They were perhaps a mile apart; the nearer man to us was also much lower, though both took up to fifteen minutes to reach the ground. I went out front in time to see an LDV man in shirtsleeves, pullover and flat cap cycling sedately past and obviously heading in the direction of the nearer parachutist. This man was one of those lucky enough to have been issued with one of the old rifles that had been rushed over from USA and Canada. Not too long after I heard, along with many others in the street who were, as usual, exchanging stories after such events, the pop-pop-pop of rifle fire as the men on the ground began shooting at the descending airmen.

Subsequent research proved that one of the parachutists was the pilot of a Messerschmitt 109 who landed near a gunsite where he was treated to a few blows before being taken away. The other airman is believed to have been an RAF pilot, but no record of him descending on that date has been found. However, a witness recalled a fighter coming down 'at Rainham' in that period, not far away. In fact, such an RAF loss occurred the day before (30 August), but I definitely saw two paras descending on Saturday the thirty-first.

More certain is the data on two other incidents involving troops on the ground in action, events that occurred in 'the heat of the action', as one record put it, absurd though this seems. Pilot Officer King was in action with his Hurricane of 249 Squadron from Boscombe Down in the early afternoon of 16 August as his section was bounced by 109s. The RAF pilot's fighter caught fire and he baled out. The same fate also overtook Flt Lt James Nicholson, who abandoned his machine with severe burns to his face and hands. Below these descending airmen a group of Royal Artillerymen were ordered by their officer to take up position and open fire on them, LDVs also joining in. As a result, King's parachute canopy shrouds parted and he plunged to his death; Nicholson, already in great pain from his burns, was struck by shotgun pellets in the rear. When he hit the earth and was identified he was rushed to Southampton Hospital, where he made a full recovery and became the only member of Fighter Command to receive the Victoria Cross, for his action in the air battle. Unhappily, he was lost in a Liberator off Burma later in the war.

Dangerous amateurism on the part of one teenage Home Guard gave me another narrow squeak only a week or so later when, following the first successful German raid on London, we emerged yet again from our shelter to witness the amazing spectacle of the late-afternoon sun blotted out by an immense, broad mass of smoke as thousands of tons of goods went up in flames in the docks. Again, passing out front to exchange tales with my pals I discovered the citizen soldier mentioned had turned out in uniform to call on the two lads next door to us. As it happened, both families used the same brick path which broadened to serve the doors set at the sides of the separate terraces. I was in awe as the youth proudly showed me his rifle, another gun from across the Atlantic. It seemed a round had jammed in the breech, and he had been unable to shift it, but instead of reporting the fault to someone better qualified to deal with it he had been marching around to show himself off.

Having explained the problem the lad set the rifle down rather smartly by the butt on the brick path, which gave the weapon enough of a jolt to set it off. The bullet discharged with a loud bang, just missing us both and striking the nearer house wall. A sliver of wood was removed from my own front door five to six yards away, and naturally, those in the street not already gossiping outside rushed out in alarm, including my mother (my dad was, unknown to us, still trapped after his working day among the great fires and general dislocation around the docks). A few minutes later a police constable arrived on his bicycle to investigate.

But this experience was as nothing when compared to the fatal experience of others who had the misfortune to run into over-enthusiastic Home Guards in this period. With invasion expected daily – or nightly – and the warning church bells rung in at least one spot to signal the *Wehrmacht* had actually landed, nerves were on edge among many of the guardians wearing LDV and HG tags. Even as far away as Scotland the fear of German landings by sea and air had put everyone on alert; at one point even an Admiralty report was issued stating a German invasion fleet had set sail from Norway.

Two miles from the RAF base at Leuchars three Home Guards were on duty at a dark checkpoint one night when they saw a car approaching. The three soldiers stood astride the road, one of them waving a red warning lamp, fully expecting the vehicle to halt so they could examine the driver's credentials, namely his identity card, which every citizen was expected to carry at all times. To their surprise, the car showed no sign of slowing down and the men were obliged to leap aside to avoid being run down. Without further ado, two of the Home Guards levelled their rifles and fired at the fast-vanishing car. One of the bullets struck and killed the driver. The car ran off the road and hit a wall. When the Home Guards reached the wreck, they discovered the dead man was known to them; he was in fact one of the organisers and pillars of the local ARP service, a Mr David Calder. Only in recent times has William Paul admitted publicly that he believes it was his shot that killed Mr Calder. The Home Guards had done their duty; it is difficult to blame them.

But in another ugly incident in Norfolk blame can surely be levelled. Alan Chadwick was a fifteen-year-old plane fan who loved to cycle to the Boulton & Paul aircraft factory field at Norwich to watch planes being wheeled out and tested. Why he chose to make such an excursion on this night is unknown. His route led him past a Home Guard checkpoint manned by two teenage soldiers who called on the approaching cyclist to halt as per instructions. But the lad failed to do so, and in the darkness neither Home Guard realised it was a lad they knew; if they had, they would have known Alan Chadwick was deaf. It was very likely he had his head down and never even noticed them. Even so, it should not have been beyond the wit of the two young soldiers to physically apprehend the boy. Instead of doing that they levelled their rifles and fired, though even their poor shooting resulted in a ricochet striking Alan in the back. He crashed to the road, dead.

In an even more bizarre incident not one but two innocent civilians were shot dead by a Home Guard. It all began when an inspector from the Ministry of Agriculture arrived to inspect a field offered for the national need by a private owner. It was near Pitsea in Essex. The Battle of Britain was at its height and, as it happened, a German aircraft had been brought down that day in the area. The owner of the field, a woman, was outside when to her surprise and amusement her neighbour informed her a German was in 'her field' at the back. Despite also being told the contrary, the woman remained adamant: the stranger behaving suspiciously with a notebook in the field was a German. The episode then gathered momentum towards absurd and tragic proportions, as in no time a small crowd of locals invaded the field to apprehend the 'German'. A real fracas ensued, the innocent official protesting his identity and business, but he was manhandled as the mob tried to cart him off, now aided by Home Guard Mr Thomas Harris. At this point another man hurried to the scene, a Mr Barnard, who had witnessed everything and began remonstrating with his irate neighbours. Mr Harris, apparently completely overcome in the excitement, lost all control and shot James Barnard dead.

Despite this fantastic occurrence, when the Ministry of Agriculture inspector Mr Nichols attempted to escape and run away the mob pursued him, throwing him to the ground and confiscating his ID card when he tried to show it to them. Then, having left James Barnard lying dead on the grass, Thomas Harris ran to join the others, and in the general mêlée he shot Mr Nichols.

Harris was charged with manslaughter, and in sentencing him to twelve months in jail the judge commented that his excellent service record in the earlier war had saved him from a heavier sentence.

In yet another example of how men under stress can and do commit acts counted as atrocities, a well-known researcher into *Luftwaffe* activity over Britain mentioned the fate of two German airmen who landed on our soil. The first, he alleged, was killed by a farmer using a pitchfork, circumstances unknown; in the second case a *Luftwaffe* aircrewman parachuted down into Wapping, in London's East End, where he was set upon by a mob and killed. Such tales were mere rumours, very difficult to flesh out with facts without proper, time-consuming investigation; if an atrocity had taken place then, like others, it would be swept under the carpet, for such things simply did not happen on the Allied side. No more of the first incident seems to have come to light, but the other has been subject to further disclosure.

Many of the airmen who escaped from the advancing Germans in 1939–40 to fight with the RAF (Poles, Czechs, French, etc.) knew little English; it is evident that in some cases even RAF pilots themselves were taken for the enemy when parachuting on to their own soil. It seemed to many English civilians in the tense days of 1940 that any figure descending from the skies must be an enemy. It was one Polish airman's bad luck to come down in an area that, while still awaiting its real baptism of fire, had already received a few bombs. This clue as to date was passed on to me by my father-in-law, who resided in the Stepney area all his life. He has confirmed the incident really happened in Wapping:

> It was some time during the height of the Battle of Britain, probably late August 1940. The All Clear sounded after one of the afternoon raids so I went out into the street and down to the riverside, which was close by, for a look round. I saw a parachutist coming down and guessed he would land less than a mile away, in Wapping. A lot of people including some Home Guards were running through our street in that direction, and a few minutes later several police cars raced by. I went back indoors to tell my wife what was going on, and later that evening I went out again and met various friends and neighbours, all of whom couldn't wait to tell me what had happened. It seems there had been a fight and the airman had been killed. Later, I heard from a police inspector friend that a number of people had been arrested, but later released.

It seems obvious that the Pole's frantic attempts to explain himself had been to no avail.

Don't Wake the Führer

General Montgomery's bid to 'knock Rommel for six' in Africa began on 23 October 1942, an attack which opened with a barrage from nearly one thousand guns. After nearly ten days of heavy fighting the German–Italian army was being ground to pieces and the German commander sent an urgent despatch to Hitler requesting permission to retire to Fuka before his forces were completely annihilated.

This signal arrived at Hitler's HQ during the night of 3 November, to be received by the duty officer, Major Fussmann. In peacetime Fussmann had been director of an industrial concern, used only to reprimanding those below him if they committed errors. Major Fussmann was about to commit a blunder himself, one that would cost him dear.

The receipt of bad and even alarming news was commonplace at Hitler's HQ, most recently concerning the intensifying of the fighting for Stalingrad on the river Volga. It was late at night and as Rommel's signal was decoded Fussmann knew that both the *Führer* and his chief of staff General Jodl had retired to bed. As is well known, Hitler kept his entire staff awake half the night while he pored over battlefield maps or harangued intimates with endless monologues. Only after he finally gave up were they able to relax and go to their own quarters. On this night, despite the urgency of the Rommel message, Major Fussmann thought it wise not to have the master disturbed.

Next morning Jodl saw the signal and was baffled since the *Führer* had only just signed an order giving Rommel no choice but to stand and fight at El Alamein. In other words, as it transpired, Hitler was unaware of the true state of things in Africa. In fact, a delay had occurred in the sending of Hitler's order and it had only been despatched the previous night; obviously it would now be read by Rommel as a response to his own appeal. Indeed, this was the way the history of those tense days would be written up, as Hitler's refusal to allow a withdrawal, typical though it would have been.

When Hitler rose at 11.15 and eventually reached his ops room he was greeted with the bad news by Jodl and immediately asked about his own order, saying, 'Why have I only just been given this report from Rommel?' He then flew into a rage, demanding to know why he had not been woken up to see the Rommel signal. When Jodl attempted to explain, Hitler cut him short, now raving and ranting over 'more stupidity and indifference!' He would make an example of this major, he would be court-martialled at once. The staff in the adjoining rooms listened to the tirade – they had heard them before.

Just three hours later the unfortunate Fussmann was facing a court-martial. That evening sentence was passed: he was to be reduced to private and posted to a labour battalion.

Tanks All At Sea

The Churchill tanks had supported the infantry across the Norman fields, through the smoke and whistling shells and bullets until the enemy had been eased out of his positions. The fog of the battle swirled about the tanks as they halted, their commanders opening their turret hatches to try to gain their bearings. This was difficult; the hot summer dust and smoke from two burning tanks made visibility poor. Normally, it could have been fatal to get separated from the protecting foot soldiers on the battlefield; the enemy were too good at infiltrating back along the ditches and tall hedgerows, small bazooka squads adept at knocking out tanks at close range and vanishing again before they could be caught.

The situation was still fluid, and it came as a relief to the tankers when the call came to withdraw, to regroup, replenish their supplies and, hopefully, brew up some tea. The Squadron Lieutenant glanced around as the fog cleared. He could see no sign of *Angler*, not for the first time the crew seemed to have gone astray. Then the British artillery began lobbing in smoke shells to cover their withdrawal. The Lieutenant made an urgent call over his B set, but no response came from *Angler*, so he ordered the turret reversed and they began withdrawing. His sergeant then spotted a Churchill crossing their front, but it was not *Angler*. The smoke screen rolled around them, but just before his tank was enveloped the Lieutenant spotted his missing vehicle – there was Smith 161 shouting and cursing from his driving hatch as they went by. The Lieutenant waved, grinning with relief. *Angler*'s engine had stalled again, but now the squadron, minus the two tanks lost, was moving back to Hill 112, once more cut off from each other in the fog.

Suddenly, swivelling in his hatch, the Lieutenant realised he had lost his bearings, so called for his driver to halt. A moment's thought and he told him to bear right, but soon called a halt again, embarrassed and hoping his men could not see his reddening face as he peered at his map, and again at what little he could see of the terrain. Then, his straining, red-rimmed eyes were startled by two figures only a few feet to the left of the tank – Germans! Two machine-gunners. For a few seconds the officer was petrified, but puzzled by the complete lack of movement on the part of the camouflage-jacketed enemy. One of the Germans held the weapon, his chin resting on the butt, his eye sighting along the barrel, while his comrade lay alongside, holding the ammunition belt. Only then did the Britisher realise they were dead, killed cleanly but remaining at their post, their expressions somehow unconnected with death. Tearing his eyes away from this macabre sight, the Lieutenant switched to channel A on his radio: 'Hallo, Peter Five, I'm afraid I've lost my bearings. Can you give me a light?'

This was not an unusual situation, but on this occasion it proved a blunder. Within seconds the Lieutenant saw a white Very light soar up a few hundred yards to the right, so he ordered his driver to head in that direction. The smoke was now more intermittent, and *Avenger* had barely covered fifty yards when, gazing about them, the Lieutenant saw another light whizz up out of the fog, this time over to the left. And a second later several vague figures darted across their front, vanishing before he could focus on them. Then, as he called his driver to halt, the radio crackled to life and the familiar voice of Alan, his immediate superior, rang out loud and clear: 'There's your light – sorry about the delay. By the way, that other one was Jerry's!'

Aghast, the Lieutenant ordered his driver hard left. Through his glasses he could now make out a German 50mm a/t gun being manhandled into a new position to fire at them. Mercifully, more smoke shells arrived to hide them before the expected armour-piercing shot arrived. It wasn't his first blunder, and, he thought, would not be his last.

In fact, the next came the same day, that evening in fact. They had been ordered to move to another sector, just a mile or so, to take part in a dawn attack. The sunken lane they entered was blocked by some supply trucks caught by enemy fire. The Germans were still sending an occasional harassing airburst over the blazing trucks and MPs were directing traffic off the road and around the fields. An MP waving a shaded torch directed the tanks into a field well shrouded in smoke from the fires, and at once confusion reigned. Tankers leapt out to try to guide their drivers in the murk, and curses echoed about the field as collisions occurred. A call went out for a guiding light, just as more German shells began to arrive among the tanks, adding to the confusion. Then, into the rapidly darkening sky leapt the blue-white beam of a searchlight.

'Driver, make for the light!' the Lieutenant yelled above the racket of the shellfire and roar of tank engines. *Avenger* leapt forward and rolled down the sloping ground, well in the lead and leaving the confusion behind.

But suddenly, an urgent call erupted over the radio: 'All Peter stations! Ignore that bloody light – it's the enemy. I say again – ignore the light! Remain where you are!'

Aghast, the Lieutenant halted *Avenger*'s headlong dash down the field in time. Bobbing up from his turret top he looked back and saw they were now isolated – a perfect target. Hurriedly, he ordered his driver to reverse back up the field.

The enemy constantly monitored all battlefield transmissions, and the British tank crews' radio net security was never good at the best of times.

Low Tide at Tarawa

None of the marines had ever heard of it. They knew of the Phillipines, of course, of the surrender at Corregidor, and naturally the disaster at Pearl. But Tarawa? One more name on a bewildering list that had streamed from the news bulletins over the past year or two, outstanding among them Guadalcanal, where the 'Old Breed', the 1st Marines, had first hit back against the Japs. By now, November 1943, the tide had long turned; the enemy had been decisively defeated at Midway and MacArthur's strategy seemed to be working. He was no marine, and could never have begun the long, tough slog back without them. There was a long way to go yet, but these men were determined that when the stars and stripes were finally hoisted on the emperor's palace in Tokyo the hands that hoisted that flag aloft would belong to Marines.

That was the kind of remark Captain Nielsen had made in the last briefing below decks where the atmosphere was a good deal more stifling.

The regiment was aboard one of the transports in the convoy taking them to the atoll occupied by the enemy, just one of very many scattered across the Pacific. They imagined a few pimples of palm-covered sand, a beach maybe like that at Waikiki where there was a service club right there on the sand, where the lucky swabs had danced to Artie Shaw's Rangers, alias Navy Band 501, who had gone off across the ocean to play jungle areas. There would be no bands or gals or anything at Tarawa, no army either with a multitude of supplies the Marines could filch.

There was a certain sergeant in the First Platoon who liked to show off his know-how, unfolding a map he took from his duffle bag just so he could point out the various place names as they came up in the news. Cape Gloucester, New Britain, Rabaul in New Guinea, etc. He would shake his head, spitting tobacco juice and swearing it would take ten divisions and ten years to winkle out every slopehead from the many islands dotted across the vast Pacific ocean.

'Don't be an asshole,' the Top Sergeant said, 'we ain't gonna do it that way, see? We're just gonna knock out some of 'em and let the rest of them Nips starve!'

Nielsen was more precise: 'This is the big Jap base at Truk, OK?' he said, stabbing his forefinger at one of the dots on the map. 'In the Carolines. And these are the Gilberts. See the ones I've marked with a red ring? They're the ones the Nips have garrisoned, part of the defensive ring, they're very important to 'em. There's Tarawa atoll, and that little bastard's Betio. Got it? Betio – that's for us, OK?'

Already proud of US Marine Corps traditions, the new boots were itching to get at the enemy, while the old hands were more cautious; they'd seen how stubborn and fanatical the Japanese were. Grizzled veterans like Jake McConnell, who'd had more stripes than a zebra, and lost them, being busted over and over in many a brawl from Shanghai to San Francisco. His profanity and know-how were legendary throughout the battalion, and never far from his side was a kid called Kowalski who looked on the thick-set, thirty-plus-year-old McConnell as a god. The kid from New York's slums had volunteered for the Marines the day after the Japs bombed Pearl. Only a few weeks later he was learning the special Marine cadences at boot camp, the recruit training depot at San Diego. Oh – this is my gun and this is for fun! In one hand the kids held their Garand rifles, in the other their private parts, this outside the tents before breakfast, their sergeant instructor's way of ensuring newcomers etched into their minds the two things he saw as most important in life. There were many more things to remember, like the great inferiority of dogfaces – common soldiers of the Army. When Sergeant Howky found one of his squad walking around with his tie folded away into his shirt front he made him do one hundred press-ups on the spot.

'What'll I call you son, DAWGFACE? Never, never let me catch you dressed like that agin – got me?'

Kowalski and the other boots never tired of hearing the tales of derring-do spun by the likes of McConnell and the other handful of tough NCOs. Especially about the Japs lining the beach at Guadalcanal, stacked like cordwood or heaps of stinking seaweed after their failed counter-attack. Or Sergeant Brown's patrol that stumbled on a Jap village encampment.

'Gees, there ah was, the kunai grass way over mah haid, an' this goddam Nip dawg was a-howlin' at me. Christ, ah thought the whole Jap army was comin' at me!'

'Well, what happened, sarge?' they chorused, mouths agape.

'Why nothin' chile, ah jus' wen' an' grabbed that li'l pooch and took 'im along with me o' course!'

Captain Nielsen was an ex-West Pointer and claimed he had escaped to the Marine Corps; aside from the briefings he had little or no contact with the men. Not like Lieutenant Hilton, who was, they felt, almost uncomfortably buddy-buddy, always anxious to hear their complaints and show off his family snapshots.

Only when they arrived off the target islands did the Marines gain their first real glimpse of the fleet accompanying their troop convoy. Cries of 'Jesus!' 'How about that!' and 'Wow!' echoed back and forth along the ship's rail as they crowded the top deck in the grey dawn light. There were the silhouettes of great battleships ('That's the *South Dakota!*' – 'Naw, it ain't!'), cruisers and destroyers parking around the troopships. They saw dark pimples sticking up out of the lightening, calm sea; not even Nielsen could point out Betio, not yet. He always did his best to keep them abreast of the general war situation – how things were in Russia, how the mighty 8th was going in the skies over Europe, and how proud he was of his battalion. Now all their thoughts centred on what lay ahead.

The whole convoy moved like some giant tableau, at slowest speed, closing in not on a welcoming group of South Sea paradise islands where a rising sun would disclose hula girls bringing countless lei garlands to dangle about them, but a dismal, grey-purple patch of ocean on which were placed the checkerboard pieces of dung infested with the yellow vermin the Americans desired above all else to wipe from the face of the earth. And everything went very still. It was uncanny, as if an unspoken signal or hand had reached out to stop the pattern of ships right there. The men's voices became muted; here and there an officer pointed at what he saw as their objectives. Some of the warships then slid silently around the islands, and all at once with a thudding roar the bombardment began. The Marines cried out as great gushes of yellow-orange and red flame shot from the gun mouths of the biggest warships. The din rolled around them, seeming to echo back and forth across the sea.

The thing that most astonished the watching soldiers was the sight of the huge sixteen-inch missiles glowing red and quite visible as they hurtled in great arcs over the sea, to land and detonate on what they now knew was Betio. Flame and smoke erupted all over the luckless lump of sand, coral and tree palms, a scene of utter destruction and desolation that had the Marines cheering and clapping as their eager minds pictured the awful hell being meted out on their enemies. And there was more for the show: carrier-borne planes now began swooping on the island. Helldivers roared down to drop their heavy bombs; between them Hellcat fighters began strafing everything, but especially the beach areas. Before long the little atoll was wreathed in yellow-grey smoke. Not a tear was shed at the thought of the Japanese undergoing the Navy treatment.

Then came the order to get ready, and the Marines began donning their gear. Stomachs began turning as the NCOs went among the men, checking, admonishing, passing out reminders: 'Be sure to keep your weapons dry, men', 'Be sure to correct your elevation, check your windage – tighten that belt!' Such instructions assumed they would reach shore and be ready for action to wipe out the miserable Japs still alive in the inferno of fire and brimstone. It was gone 03.30 hrs and their spotty green and sand suits were staining with sweat as they tried to adjust pack straps, move grenades and ammo pouches for more comfort, shake water bottles and make feeble, last-minute jokes. They had put on clean underwear to lessen the risk of wound infection – so Lieutenant Hilton alleged.

Then, at long last, the final salvos slammed out from the big boys, though the destroyers had moved in closer and were still banging away with their five-inchers. An officer blew a whistle, and the first Marines began scrambling over the ship's side as the landing craft drew alongside. They'd rehearsed it all, yet there were always accidents – broken legs as overladen men lost their balance and toppled into the water or back-first on to a heaving deck. This time one Marine got his boot caught in the nets as he tried to drop into the landing craft. He hung upside down, swinging this way and that, until freed without injury. But then another unlucky Marine fell between the craft and the ship and sank like a stone. The 2nd Marines had suffered their first loss of the day.

By the time the laden, flat-bottomed craft with their Navy crews set course they were one mile off the smoke-shrouded shoreline of Betio. At 700 yards, to the amazement of every Marine, the throbbing engines wound down to a gentle purr and the ramps crashed down into four feet of water. The Marines' amazement turned to anger and curses flew at the swabbies in the rear of the craft. Not that it was of the slightest use; the many planning conferences from General MacArthur downwards had failed to allow for low tide at Tarawa Atoll.

'Semper fi you lucky marines – get the lead out!'

The NCOs raged at the Navy and Marine staffs' incompetence but recovered swiftly to get their men out of the landing craft. They leapt and fell into the gentle swell, to begin the long walk to shore, cursing volubly but with humour – for so far not a single bullet, mortar or artillery shell had come at them. The sea sucked at them, increasing their weight. Some of the waves that looked so graceful lapped past the armpits of shorter men as, rifles and BARs and machine-gun parts held high, they walked slowly ashore, the temptation to start dumping gear already with some of them.

Not a dozen yards from the now empty landing craft, just as the sailors revved their motors to withdraw, the Marines heard the first Jap machine-gun rattle and the first swathe of lead swept across them, knocking men down like skittles into the sea. In seconds the surprised troops heard a veritable chorus of Jap automatics blasting from the intact bunkers craftily hidden under masses of logs just above the shoreline. As the smoke cleared the surviving enemy came to life and sighted their easy targets. The slaughter began. For the Americans it was the greatest agony to see the muzzle flashes of the Jap weapons, yet be bogged down by the terribly slow wading through the sea. Marines fell on all sides – novices, NCOs, even Captain Nielsen, who fell on his knees, clutching his throat, his encouraging calls strangled in blood until he vanished under the waves which were reddening about him.

The din was saddening, yells of rage, frustration, anguish and pain mixing with the hoarse bawling cries of the surviving NCOs to encourage their troops ashore. Every second brought death as the Marines heard the last cries of their buddies around and behind them. They forced themselves on through the water, tears in the eyes of some, the first shock of battle proving too horrible, far beyond their recent imaginings of a triumphant rush up the sandy beach to wipe out any remaining enemy before planting the Stars and Stripes on the highest point of the God-forsaken island. Now everything seemed to vanish. It was impossible any of them would reach the shore alive; most of the boys who had never seen an enemy soldier or fired a round in anger were vanishing in the grey-green waves that lapped that still-distant shoreline. There, the white foam brushing the sand had already been tarnished with bits of debris from the American bombardment. Soon it would turn yet more colourful with American blood.

Somehow, a handful of Marines reached the shore, among them the battalion major who urged them off the sand and among the debris beyond. They raced on a few yards and fell dripping to the ground. Bathed in salt water and sweat, breathing in gasps, some grazed by near misses, they gaped about them and out to the sea where the remains of the unit were still struggling ashore. Suddenly, a crack, and one soldier slumped sideways. 'Somebody get that son-of-a-bitch!' the Major yelled, and the six men about him swung round to blaze away at the cut-down trees behind them. A brownish figure fell to the ground without a sound. Then they moved left to outflank the nearest Jap machine-gun nest, and at once saw one of their cursed enemies leap across a gap between great heaps of debris to vanish in another bunker hole. Well, the Marines carrying the flame-thrower had somehow survived, one man with a twin-pack tank of fuel, the other brandishing the hose and nozzle. A squeeze on the trigger and a gush of brilliant, liquid fire arced out to encompass the Jap bunker. A scream, and a khaki figure appeared, flaring up like celluloid,

US Marines wade ashore in yet another Pacific island assault, this time the Tarawa atoll.

Tough battles with many casualties resulted once on Betio Island.

dead before he hit the blackening sand. In this fashion were the Jap defences rolled up on Betio, by small squads of survivors lucky to be alive.

The blunder of the tides had cost the Marines up to 40% casualties on Tarawa, the irreplaceable NCOs suffering as much as the officers. Hundreds would never proudly strut the streets of San Diego in their Marine greens again.

Ruin befalls a South Sea island paradise.

Then came the disaster at Peleliu, where the 1st Marines suffered appalling casualties in another probably avoidable blunder.

It was not the American way to think defensively, and certainly never the Marine way. Aggressiveness and the good old charge ('Up an' at 'em!') and how to shoot were the mainstays of Marine recruit training, rather than the craft of soldiering. This never changed and brought heavy casualties, the needless loss of not only young lives but the experienced NCOs that broke up regimental organisation. These things the British discovered when they fought alongside the US Marines in Korea. The Americans preferred to huddle in shallow holes under severe Chinese bombardment. These useless little foxholes were surrounded by rubbish and bits of barbed wire, of menace only to the defenders; virtually un-protected, the Americans took heavy casualties. When their positions were taken over by more thoroughly trained troops of the Black Watch their commander at once had them clean up the area and start digging proper bunkers for shelter from Chinese fire. As a result they suffered not one casualty from that form of assault.

Hanawa's Counter-stroke

By early 1944, two years after the disasters in the Far East, the tide seemed to have turned for good in favour of the Allies. The Americans were leap-frogging across the Pacific, the Australians containing and eliminating the Japanese threat in New Guinea, while on the massive land front of Burma the danger of an enemy invasion of India seemed gone for good.

The Japanese thought otherwise.

General Hanawa had laid his plans well for a counter-stroke that would not only stop the British advance cold in Burma but destroy their divisions so that a new 'March on Delhi' could begin. To achieve this aim the six to seven thousand troops of his attack force had been liberally issued with orders, maps and diagrams outlining Hanawa's plan, and an exact schedule for achieving the various objectives. Indeed, so confident was the Japanese command that it had even passed a copy of this assault timetable to Radio Tokyo; as a result, the silken tones of 'Tokyo Rose' pronounced 'victories' over the coming days according to the script provided, which was quite out of synch with reality on the battlefield. 'Things are all up with the British in Burma', she informed her listeners. Because the Japanese made a habit of taking such plans into battle with them, their enemy soon discovered this schedule and ensured its disruption.

Initially, the Japanese assault began well. The enemy XVth Corps would disintegrate as had the former units in 1942; the headlong flight of the disorganised British forces westwards would make them ripe for piecemeal destruction by concentric attacks from flank and rear. Again, Japanese confidence in this scenario was such that their soldiers were ordered not to fire on Allied transport, which was to be preserved for capture and use by the victors in their drive into India. Furthermore, the Japanese took no artillery into battle – it would only impede swift movement; instead, they sent teams of gunners ready to use captured British guns. The British 7th Division would have to retreat through Ngakyedauk Pass, where it would be ambushed and destroyed, after which all the Japanese forces would fall on the 5th Division as it tried to escape across the Naf River. Sakurai Force would then take Chittagong, where the local population would, through the instigation of the Indian National Army, rise up to attack and generally impede the British.

The other Japanese detachment, Kubo Force, thrust north to Goppo Bazaar, closing the roads before swinging west to cross the difficult Maya range where they were faced with precipitous hillsides without tracks. This did not bother them. They climbed and hauled their machine-guns and mortars and supplies, scrambling up the cruel slopes like ants, determined to succeed, and finally bursting out across the Bawli–Maungdaw road to take the various administrative area units, complete with headquarters, by surprise. The relatively lush lifestyle of these British troops was suddenly shattered as hundreds of yelling Japs came rushing at them out of the jungle. The enemy blew bridges and attacked the headquarters, causing mayhem and panic in accordance with their timetable. All was going well for General Hanawa.

Crisis loomed for the British C-in-C, General Slim, as he received a stream of reports from the beleaguered admin boxes of his 14th Army as the victorious enemy troops poured into the highly vulnerable areas containing the British supply dumps of petrol, food, ammunition and vehicle parks. Desperate hand-to-hand fighting ensued, as on that first night the Japanese soldiers succeeded in rushing the main hospital dressing station, where they bayoneted and shot the wounded in their cots, lining up the medical staff and executing them before forcing some Indian orderlies to take away their own wounded to safety, after which these bearers were shot. A battery of British five-inch guns was blazing away at the enemy at only 400 yards' range; when asked by signal how the battle was going, they replied, 'Fine. But can you send us some bayonets?' The atrocity at the hospital would be avenged.

The Japanese command blundered completely in their battle assumptions, and the collapse of their march into India now began. For a start, the Allied forces did not flee in panic. The British, Indian and Gurkha troops stood firm, and by mid-February General Hanawa knew he had miscalculated. To his loss of face with his superiors was now to be added the complete annihilation of his forces. Four Allied divisions swept down on to his crumbling army, 'like a hammer on an anvil' as General Slim put it later, destroying the enemy almost to a man. Of the Sakurai Force of 7,000 soldiers, 5,000 bodies were counted. Many hundreds more wandered off to die of exhaustion, wounds and starvation in the jungle.

The British and Allied forces in Burma had finally exorcised the myth of Japanese invincibility on the ground, while in the air the enemy air force and their latest fighter types were driven from the skies. This Japanese error had a profound effect on the war in Burma, and beyond.

The Sicilian Pillbox

At the start of the campaign in Sicily, in July 1943, a small episode of little or no significance to the main battles on the island occurred.

The British and American armies under Generals Montgomery and Patton were to land on Sicily two months after the Axis capitulation in North Africa, where a quarter of a million soldiers surrendered, some 125,000 of these German. Coming as it did on the heels of the disaster at Stalingrad, the loss of yet another whole army came as a second terrible blow to Hitler.

There were only two German divisions on Sicily, one of them the tough Hermann Goering *Panzergrenadier*; the other six were Italian, most assigned the role of coastal defence and ripe for surrender before the invasion fleet came over the horizon. The two-pronged Allied assault would take on the nature of a race between the rivals, Patton and Monty, to be much written up later. Many small encounters would never be recorded, save perhaps in abbreviated form in unit histories. One such occurred when two small parties comprising British commandos and pioneers were landed on a remote part of the island coast in order to reconnoitre any Italian resisters. Little opposition was expected in this pre-dawn landing as the soldiers scrambled ashore well ahead of the main armies then about to begin disembarking from their transports offshore. Although these were accompanied by warships, there was no pre-landing bombardment. The invasion morning produced something like an anti-climax, especially for the tough commandos who in their young zeal were fired up for action.

Obviously, the Germans had concentrated their own force inland, leaving their supposed allies to resist on the coast, though having little faith in the Italian soldiers putting up much of a fight. As the commandos climbed the bare slopes, weapons at the ready, the troopships at sea began disembarking their loads. The commandos' enthusiasm soon evaporated as they encountered not a soul, and as they reached the clifftop, sweating and tiring from the climb, their officers commiserated with each other on the disappointment they shared. No commando had fired a shot, no pioneer had seen a chance to blow up any enemy forts and bunkers.

The two squads then pushed on along the clifftop ridge, until in a sudden dip they encountered an enemy pillbox. Uncamouflaged, its dirty-looking concrete sat among the sandy soil and scrub grass, with a steel door visible at the rear, its weapon slits placed for all-round defence. The two British parties had dropped to the ground to survey this menace, both officers peering through binoculars, trying to decide if the post was manned. No weapons poked through the embrasures. Finally, the commando lieutenant remarked, 'It's OK, old chap, we can deal with this.'

'Oh?' the pioneer officer responded. 'It's one for us, I believe.'

So they tossed a coin. The pioneer won and brought his men forward with their explosives to set charges around the structure as the commando officer withdrew in disgust with his own troops.

Suddenly, all the British soldiers were startled to see a solitary figure in green uniform appear beside the pillbox. It was one of the Italian defenders. He peered at the invaders briefly before vanishing through the steel door again. Not a moment later a white rag tied to a stick was poked out of the doorway. The British watched with mixed feelings as several Italians, minus equipment, stepped tentatively outside. The two British lieutenants grinned and cursed mildly.

The commando officer sat down to open up his ration pack and his men started to brew some tea while their engineer comrades got on with the job. The commando officer, grinning, now suggested 'tickling up' the Italians with a Bren. His opposite number obliged, picking up their light machine-gun to send a burst of fire over the heads of the startled Italians, who rushed back into their bunker. A moment later they fired a few token shots from their embrasures, this act finally sealing their fate.

'That settles it,' the pioneer officer remarked, and he ushered his men off with their explosive charges. The pillbox door had been left ajar so that the white flag could continue to be waved in surrender. A few more rounds changed that. The door was slammed shut and the pioneers got on with their task, laying charges at intervals round the bunker and with-drawing hurriedly.

The engineer officer had never been in any doubt as to his proper course of action: every enemy fortification found had to be destroyed, with or without the enemy within. He now stood erect, contemptuous of any possible Italian fire, announcing that the commandos would now see a demonstration in the art of demolition. The wretched Italians, mean-while, unaware perhaps that their last moments were at hand, were jabbering together inside what was about to prove their steel and concrete coffin.

And so it proved. The enemy soldiers' arguments among themselves on the best course of action were cut short very abruptly as the charges were detonated and the whole structure, complete with occupants, was reduced to rubble in an explosion that proved most satisfying for the onlookers, who then proceeded to enjoy breakfast as they admired their handiwork and watched the troop-laden craft approaching the beaches.

Razing Royan

As is well known, plenty of bombing blunders occurred as thousands of Allied and enemy warplanes scoured the fronts. Even as late as January 1945, when one might have thought liaison between all sections of the military had been perfected, there occurred one of the worst episodes involving RAF bombers and French citizens.

During the night of 4/5 January two formations of 100 and 200 bombers dropped 1,651 metric tons of bombs on the little French port of Royan at the mouth of the Gironde estuary. The region had been, and indeed still was, part of the German 'Atlantic Wall' fortifications, but once again inadequate intelligence led the British staffs to assume the enemy troops still holding out were actually in the town itself. By then, of course, the battle for France was long over, barring a few stubborn pockets of resistance. Why these enemy forces were not left to starve or wait for the main surrender later on is unknown – once more the British used a sledgehammer to crack a nut. The bomb tonnage dropped on the town of Royan exceeded that loosed during the 'thousand-bomber raid' on Cologne in 1942 by 200 tons. The 354 Lancasters hitting Royan added fourteen tons of incendiaries to finish the job. Between three and four thousand French citizens were still living in the town, but not one German was present. Half the civilians were killed or buried in the debris.

How did this needless error occur? It seems that the message from Supreme HQ Allied Expeditionary Forces did not reach the French commander with the US 6th Army outside the town until too late, because the message was in French and the American signalman could not understand it. It took the Americans four hours to translate and decode the signal before passing it to the one man who might just have been able to avoid the disaster.

This great war saw many more such tragedies, not least the destruction of the élite British 1st Airborne Division at Arnhem, a disaster almost meant to happen given the state of mind of most involved in that epic on the British side – and among them one must include the Army commander, Field Marshal Montgomery.

The SOE in Holland

German Intelligence – the *Abwehr* – showed incompetence bordering on the ludicrous in its efforts to infiltrate spies into Britain during the early part of World War II. For example, in one case an agent was landed on the east coast of Scotland and went to the nearest small railway station clutching a suitcase containing a radio transmitter and some sausage. To suddenly appear in the dawn hours as a stranger at a lonely Scottish wayside station was suspicious enough; to open a suitcase and begin eating his German sausage when aboard the train for London capped it. Long before reaching its destination the train had been boarded by detectives who, on reaching London, had the would-be spy in custody.

By way of contrast, the *Abwehr* carried out one of the greatest counter-coups of the war on its 'home' territory – Holland. This intriguing, in fact fantastic, story has been told more than once; in the context of this work an outline will suffice in order to point out a small but very significant blunder on the part of MI6, and subsequently the disaster involving SOE.

The German invasion of Holland on 10 May 1940 sent the Dutch royal family and some trusted officials and officers to London. It was dis-covered that Dutch Intelligence had been thoroughly incompetent and had failed to set up a network of agents to operate during the enemy occu-pation. These officers still in Holland were in disgrace. They gave an undertaking to the occupiers not to indulge in anti-German activity, and in most cases stuck to it. The Dutch government-in-exile in Britain there-fore had to begin again from scratch in setting up a fresh intelligence department, naturally approaching the British, who insisted (not unnat-urally) on controlling everything. It was then that the Dutch officer appointed discovered something of the true nature of the game he was entering. As a straightforward Army man, he found himself in the hands of professionals who were devious, cunning and ready to hoodwink or probably double-deal anyone save their own kin.

It was MI6 who, anxious to know everything about the German occupation in Holland and their invasion preparations, sent in a young Dutch naval officer called Van Hamel who had come to their notice following various valiant acts he had performed around the Dunkirk evacuation period. Van Hamel was successfully parachuted back into Holland in August 1940 in an attempt to rebuild the British spy network ruined by the incompetence of Messrs Best and Stevens in the 'Venlo Incident'. At this time the German security apparatus had barely got itself into the saddle in the occupied countries. In Holland the *Gestapo* and SIPO (Security Police) were under the command of one Joseph Schreieder and were working quite separately from the *Abwehr*. By then the deadly rivalry between the two had been established following the creation of the Nazis' own SD; the 'accord' ostensibly hammered out between Admiral Canaris for the *Abwehr* and Reinhard Heydrich of the SD never worked. If it was thought the SS–SD, with the *Gestapo*, could handle the political side of counter-espionage, leaving the military side to the old established *Abwehr*, then this proved a fallacy. The two facets were too often linked.

Van Hamel proved very successful in setting up a working spy network, with the most valuable assistance of a *Luftwaffe* mechanic he had met before the war. The German apologised for his country's invasion, then proceeded to supply a stream of documents, including plans of German airfields. Much was radioed to London, but by October Lieutenant Van Hamel needed a rest and asked MI6 to honour its promise to extract him when necessary. The British refused, apparently insisting that all its agents stayed in the field. Exchanges continued, with MI6 procrastinating, but suddenly ordering Van Hamel to be at a certain lake rendezvous in three days for pick-up by seaplane. It was short notice for the agent, but he arrived with two helpers to reconnoitre the lake, which was near a village, the three posing as bird watchers and cycling around the area. This incurred the suspicion of the local policeman, to the extent that when the day for the pick-up came Van Hamel and his friends were already under arrest and the lake surrounded by German troops with flak, searchlights and security officers. The seaplane that arrived days late was Dutch, as was its crew, in the pay of MI6, and as it began circling the lake the Germans switched on their searchlight and opened fire. Shaken, their plane holed, the Dutch airmen just managed to escape back to England.

The Dutch police, the agents belatedly learned, were anxious to co-operate with the enemy; indeed, some of the Dutch officers had already been pro-Nazi before the invasion, in keeping with the largest fascist

Claude Dansey, cunning, ruthless executive head of MI6 in World War II.

Lieutentant van Hamel, a brave Dutchman, successful spy but shot by the Germans in June 1941.

A Dutch Fokker float plane as used by MI6.

movement in that country outside Germany. Having observed the 'bird watchers' carting a suitcase about with them, the village policeman had made the fact known to his superiors; as a result the German police, with Dutch help, had had the area thoroughly searched until the important item was found – by a Dutch policeman. The Dutch area police commandant was a pro-Nazi and had pursued the case with vigour, all the better to ingratiate himself with his Nazi masters. From this episode MI6 learned one valuable lesson: as a rule the Dutch police could not be relied upon to help. Not that at first they had any idea of the cause of the disaster, so they persisted in making foolish blunders in one crucial direction that seemed to belie their reputation as experts. Van Hamel's papers were poor forgeries, and this was evident to the Dutch and German police who at once noticed the worst blunder: the prisoner's date of birth was shown as 29 February 1915 – a non-leap year if ever there was one.

Van Hamel and his two helpers were taken off by the Germans, and when little progress was made in the interrogations the ringleader was removed for more specialised 'treatment' by the SS, who used both psychological and more direct methods to try to extract everything. But Van Hamel was brave and stood up well to the barbaric handling, repeating over and over again how he was serving Queen and country and in any case was unable to tell them what they wanted to hear because he had made a vow of silence, rather like a nun or a member of the Mafia. When facing a military tribunal this stand impressed the German court, some of the officers allegedly saluting him and, when the death sentence was pronounced, walking out in protest, which seems unusual. It was the normal penalty for spying in wartime and had been and was being carried out by the British. The German SIPO chief, Joseph Schreieder, was openly criticised by the court for his failure to produce results from the interrogations.

Schreieder had been shocked and embarrassed by the discovery of a British spy ring operating under his nose for two or three months, and had been obliged to allow the *Abwehr* ace sleuth Major Hermann Giskes into the case. Though two separate agencies, in this operation the two managed to achieve co-operation, and it brought results far beyond any expectations. This came about as a result of the intervention of the new Special Operations Executive, which soon followed MI6 in despatching agents to Holland. The myth grew up later that this sprawling agency sprang to life through a memo of Winston Churchill, which recommended that occupied Europe be set ablaze through sabotage to make the Germans' life a misery. In fact, studies had already been carried out along such lines before the war, though, as in other areas, it was Churchill's prodding that helped things along, even though the much-ridiculed Neville Chamberlain actually began the agency before his death late in 1940.

Whatever blunders were made in the MI6 forgery department, the senior secret service acted more professionally by far in other ways. Following the discovery of Dutch police collusion with the occupiers (some Dutch policemen were, however, patriots), MI6 acted more circumspectly, its radio operators in Britain better trained in the game which meant life or death to agents in the field. By contrast, SOE began its operations in cock-eyed fashion, its whole organisation riddled with incompetence, amateurism and a shocking lack of security, to mention just a few of its faults. Its Dutch section was split against itself. The first agents trained rebelled against their chiefs and were despatched to Scotland (for disciplinary reasons). The section was intrigued against by the far more devious MI6 personnel, and when the head of a Dutch underground organisation reached Britain later he was appalled to find a bunch of bureaucrats living a comparatively lush life in London and fighting among themselves. The fantastic lapses and oversights committed by SOE continued, enabling Giskes and Schreieder to totally hoodwink London into believing it was running a successful resistance movement in Holland, in much the same way that the British Double-X Committee fooled the *Abwehr* into believing it had a spy ring operating in England throughout the war.

The complications in London seemed endless. The Dutch wished to run their own show in Holland; the British assisted them, but in reality controlled everything vital. Far too many departments became involved, three or four all told, working without central direction or cohesion, often against each other's best interests, and in fact, in the eyes of some, quite needlessly. For it was suggested that Holland, with its dense population, was a country quite unsuitable for acts of sabotage, which was SOE's main theme.

Not that the twenty-five-year-old Van Hamel ever learned of the mess being made behind him. He was shot in June 1941, by which time things had moved on considerably. The agents being parachuted or sent in by motor boat were being rounded up by the Germans. The next brave Dutchman to fall into enemy hands, by the name of Lauwens, continued to believe in the invincibility of the British, even after his capture, asserting to himself that the regular parade of other seized agents in the 'Orange Hotel' jail were simply being sacrificed by SOE as part of some amazing triple-bluff. Lauwens agreed to transmit for Major Giskes in the belief that by omitting his security check the operator in London would realise he was in enemy hands. Indeed, even though Lauwens continued to get away with this ploy, even with a German operator at his elbow and (at first) a room full of excited Germans, SOE did not once catch on, and from then on were servants to the Germans' whims. The new German firm of Schreieder and Giskes set up Operation 'North Pole', by which they invited London to despatch flight after flight of agents and supplies at arranged rendezvous points, ready and able to accept everything sent. At one point the chiefs of SOE in London were despatching agents and supplies nightly. In fact, to give but one example, in one night's drop alone eighteen tons of arms and explosives fell into the hands of the waiting Germans.

Although the new co-operation between *Abwehr* and SIPO worked well, the latter gaining confidence and expertise and even outshining the more experienced Giskes on occasion, none of the Germans' successes could have been achieved without their constant use of 'V-men', trusted Dutch traitors and *agents provocateurs* who infiltrated everywhere and sent so many brave Dutchmen to the torture chamber, the firing squad or concentration camp. The episodes surpass spy fiction. The Germans kept very busy racking their brains to avoid giving things away in the constant radio game. For example – and this is an exact parallel of the case involving the British double agent Eddie Chapman, who was sent in by parachute by the Germans and carried out an act of sabotage against the de Havilland plane factory with the help of MI5; the event was duly allowed some space in the press, the Germans swallowing the fiction – SOE asked one of their groups in Holland to blow up a German radio-radar site. Schreieder and Giskes obliged, arranging a small explosion and the firing of blank ammunition to simulate a battle. This episode was reported in the Dutch papers, London SOE gaining satisfaction thereby.

No matter how many warnings the brave Lauwens sent to London by radio, SOE seemed to notice nothing amiss. It is stretching credulity, but the *Englandspiel* went on for over two years, by which time it had become rather routine, almost boring for the Germans. It had, however, by 1943 taken on greater importance, for the Germans at the top level believed their enemy in Britain was using the Dutch operation as some cover connected with invasion plans. The idea the Germans would believe for one moment that Holland could be the target for D-day is erroneous, but the huge success brought about by 'North Pole' attracted both Himmler's attention and a visit from Minister Goebbels to view a real-life enemy agent (there were always plenty to show off), and to hear how the game was progressing. Hitler also closely followed these cases. Not until later in 1943 did the British and Dutch of SOE begin to believe things were unwell with their game in Holland, so it was finally wound up. Belatedly, over fifty agents would pay for it with their lives, Giskes having the nerve and humour to send a sign-off message to London in English from his own side.

After the war, an inquiry concluded that 'errors of judgement' had been made in London, while the post-war Dutch authorities seemed to conclude that the lives of their own people had been cynically sacrificed in some British double- or triple-bluff. Even if that were true, the manipulators could only have been MI6, and the blunders of SOE were real enough. From its own operations, MI6 lost only three agents.

As executive chief of the German security police, Joseph Schreieder was held responsible for allowing up to twelve of the prisoners to escape. Rauter, the Nazi boss in Holland, wanted him to be put before a court, especially when it was discovered how lenient he had been in permitting captives to be held in comparatively luxurious conditions in the old monks' training college converted into a prison at Haarlem. There the prisoners were kept under Dutch SS guard in rooms fitted with radios, with sheets on the beds. When this kind of report reached London via escapees it was flatly disbelieved. In the event, Schreieder escaped the court, but his powers were reduced and he was no longer allowed access to prisoners.

The *Abwehr* in 1944 suffered the loss of its chief, Admiral Canaris, who was arrested following the failed bomb plot against Hitler in July 1944. But Major Giskes also escaped lightly. He was not arrested and continued good work from a new base in Belgium, also taking a hand in crushing the huge SOE circuit called PROSPER in northern France. Therein lies another blunder by the British, an incredible story in which SOE managed to get itself completely outmanoeuvred by both the SD and its deadly rival and part mentor, MI6.

Having failed to win the chairmanship of the SIS late in 1939 when the incumbent 'C', Admiral Cummings, died, Claude Dansey became the effective 'field exec' under the new chief, Sir Stewart Menzies. Dansey was a totally dedicated and ruthless spymaster who, it seems, was perfectly ready to sacrifice Allied lives to win his own game, which in this case was to penetrate the SD in France. Sometimes referred to as 'Uncle Claude', Dansey, deprived of funds, had set up his own 'Z' organisation before the war, recruiting businessmen and others who were based in or travelled on the continent to spy for him, paralleling the network of the regular SIS. The SIS never seems to have forgiven the politicians for stealing one of their sections as a basis for the new SOE, but Dansey ensured the new spy and sabotage organisation was fully monitored. SOE was obliged for some time to use MI6 communication facilities and never broke free of Dansey's surveillance.

Claude Dansey was cunning and determined enough to effectively run his own show without regard for his chief, Menzies, and having met one Henri Dericourt, a French pilot adventurer, Dansey decided to use him for his own ends. Dericourt had by chance met the SD executive in Paris, Karl Boemelburg, before the war when Boemelburg was in France, ostensibly to help the French police root out expatriate German Red terrorists. The authorities in Paris finally woke up to Boemelburg's real business, which was spying, and he was expelled. When the *Wehrmacht* occupied France, Boemelburg and his SD police moved into the Avenue Foch in Paris, Dericourt once more popping up to renew his acquaintance. A few months later the Frenchman reached London where he at once told MI5 he was in touch with German Intelligence. The Security Service recommendation was that he should not be employed; Claude Dansey thought otherwise. Dericourt was allowed to be snapped up by the new SOE, who were unaware he was already in the employ of a man said later by several leading figures of the British Intelligence establishment (including Hugh Trevor-Roper, Lord Dacre) to be 'evil'.

As GILBERT, Dericourt was sent back to France to act as 'movements officer', arranging the comings and goings of the hundreds of agents and vast quantities of supplies sent to the PROSPER ring in northern France. But every single one of these drops and pick-ups by RAF planes was known to Boemelburg and his deputy, Josef Kieffer, through regular meetings with Dericourt. Dansey, too, was well in the picture, having his own link to Dericourt. When the first reports of GILBERT's double-dealing reached SOE they dismissed them, certainly never realising he was actually controlled by Dansey. As a result, their whole organisation in northern France was wiped out.

Dansey made certain his man monitoring the SD in France was protected, and when it was all over Dericourt found himself honoured with various awards, including the British DSO, which however, was never gazetted and was withdrawn. When at last, after the war, the French themselves decided to press charges of treason against Dericourt – not to mention the matter of hundreds of agents arrested, tortured and executed – Dansey's MI6 hounds so undermined the prosecution witnesses (including former SD and *Abwehr* men) that the case collapsed. Dansey had shown great delight on hearing of PROSPER's collapse in 1944, though SOE was not wound up as a result of its ineptitude.

The then head of SOE refused to believe that GILBERT had been a double agent, going so far as to send a memo in December 1945 denouncing all those who had doubted him. Only later did he admit incredulously he had been deceived. The truth was that in matters of double-dealing and deceit the chiefs and staff of SOE were mere bungling amateurs, as proved by Claude Dansey and others of MI6. It would have seemed incredible, unbelievable, to the British public in the 1940s and later that rivalry between their secret services could exist to such a deadly extent.

Karl Boemelburg was transferred from the lush environs of Paris in 1944, following the triumphs over SOE, unaware all along that his man GILBERT (later called CLAUDE, perhaps appropriately) had also been working for their far deadlier opponent, MI6. In fact, Dericourt himself had thought Dansey and his men simply part of 'British Intelligence'; even the *Abwehr* and SD never seemed to grasp the fact of quite separate, rival organisations. In that respect they paralleled the *Abwehr* and SD who in Paris worked to get in each other's hair, sparks flying between the two agencies.

From all these wartime machinations the British MI6 emerged the winner, and, as one former member remarked much later, 'if you're going to get involved in these things, you must never admit anything afterwards'. That, generally, has been the way of the British, though in more recent times a younger generation has sprung up less able to 'keep their mouths shut', seeking in well-publicised cases to feed ego and bank balance by disclosing secrets and betraying the code of silence which has always been the hallmark of the best and most secret services.

Boemelburg, sent to ensure Marshal Pétain's security at Vichy, went into hiding once the war was over. He was said to have obtained employment as a humble gardener near Munich, later taking over the care and maintenance of his employer's library. His boss, Helmut Knochen, was executed for the killing of British SAS soldiers. Claude Dansey died of natural causes in 1947, while his protégé Henri Dericourt went on to become a pilot, having faked his log book entries. He became involved in drug smuggling in the Far East before dying in a plane crash in 1962.

The Submariners' Lot

Winston Churchill once remarked to crews of the Eighth Flotilla in the Mediterranean in 1943 that they faced grimmer perils than any other branch of the services. This they knew, for no fewer than fourteen submarines had been lost in that theatre the previous year, seventy officers and 720 rating comrades vanishing with them. Some of these boats had been sunk by enemy anti-submarine craft, others had struck mines. And submarines faced other dangers peculiar to them: the risk of being run down at night if on the surface, and that of misidentification. The world's largest serving submarine, the French *Surcouf* of 2,800 tons displacement, for example, was ordered to the Pacific following the Japanese offensives in December 1941. Setting off from Bermuda and carrying, in addition to its French crew, several British liaison officers, the boat was due to pass through the Panama Canal, en route for Tahiti. *Surcouf* never reached the Canal Zone. The American freighter SS *Thompson Lykes* radioed that during the night of 19/20 February it had struck and sunk a large submarine. There were no survivors among the 129 men aboard.

Coastal Command aircraft routinely patrolled the Bay of Biscay, searching for enemy submarines en route to operational zones in the Atlantic or returning to their bases in France. By 1942 some of these planes carried the new anti-submarine searchlights, and during the night of 11/12 November a twin-engined Wellington illuminated a submarine on the surface. The pilot dived to the attack, its load of depth bombs straddling the sub, which was claimed as probably sunk. It proved to be HM Submarine *Unbeaten.*

A similar case of misidentification, but along more bizarre lines, occurred in the spring of 1944. As part of the aid being given the Soviet Union, the Royal Navy offered four submarines: *Sunfish, Unison, Unbroken* and *Ursula.* Russian officers and crews arrived at Rosyth to collect these gifts, suspicious and full of questions. Submariners of the Royal Navy had already had contact with the Soviets – a few British boats had been sent to operate from a north Russian base. Climatic conditions were

HM Submarine *Sunfish*,
gifted to the Soviets,
then sunk by the RAF.

so bad that little could be achieved in terms of operational success, and the Britishers' experience of their Russian hosts was mixed. For a start, the accommodation provided – a block of flats – was 'indescribably filthy'. When permitted to look over some Soviet submarines, they found them 'incredibly smart', but the Russian captains and crews seemed amateurs in operational techniques. This showed following the Russians' departure in the British boats from Rosyth.

The Soviet officers had been advised of and co-operated in planning their route home, but in the event the same degree of incompetence showed. Somewhere between Scotland and Norway a patrolling Coastal Command Liberator crew spotted a submarine on the surface, moving north-east. The RAF crew had been warned of the four Soviet-manned boats moving through their patrol area, but this sub had to be a U-boat; it was far from the course laid down for the Russian crews. The Liberator attacked, its depth bombs fell on target, and the sub vanished beneath the grey sea. The submarine subsequently proved to be the ex-RN *Sunfish*.

Extraordinarily, the US Navy's submarine fleet suffered much the same problems as did Doenitz's U-boats: torpedoes ran too deep, whatever the settings made, passing harmlessly under their targets; too often they exploded prematurely, or sometimes not at all – even after striking the side of a Japanese ship. The chief fault, as with the German weapons, lay in the new magnetic pistols which were designed to detonate the explosive beneath the hulls of enemy vessels, in this way doing the most damage. Additionally, the earlier American torpedo warheads contained only 500lb of Torpex; the Japanese used 900lb.

American sub skippers took their boats long distances across the Pacific to search for enemy shipping off the coasts of Japan. The old rules governing submarine warfare had soon been abandoned, and the notion that subs should act as escorts to large surface warships and only attack enemy war vessels was quickly dropped. A week after the attack on Pearl Harbor the US submarine fleet was ordered to commence unrestricted undersea warfare against all enemy shipping. But over a period of nearly two years it became the unhappy lot of many sub crews to spend hours stalking Japanese targets, only to find that following perfect set-ups their torpedoes failed them. As one veteran skipper who survived put it later, 'Whenever I conned our ship into position to fire torpedoes, there lurked in my subconscious mind the dark memory of betrayal by imperfect weapons.' In these circumstances the frustration and rage of both American and German sub crews is understandable, especially when the men manning enemy vessels spotted the tell-tale streak of torpedoes passing harmlessly beneath them, or were amazed by sudden explosions in the sea far from their ships. This could and did lead to escort vessels tracking down the culprits beneath the waves; US sailors died as a result, with no victory to balance their loss.

Eighteen months after Pearl Harbor, American subs had fired over 2,700 torpedoes, hundreds of these malfunctioning due to the defective Mk 6-type magnetic pistols. The officer in charge of such developments refused to acknowledge any fault in his department, and rather uncharacteristically those admirals above him took no action, constantly reassured that neither magnetic pistol nor the (in fact) badly designed firing pin were to blame for the sub crews' failures to score. Not until well into 1943 were steps finally taken to cure the problems. The Germans had been much swifter: four responsible officers were court-martialled within months. As for the Royal Navy, the magnetic-type detonator had been rejected as imperfect, and no problems resulted from that source for the British.

Luck seemed to disfavour the Americans, whose submariners also suffered the tragedies of misidentification and accident through error.

After Pearl, a number of old R and S boats were pushed out into the Pacific to guard against another Japanese attack, primarily around the Panama Canal. Several submarines returned from this first patrol in January 1942 with no result. The Japanese did indeed (it was learned later) have a plan to attack the Panama zone, but never put it into practice. This involved the use of one of their giant 5,000-ton submarines, each of which carried three seaplanes. The US sub *S-26* returned to Balboa harbour where it met *S-21*, *S-24*, *S-29* and *S-44*. All had successfully passed under patrolling US Navy and Coast Guard planes, forced to use flag signals and twelve-inch searchlights to ward off attack by these friendly fliers. As the bridge crews entered harbour they exchanged greetings, but when night fell the amazing news came that *S-26* had been sunk with all hands. The cause of this tragic error was soon established.

It was customary for submarines to be escorted out of and back into

USS *Halibut* returns to Pearl Harbor from its ninth war patrol, 15 May 1944. Many other American subs were less lucky.

harbour by small naval craft, in this case a converted yacht given the Navy number PC-460. On this evening the escort, having completed its duty, went about to resume normal patrol in the ocean, a signal to this effect being made to the submarines, though it transpired that only *S-21* received it. It was now pitch dark, and no sooner had the escort skipper ordered the helm swung and his ship turned to starboard than it collided with *S-26.* The submarine's hull was rammed by the sharp bows of the naval yacht, against the torpedo room, and *S-26* swallowed sea water by the ton, flooding too fast for a single man to escape, wallowing down 300ft to the bottom.

Ill luck and blunders forever added to the hazardous nature of the American submarines' service in the Pacific. In March 1944 *Tullibee* made a night surface attack on a Japanese convoy off the Palau islands, firing two torpedoes from the bow tubes, one of which refused to settle into its assigned course at the enemy target ship. It was not an unknown phenomenon. Describing a full circle, the torpedo struck *Tullibee* and blew the sub to pieces. Only one sailor survived. He was picked up by the Japanese and spent the rest of the war in a POW camp, eventually being rescued after August 1945.

In fact, in a six-week period in autumn 1944 the US Navy lost eight subs. But as the Japanese Navy was steadily annihilated losses subsided. American forces shrank the enemy perimeter nearer Japan and air bases were set up near enough to the Japanese home islands for air power to take over the lion's share of sinkings. Submarines spent many days on picket, waiting to rescue over 500 airmen downed in these operations. But the errors that brought death to fellow sailors never ceased. In January 1945 USS *Guardfish* mistook the salvage tug *Extractor* for a Japanese I-class submarine. The tug was destroyed with all hands by torpedo.

Get Rommel

Late in 1941, there occurred in North Africa one of the briefest but most dramatic skirmishes that, if good fortune had favoured the attackers, might well have changed the course of the war in that theatre. The operation itself would never have gone ahead had Intelligence provided more accurate information. As things turned out, the Britons involved went into action blinded by false hopes. Almost every man of the attack force was killed, wounded or captured.

By the summer of 1941 the small German army in North Africa under General Erwin Rommel had put paid to British domination, an upper hand gained by a brilliant victory over the large Italian army which had invaded Egypt the previous year. Despite his demonstration of superior

General Erwin Rommel,
tactical wizard of the
desert war.

leadership and tactics, Rommel's forces suffered heavy losses and had failed in repeated attempts to capture the 'pivot of North Africa' – Tobruk, an important coastal base and port. Despite this, the British and Commonwealth Army had suffered severe and humiliating reverses. The despatch of troops to aid Greece could not excuse the failings of the desert generals.

'Rommel's very name and legend are in the process of becoming a psychological danger to the British Army.' That was the verdict of staff officers in Cairo, and in due course Winston Churchill would himself pay tribute in public to the enemy's new star in the desert war, a war that Rommel himself saw as of the greatest importance to Britain and its Empire, a fact of lesser note to the *Führer*.

Having reluctantly relieved General Wavell of his overall desert command, Winston Churchill replaced him with another old India hand, General Auchinleck. It was the 'Auk's' duty to drive back Rommel's German–Italian army and lift the siege of Tobruk; an offensive was planned to begin on 16 November. By an extraordinary circumstance, each side learned of the other's plans in advance. First, a nurse working in a British military hospital in Jerusalem got wind of the coming operation from loose talk from patients and others, and since she was a German agent this reached the *Abwehr*. The Italians, too, had even better (it is alleged) intelligence behind the British front, probably in Cairo and Alexandria. Then the Germans captured a British sergeant, on whom was found a plan of the German dispositions, plus something quite fantastic: a copy of a sketch actually made by General Rommel outlining the tactics to be followed in his own offensive due to start on 23 November. This revelation – that the enemy should have such inside knowledge of their plans, almost as if provided by Rommel himself – came as a bombshell to the Germans. Great speculation and investigations began into the source of such a leak. Indeed, that mystery and others led to the Germans believing their enemy had spies at the highest levels in their own leadership. Even historians writing long after the war ended attributed British 'know-all' to spying; only later did much become clear when the Ultra secret was divulged. Even so, the 'Rommel sketch' did not come via that source and made no difference to the outcome of the battles that followed.

To augment their own offensive the British decided to mount more raids behind the enemy front, to disrupt communications, destroy aircraft on desert landing strips and generally create a sense of unease and alarm. But now a far bolder scheme was hatched by daring minds; why not try to cut off the head and nerve centre of the enemy army, the brain that was bringing the British such tribulation in Africa? Thus was born the scheme to kill or capture General Rommel, who was to be found, so it was believed, in his headquarters near Cyrene, at an Italian settlement called Beda Littoria. The Long Range Desert Group would drive 300 miles behind the enemy front to capture Jaolo Oasis, then on to the Gulf of Sirte to attack enemy transport and generally create alarm and despondency. The SAS were assigned the job of attacking enemy airfields.

Intelligence had been gathered by a brave Britisher with Arab assistance; Colonel John Haseldon had been roaming about behind enemy lines disguised as an Arab. Most Arabs were naturally opposed to their Italian colonial masters, but had been forced to bow their heads before the power of the occupiers, who were intent on maintaining Mussolini's North African empire. As an officer of the Libyan Arab Force, Colonel Haseldon spoke both Arabic and Italian, and was doubtless well acquainted with the ruins of Cyrene which had once been magnificent Grecian buildings, long ruined by earthquake. Both he and his Arab spies had noted the larger building in the nearby village of Beda, with its car park full of German vehicles, and, of course, the comings and goings of high-ranking officers. It was an area well suited to a raiding party, set among dark cypress trees and not far away from ravines and caves.

The plan to get Rommel had been handed to Major Geoffrey Keyes and No. 11 (Scottish) Commando; of some one hundred men well trained for such hazardous activities only half were chosen. Major Keyes was the eldest son of Admiral Sir Roger Keyes, a hero of the earlier war who had led a naval assault into the German U-boat base at Ostend, sinking blockships packed with cement to bottle up the port. For his second-in-command, Major Keyes chose Captain Campbell, who spoke fluent

Major Geoffrey Keyes, awarded
the Victoria Cross for failure.

German and Arabic. The commando force based in Egypt was known as
'Layforce', after its commander, Colonel Laycock; his unit had been
depleted owing to the number of men needed to fight at the front. Many
of the Army regulars were and always had been opposed to such small,
independent élites and never missed a chance to snatch back men even
temporarily unemployed 'between ops' at base. But when the plan was
put to Laycock he expressed great pessimism; used as he was to
dangerous ventures, this one seemed suicidal. Major Keyes asked him
not to spread his gloom further; Laycock agreed, and suggested he go
along as observer as far as the proposed landing site on the coast. For it
was planned to transport the raiders in the two submarines *Torbay* and
Talisman.

Colonel Haseldon returned to Alexandria on 27 October to brief the
raiding force as to the location of Rommel's HQ and what help he and
his Arabs could provide. He was then returned to the target area by air,
parachuting down outside Beda. On 10 November Major Keyes set sail
with his force in the two subs from Alex, only briefing the troops when
they were two days out into the Mediterranean. Along with the raiders
were a Palestinian to act as interpreter and two Arab Senussi guides who
carried a letter from their exiled leader Seyed Idris, who requested his
people under occupation to help the British. Despite this, in the event
Arabs would prefer a 'bird in hand' to promises, and English pounds or

Italian lire. The commandos also took fourteen rubber dinghies, the handling of which was assigned to a few men of the Special Boat Service.

After successfully parachuting back into Cyrenaica, Colonel Haseldon went to the house of a friendly Arab where he borrowed a horse to travel on to Hamma on the coast, there to await the arrival of the two submarines, which actually arrived the same day. The sub skippers kept their boats submerged until dark. When they surfaced they discovered the bad weather had grown worse; a gale was running and heavy seas swept over the subs' casings. In short, the omens did not look in the least promising. To launch flimsy little 'folboats' into such conditions seemed madness and Colonel Laycock's worst fears seemed justified. In fact, though the normal weather for the time was dry and cold, there now developed a worsening storm which should have brought cancellation to the operation. But Major Keyes opted to go ahead, feeling no doubt that having gone that far, and with their guide having signalled from shore that all was well, he had no option.

The commandos began shoving and hauling their collapsible dinghies out of *Torbay*'s hatches as her skipper eased his boat inshore, but the seas and breakers were so great the sub was rolling badly and two men were swept overboard. It took an astonishing six hours of persistent battling to get seven of the dinghies ashore. The soldiers collapsed on the beach, soaked, cold and exhausted.

On *Talisman* the bridge crew had watched and waited anxiously, aghast at the long delay. Colonel Laycock was on the point of calling off the operation when the signal flashing success appeared from *Torbay*. With something over three hours of daylight left Laycock agreed to take the risk. *Talisman* was nosed toward the shore and actually touched ground as the rest of the dinghies and commandos were launched. Seven folboats and eleven men were swept overboard by the fierce seas. *Talisman*'s captain decided conditions were impossible and ordered a withdrawal. Only seven more commandos reached the beach safely, among them Colonel Laycock.

Apart from the attempt on Rommel, Major Keyes planned to attack the Italian HQ at Cyrene and destroy their communications centre at Apollonia. But in view of his depleted strength (both Senussis had vanished in the landing), he decided to concentrate on the 'Rommel villa' and also destroy the power pylon nearby. On meeting Colonel Haseldon he was able to borrow two Arab guides, learning, perhaps to his surprise and disappointment, that Haseldon would not be accompanying them on the raid. Everything seemed to be going wrong. The raiders would have to hole up before dawn came and spy out the land through the following day. The rain continued to pour down and the ground turned to mud, the troops certainly feeling luck was against them as they plodded off for shelter, trying hard to keep their weapons and explosives dry.

In fact, the daring Britishers' luck was even worse than they suspected, for despite all Colonel Haseldon's spying Rommel was nowhere near the area and had never used the two-storey building in Beda as his permanent HQ, only paying occasional visits. Indeed, since August Rommel had been near the front, directing the battle in the manner his opponents should by November have recognised. For Rommel was above all a battlefield general. He had found his true niche in the 'desert sea' where fluidity of movement enabled him not only to make lightning decisions but to know the units of his *Deutsches Afrikakorps* (DAK) were well capable of carrying them out. There was never any sign of plodding; Teutonic methodism in the desert war was astonishing and rapidly applied improvisation had become the hallmark of German warmaking. Through successive periods in that conflict such measures were in large part forced on Rommel by the increasing toll of his supply ships, sunk by the Royal Navy and RAF, mostly operating from the island of Malta. None of Rommel's hopes for the British bastion's elimination bore fruit.

By mid-November, General Rommel was using Cantoniera Gambut (between Tobruk and Bardia) as his field HQ. It has to be said that at this stage of the desert war Rommel's likeness was nowhere near as well-known as it was to become later. In fact, his face has become much better known through post-war publications. So perhaps in 1941 some small excuse can be made for the failure of British Intelligence, or rather Colonel John Haseldon and his Arab spies, to recognise the chief of the newly designated *Panzergruppe Afrika.* Only one commander of sorts used the headquarters at Beda Littoria as his base in that period, and he was Major Schleusener, Rommel's quartermaster general, and even this commander was absent from the building at the time, ill in hospital at Apollonia with dysentery, a complaint rife in the desert and shared by his deputy's adjutant. As for the former, he too was on his back in the same sick bay, with inflammation of the lungs. Therefore not one of the top staff of the *Afrikakorps* were available for the Keyes raiders.

Two officers standing in for those higher up were, however, in the building when the British attacked, the acting QMG Captain Weitz and a Major Poeschel, together with about ten other staff, including NCOs. According to post-war German testimony, which is certainly the only reliable source on this aspect, these men were normally in their cots before midnight, leaving one man in a guard tent outside the front of the building and another inside the front hall. The latter soldier was unarmed, but for the regulation bayonet hung from his belt.

Colonel Laycock remained with three men at the landing site to cover the withdrawal while Major Keyes went off with twenty-five commandos, Colonel Haseldon and his Arabs in the lead to point the way to Beda; not long after, Keyes and his commandos were left to go it alone. (One German account tells of Haseldon being too precious for MI5 (*sic*) to risk losing, suggesting he decamped at an early stage.) Haseldon lent them one of his guides, but this one insisted on leaving long before reaching the village, evidently fearing harsh treatment if caught by the enemy. Major Keyes had only a rather poor map and a compass, and was obliged by the onset of daylight to disperse his men among the scrub where, during the following day, they were discovered by Arabs. Farcically, in view of Colonel Haseldon's previous work, Keyes was now obliged to begin haggling with the Arabs in order to obtain more help in finding the German HQ. Incredibly, he was forced to cough up 1,000 Italian lire before the natives would agree to help.

When night came again the new guides led them to a cave filled with the stench of goats, and next morning Keyes set off with a small party to recce the German HQ, being driven back to his hideout by torrential rain. Instead he sent an Arab boy to do the job, and when the lad returned Keyes was able to draw up a sketch plan that proved accurate. At six o'clock Major Keyes set off with Sergeant Terry to reconnoitre the German HQ, whereupon one of the commandos left behind with Captain Campbell tripped over a tin can. It was one of those silly yet alarming episodes usually reserved for film fiction. The racket set the local dogs barking, which in turn caused one of the nearby inhabitants to start screaming, and in no time an Italian officer with an Arab soldier ran out from a nearby hut to investigate. The commandos were rooted to the spot, weapons ready to fire, when Captain Campbell called out in his best arrogant German. Fortunately the Palestinian had survived the terrors of the landing to translate, and in the gloom the enemy were satisfied that the men were indeed a German patrol. They returned to their quarters.

Unfortunately for the historian, the details of these events vary according to which source is consulted. Surprisingly, little or no attempt seems to have been made to track down any survivors among the 'other ranks' of the commandos, and while details from the German side must be considered accurate due to the efforts of one well-known journalist-historian, from the British side successive writers seem to have relied on hearsay, inaccurate accounts and film fiction in which crashing action is engineered as box-office entertainment, with the British triumphant. In Desmond Young's well-known biography of Rommel first published in 1950, for instance, the author quotes Major Kennedy-Shaw, who wrote in *Long Range Desert Group*: 'Standing back from the road amongst the cypresses, a larger, two-storied building, dark and rather gloomy. In this house, in 1941, lived Rommel.'

The German journalist writing under the name Paul Carell provided much in the way of gripping, interesting detail in his war accounts. But in writing of this British attempt to catch Rommel (published in 1958), he was quite stuck for details due to the paucity of information available from the other side. Indeed, Carell mentions the somewhat surprising fact that at that time the most detailed account of the raid had appeared in the little pocket magazine *Men Only*, a publication of that period best

The villa used by German staff at Beda Littoria in Libya, mistakenly believed to be Rommel's HQ in World War II.

known for one or two girlie photographs. This feature came out in January 1957 and included the claim that the German-speaking Campbell called the sentry out from the building entrance, whereupon Keyes shot him. Then, 'Keyes, Campbell and Terry leapt over the dead man and wrenched open the door of the first room. They were faced by a blinding light. The German officers seated round the table stared motionless at the intruders. Without a word, Keyes mowed down the best men of the German Supply Service with a burst from his tommy gun. They went into the next room and once more tore open the door (?). But here the lights had already been switched off and they were met by concentrated revolver fire. Keyes was hit by five bullets but Terry jumped forward and fired a few bursts into the room.'

Carell then states that, 'according to the British official account', Campbell, realising that his commander was mortally wounded and that he had been hit in the leg, ordered Lieutenant Cook to take the party back to the beach. No mention is made of what the rest of the commandos were doing while this went on, and one is left with the impression that once the brief fight in the house was over and the two leaders were put out of action the commandos ran off, having achieved nothing. 'There are many similar versions and they are all very dramatic. The British are always depicted as bold and contemptuous of death and the German officers as paralysed with terror.' Carell then claims to have discovered the truth from surviving German witnesses, and one has to accept this in some respects, though again aspects of it are guesswork.

How the action really began is unknown, as according to one version Keyes and Campbell, failing to gain entry at the front of the house, went round the back, where they found a locked door. It seems certain that the following sequence is reasonably accurate. Captain Campbell bawled in German for entry, and the guard inside obliged, opening the door to be grabbed by the raiders. Keyes' pistol was thrust into the man's midriff and a struggle resulted as the German tried to deflect the gun barrel and call for help. Here occurs one more deviation, for a German of the QMG's motorised detachment had indeed been sheltering outside in a tent. Matthe Boxhammer from Malling in Bavaria was alerted, rushed to investigate, and was shot down by tommy-gun fire. The sentry in the hallway survived to relate these details, as did other Germans present. But in the struggle with Keyes the German crashed back against the door of the munitions office where three NCOs had retired to their cots. It seems that the staff had been passing the time while a storm raged outside, thunder, lightning and heavy rain providing a kind of film-set backdrop to this dramatic action. The men had gone to their rooms and most were in bed by midnight. The kerfuffle in the hall roused the NCOs; Sergeant-Major Lentzen and Sergeant Kovacic leapt from their cots, grabbing up their Lugers. Lentzen wrenched open the door, raising his gun to find a target just as the Britishers hurled two grenades which sailed over his head to blast Kovacic to death. In that instant Lentzen fired, and it seems fairly certain that it was these slugs that struck Major Keyes in the chest. As for the third NCO in the office, he had luckily been slower and had dropped off his bed onto the floor, escaping the worst of the bomb blasts.

Meanwhile, in those first seconds the German orderly officer *Leutnant* Kaufholz rushed out of his upstairs room and emerged on the stairs, pistol in hand, allegedly seeing the Britishers by the light of the exploding grenades, splinters from which had penetrated the back of the guard in the hall. This part of the story is again controversial, for elsewhere one learns that Keyes had thrown the grenades and slammed the door shut before they went off. Kaufholz fired, as did Campbell, a German bullet striking him in the shin, rendering him *hors de combat*. Kaufholz died on the stairs.

The fate of the raid was decided when both leaders were put out of action. Keyes is said to have given a cry of pain, complaining, 'Damn it! I'm hit!', slumping to the floor as more Germans ran out onto the stairs. Sergeant Terry was now the leader, according to Carell, with two privates, and was startled by a burst of machine-gun fire outside. At the same time, more commandos had gone to the rear of the house but were unable to find entry, due to a somewhat amusing reason they could not have realised. The rear door led to a small office packed with office equipment; beyond that was a small hatch to some spiral stairs and a cellar where two more Germans had their bedspace. One of these was an 'elderly' corporal who, sick of draughts from the unlockable back door, habitually piled a cabinet and can of water against it to keep it shut.

If some of the commandos did try this entrance (and it is uncertain if they did), then they were diverted by the firing that came soon afterwards. Investigating, or perhaps fearing a trap, they ran back towards the front of the building. Campbell is said to have dragged his dying leader outside, ordering some men to destroy the power pylon nearby. But the fuses and explosives had been ruined by rain, so grenades were used instead. This cut off all electric power in the German HQ.

All this, apart from the sure fact that both Keyes and Campbell were struck down inside the house, remains to some extent speculative in view of the many contradictory versions given. For example, in one version given by a supposedly worthy historian some twenty years after the event, the two commando leaders first tried one door and found an empty room, but on opening the next were confronted by ten Germans wearing helmets! One assumes from this the enemy were ready and waiting for them, a surprising fiction from a historian who then states that the two Britons slammed the door shut and Campbell primed grenades which were thrown among these carefully counted Germans who had the presence of mind to open fire and disable Keyes. Another British account has it that Campbell, after leaving the building, went back inside to find it in darkness and silence, and that when he emerged again he was shot in error by one of his own men.

Naturally in such a swift and perhaps overlapping sequence of events confusion arises. *Leutnant* Jaeger slept in the room beside the munition NCOs, the concussion from the exploding grenades tossing him out of bed. In panic he leapt through the broken window in his pyjamas, to be riddled with tommy-gun fire. This shooting may have brought Sergeant Terry rushing outside, and possibly the men at the rear round to investigate. But the mayhem created by British commandos upstairs in film versions is fiction. Major Poeschel rushed onto the landing, as did other officers. He ordered them to lower their torches; they were deterred perhaps by the firing outside. In this brief interval the commandos placed bombs in the car park, and in the meantime the other group sent to attack the Italian communications centre had succeeded and withdrawn. They would all be captured later.

According to Carell, when the Germans upstairs finally came down into the hall they found Keyes still lying there and dying. He would be buried with full military honours beside the four Germans killed in the raid: Kaufholz, Jaeger, Boxhammer and Kovacic. There were no other German casualties. Tales of high-ranking German staff officers being killed were a British fiction to try to salvage some triumph out of disaster. Again, another tale tells how Rommel had only just been missed after all, having left to attend the wedding of an Arab Sheikh, returning to his headquarters at four in the morning. This, too, is pure nonsense.

When Captain Campbell was tended by a German doctor called Junge, the latter was under instructions to try to prise information from the prisoner. Junge failed, learning shortly afterwards that the commando officer spoke good German. Once again, one version alleges Campbell's leg had to be amputated. Junge stated he kept it in plaster for two weeks, trying to save it, until the prisoner was removed by air to an Italian hospital. Junge confiscated the prisoner's 'sand creepers' (plimsolls), wearing them for the rest of the war.

The fleeing commandos hid among the Arabs, not daring to try to get back to the rendezvous on the coast at once. Next morning German police and troops began a thorough search for the fugitives, failing to find them. But success came when an Italian *carabiniere* arrived to assure the baffled Germans he could find the Britishers. And he proceeded to do just that. He had an Arab girl brought to him and told her to spread the word that for every Britisher discovered her family would receive eighty pounds of corn and twenty pounds of sugar. Before long the German MPs were being led back to the very huts they had already searched. 'Eventually,' states Carell, 'the entire commando fell into German hands.' This is not quite true, though most of the bedraggled survivors clad in Arab rags were taken. None was shot, according to Hitler's standing order. Rommel had them treated as ordinary POWs. Only Colonel Laycock and the redoubtable Sergeant Terry escaped the enemy dragnet, to appear in 8th Army lines forty-one days later.

Blume in the Devil's Garden

After Rommel was checked before El Alamein in the summer of 1942, this master of the war of movement realised to his chagrin that he had been forced into positional warfare, a situation he abhorred, especially since he knew full well that his opponent, the British 8th Army, would soon, owing to its shorter supply lines, be in an overwhelmingly stronger position. In these circumstances Rommel ordered his 'Devil's gardens' to be planted in the terrain before his five infantry divisions (one German, four Italian). Widespread minefields were sown to deter or at least seriously hamper a British attack.

In no other theatre of war were so many deadly eggs buried on the battlefield; German, Italian and British mines of all types were planted in their millions. Both Rommel and the new British commander, General Bernard Montgomery, knew there could be only one method of assault against the German–Italian army, a frontal attack, for with the sea on his right flank and the impassable Qattara Depression to the south, no other option lay open. The 8th Army faced a vast carpet of deadly anti-tank and anti-personnel mines arranged in eight boxes before the Axis army.

In the laying of mines the engineers of both sides became cunning and fiendishly ingenious, planting these killing devices in the unlikeliest of places to catch their enemy. For example, the retreating Allied troops left an explosive charge in a toilet at Mersa Matruh, just inside the Egyptian frontier. It was attached to a plug and killed a corporal's best chum, an orderly for the battalion commander. The small, undemolished hotel at Mersa was a haven for relaxing German and Italian officers and was booby-trapped to receive them. Corporal Karl was a member of an engineer combat group, so, his hatred for the enemy aroused, he set about dreaming up new ideas for his own booby traps. The trapping of door handles was too obvious a ploy. Karl was more subtle: he arranged a wall picture to hang askew, reckoning that only an enemy officer would bother to straighten it – and that would be the end of him.

The German minelaying teams used truckloads of French and Egyptian mines as well as their own – everything they could lay their hands on, including *Luftwaffe* bombs. Barbed-wire fences were erected using old iron posts and sawn up telegraph poles, these barriers placed before the front-troop foxholes and dugouts. Before them were laid mines in horseshoe patterns, first in line the simple T mines, placed in twos and threes atop each other. If the enemy minesweepers found the first and tried to remove it, the second exploded, and if by chance the second was revealed by careful sweeping, then the third went off. Italian grenades were tied to T mines, as were *Luftwaffe* bombs, designed to go up if the mines were lifted. These were put down in chessboard patterns, sometimes covered with battlefield debris connected to tripwires in spider fashion. Bits of destroyed vehicles and lumps of wood were wired up to concealed bundles of artillery shells that formed huge charges of explosives. Rommel decreed that his 'gardens' were not to be made 'live' until all the work was finished and the engineers withdrawn behind the barriers. Many days were spent under the boiling sun in these dangerous labours; by night the work took longer, and in the darkness one small error could spell disaster.

It was not unusual for the German teams to lay one thousand mines in one night, the ordinary infantrymen amazed at their cool nerve and audacity. But sometimes even the experts made mistakes, forgot details or lapsed in concentration. A certain Sergeant Blume of the 2nd Company liked to scare infantry comrades watching from the safety of their holes when he laid live French anti-tank mines. These mines, unlike their German counterparts, only reacted when a pressure of seven hundred pounds was exerted on them. Just for fun, and to both impress and terrify the amazed infantrymen not far away, Blume marched back and forth across the rocky sand of the desert where he had just helped to lay dozens of the French mines, confident he was perfectly safe.

This bravado cost Blume his life. He had quite forgotten that interspersed among the French anti-tank mines were German S mines, designed solely as anti-personnel weapons that went off at the slightest touch.

Rommel's Wanderings

Right as it is to highlight the battlefield genius of General Rommel, there were occasions when even he blundered. In one episode at least he was condemned by one fellow officer of rank for needlessly squandering lives in pointless, repeated attacks on Tobruk. Others found him exasperating through his habit of 'swanning' off across the desert in his Mammoth, a captured British command vehicle, often alone but for his driver and one aide. On one occasion they became lost and out of fuel, and it was by the most amazing luck that another officer of his staff out searching for the commander found him, for Rommel had been completely out of touch with his own HQ.

This kind of predilection for mounting personal reconnaissances of the battle situation also brought him into much more dangerous scrapes. On one occasion he found himself driving through a British formation, almost close enough to touch the other vehicles. Fortunately, the dust and sand billowing around them enabled him to get away with it. That kind of thing happened more than once. In another farcical incident the battle-field master peered through his binoculars at the horizon and excitedly told his aides that an enemy formation was coming in to surrender. When they too used glasses to investigate they saw nothing, but despite all their queries and assertions Rommel insisted he was right and sent men in a vehicle to investigate. Not only that, he had the pilot of a light plane fly over to accept the enemy's surrender; the bemused airman could see nothing but camel grass. The CO had been the victim of a desert mirage.

But Rommel's fast thinking and capacity for making lightning decisions marked him out as very different to his opponents, and when once again he blundered on the battlefield during one of his personal forays he had, as always in that period, the cool nerve to improvise his way out of it.

Rommel, quite unexpectedly, though the situation was hardly untypical of the fluid desert war, came across a British field hospital. Sometimes such installations changed hands several times in one day. When he strode with an aide into the large tent he found not Germans stiffening to attention but British staff and patients. Quick off the mark, Rommel let it be known they had been overrun and proceeded to inspect them, even assuring them that extra medical supplies were on the way. He then strode briskly out of the tent. There were one or two Britishers on guard, but they were too hoodwinked to wake up until the enemy commander had driven off hurriedly in a cloud of dust back towards his own troops, doubtless congratulating himself on another lucky escape. His own men often thought he had the devil's own luck, especially when he showed such contempt for enemy bullets in hot spots.

Cobra Attack

In July 1944, USAF medium bombers saturated the assault battalions lined up ready to launch Operation 'Cobra' in Normandy. Alive to the dire possibilities, the American ground commanders had arranged with their air force colleagues for clear marking and for the bombers to fly south at right angles to the front line. Instead, for some inexplicable reason the bombers came in from the west, over the American troops' right flank, and deluged them with high explosive and fragmentation bombs. Among those killed was the American commander of the assault division.

Hard Liquor

One American writer has recorded that 'very heavy drinking of hard liquor had been a notable custom in the peacetime US Army'. One famous general and his wife were (he alleged) well-known drunks. Disturbing rumours of widespread drink problems around training bases were countered by the findings of an investigation which announced there was no problem. Still, US Army public relations officers were obliged to take steps to conceal such facts. After the Americans entered combat in North Africa it is said that their British comrades of 1st Army were 'horrified' by the drunkenness rife among their allies. One British officer recorded that the two armies were kept apart, as 'an army that is drunk all day is no good to be associated with'.

The same problem of soldiers obsessed with the need to escape via drink resulted in more deaths through liquor in the European theatre for the Americans than by communicable diseases. In one memoir an ex-soldier confessed he and his buddies 'got blind ass-hole drunk every chance we got'; they used canned fruit, potato peelings and distilled sugar to brew a mix they called 'swipe'.

Men involved in hard battles will often guzzle whatever drink falls into their hands, but some Americans made the ultimate blunder, not simply allowing their service experience to turn them into drunks, but making the kind of error that cost them their lives.

As the Allied armies swept across France they sometimes overran 'buzz bomb' sites where unused V1 'doodlebugs' were to be found. Also discovered were stocks of fuel for the reaction motors that propelled the weapons. One sniff was enough to send some Yanks into a drinking session – on pure methyl alcohol.

They died.

Indianapolis

In the last days of World War II, long after the surrender of Nazi Germany, there occurred in the Pacific a disaster that cost the lives of hundreds of US sailors, a blunder that could have been avoided and a tale taken up, perhaps with the usual amendments, by Hollywood film producers later.

The American heavy cruiser *Indianapolis* was sailing independently when it was struck by torpedoes fired by a Japanese submarine. It was 30 July 1945, and the hit was perhaps the last successful action by the enemy's navy, only a few days away from the launch of the *Enola Gay*, the B-29 Superfortress that would drop the world's first atom bomb on Japan. Many of the American sailors survived the sinking, taking to their life rafts; others swam off in lifejackets, all of them confident of early rescue. Four days passed, and not one American rescue ship or plane came.

By an extraordinary series of omissions, none of the appropriate US bases or offices became aware the cruiser was overdue, or even that it had been attacked. During those four days adrift in the Pacific 500 sailors died, many slowly from hunger, thirst and madness, others more quickly when sharks intervened. It was the greatest loss of life ever suffered at sea by the US Navy.

Birmania *Explodes*

Despite all his great expertise on the desert battlefield, General Rommel soon discovered it could count for little in the long run if his army failed to receive the necessary supplies. By and large, apart from one period when the *Luftwaffe*'s Xth Air Corps subdued the island base of Malta, those supplies never reached Rommel in sufficient quantity, which was why the German soldiers placed such reliance on the capture of British supplies, trucks and even guns. In terms of personal sustenance, the Germans never had it so good as when they managed to overrun British supply dumps which were scattered all over the desert in North Africa. By German standards, the British were profligate in supplying their troops with not only the basic rations, but delicacies and luxuries such as canned peaches and cigarettes by the million; it is doubtful that there was a single man in the *Afrikakorps* or other German units who did not taste a Players cigarette, though the favourite seemed to be Senior Service. Bully beef was commonplace; something similar supplied to Rommel's men was dubbed *alte mann*, meaning 'old man'.

As for the soldiers themselves who set sail from Naples en route to Rommel's war, many of them had never even seen a ship or the sea before. It was all a grand adventure – until they began to receive warnings of the great hazards awaiting them in the Mediterranean, a sea where the British were – despite the far larger Italian Navy – the masters. Submarines, bombers and torpedo boats reduced the chances of reaching Tripoli or Benghazi by more than half. Problems had soon arisen in the arrangements made with the Italians, who supplied many of the transports for the four-day trip. Half the accommodation was reserved for the Germans, the rest for Italian personnel, but when the Italians suffered heavy losses during the first half of 1941 and more Germans were sent, Rommel found this arrangement unsatisfactory. Thousands of Germans were lost. But disaster came in a different form through a bad blunder made by the German ammunition supply organisation.

On 4 May 1941 the large Italian liner *Birmania* lay in Tripoli harbour, having somehow survived the sea crossing. *Korvettenkapitän* Meixner had just arrived to meet the shipwrecked captains of the *Arcturus* and *Leverkusen*, both German ships sunk by the British. Meixner was the chief of the German Naval Transport Command in Tripoli. Captain Morisse had kicked off his shoes on abandoning ship, descending the gangplank barefoot, and would be seen later in the posh Hotel Uadann in that state, as well as about the port, still without footwear since he claimed he could find nothing to fit him. The *Birmania* carried ammunition so the crew was mightily relieved to have survived the crossing, though aware more trouble lay ahead. And the danger certainly was far from over: long-range British bombers could catch them in harbour, before the dangerous cargo was unloaded. In the event, it was German negligence that brought disaster.

Responsibility for unloading such cargo lay with Captain Morisse's former first lieutenant, a man called Hoppe. The two met near the quayside to liaise and enjoy a drink of gin. As Morisse took his leave there was a tremendous explosion aboard *Birmania*, and he leapt back into the cover of the military headquarters just as a second detonation took place and black clouds of smoke billowed up into the sky. Foolishly, the port controllers had allowed the Italian auxiliary cruiser *Città di Bari* to tie up alongside. This vessel was laden with cans of petrol and also blew up. Unloading with the help of Arab labourers had begun when disaster struck *Birmania*, bringing carnage: twenty-eight Germans were killed, thirty-eight wounded; forty-two Italians also died, with fifty wounded;

and the labourers suffered 150 casualties. Captain Hailer was on the quayside, supervising the unloading. He was struck immobile with shock for a few seconds as the complete stern of the 10,000-ton liner came hurtling down on him. Blacked out, he was protected from the rain of smaller debris that followed.

Experts soon discovered in their inquiry that *Birmania* had been carrying a load of German anti-personnel bombs among its cargo. These 20lb weapons were held together in groups of ten by a single strip of tin onto which a small explosive charge was attached, intended to become live as soon as the load was dropped. After this, it took just two to three seconds for the heat from the explosion to eat through the holding strip, which allowed the bombs to fall independently. The detonators on these loads were so sensitive that the slightest touch would cause the bomb to explode immediately. The bombs were designed for use against enemy columns and other targets out of cover, and were being supplied to the *Luftwaffe* in Africa for the first time. Those sending the bombs had failed to allow for the highly sensitive nature of the weapons; they had not been packed securely in the right type of crates. The bomb strips were lying almost loosely in their boxes, and as soon as these containers were craned aboard the weapons became even more dangerously movable. Some of the bombs had even turned over in their boxes, their detonators made 'live' in the process. These lethal eggs were the companions of other weaponry aboard *Birmania*: heavy bombs.

Rommel's chief of supply, Captain Otto, had left the ship only minutes before. He hurried back to the disaster scene to learn more alarming news: two more Italian ships carrying the cursed weapons were about to dock. Captain Meixner ordered them carefully berthed at a wharf and their anchors gently lowered. Meanwhile, as soon as news of the disaster reached Berlin, Goering flew into a panic, ordering both ships to be put back to sea and sunk – 'In no circumstances must men's lives be endangered.' Meixner was in a fix. He knew the general munitions cargo remaining aboard the heavily damaged *Birmania* was urgently needed by Rommel. Meixner was no coward: he had commanded a German warship in the earlier war, ramming and sinking an Italian destroyer. Later, he studied to become a lawyer, but as a lieutenant commander had been called back into the *Kriegsmarine* when the next war came. He had become an instructor involved in preparations for Operation 'Sea Lion', the invasion of England. In North Africa he had worked closely with Rommel, having the courage to tell the general to stop interfering in his supply business. Meixner decided to risk Goering's wrath and call for volunteers to try to unload the lethal cargo remaining.

Captain Reinen was another skipper without a ship. His boat, the *Menes*, had also been torpedoed. With Meixner's adjutant, Lieutenant Kruger, and ten more German volunteers, Reinen went back aboard the ruined liner and like bomb disposal men they began the almost suicidal task of removing the killer eggs. On their first day, working slowly for hours, they found six live bombs, the next day nine, and on their third day four. It took five days to unload the cargo and a total of twenty-two live bombs were found. All through this period firemen had stood by with hoses ready for the worst; sixteen times they had removed themselves from the worst danger area while the two officers defused bombs. Captain Reinen and Lieutenant Kruger each received the Iron Cross 1st Class.

Naturally, no word of this event reached the ears of the German public, any more than did news of another disaster in that theatre, the loss of the *Preussen* off the island of Pantellaria. This vessel was carrying 6,000 tons of ammunition, 1,000 tons of petrol, 1,000 tons of food supplies and 300 vehicles, including tanks. Among the load of ammunition were the first 4,000lb bombs for the *Luftwaffe* and 21cm guns for the *Afrikakorps*. Also aboard *Preussen* were 600 soldiers and a crew of sixty-four; 200 of the troops were lost, as was the complete cargo. But this disaster could be laid at the door of the British, the RAF, and specifically a single Blenheim medium bomber.

As one German commented later, were there tombstones to mark such losses; the Mediterranean and its harbours would be paved with them.

The Slippery Brockmann

Leutnant Pfirrmann was in command of the 2nd Company of Rommel's 361st *Afrika* Regiment. It was November 1941 and a patrol of the unit had just returned from a raid against the enemy, minus their tough and redoubtable Sergeant Brockmann. He was missing after a skirmish with the enemy, and he would be sorely missed. Brockmann was one of a number of ex-French Foreign Legionnaires now in Rommel's army, all tough, resourceful and somewhat scornful of their new comrades in the regular German Army. They tended to be rather wild, independent types, difficult to handle, and therefore most were organised into their own special unit with carefully chosen officers to command them. Brockmann was especially known as an 'organising genius'.

About seven months later, the British desert army was yet again in crisis, its field commander General Ritchie confounded by Rommel's tactics, the fall of fortress Tobruk imminent. At that time, despite being on the brink of one of their greatest triumphs, every man in Rommel's army was alive to the danger of sudden attack behind their lines by British raiders. At a desert landing ground south of Derna a group of *Luftwaffe* officers of the Stuka and Messerschmitt squadrons based there were celebrating the birthday of *Leutnant* von Rantzau. The chat over drinks and cake had turned to more serious topics; the airmen were discussing lofty questions, of God and the universe. They proposed and argued, their thoughts temporarily divorced from the war and what the next day might bring.

Not far away, in the pitch black of the night, raiders of the Long Range Desert Group had eased slowly forward towards the German air base in two trucks. Debussing, Captain James Bray gave them a final briefing: they would now split into two groups, destroy aircraft, fuel and bomb dumps, cut telephone wires, and bring back at least two prisoners. They were a mixed bunch and included both Frenchmen and anti-Nazi Germans. One of the truckloads of men that went on was commanded by a French lieutenant; beside him one of the commandos of German origin volunteered to go forward on foot, since the officer seemed rather hesitant and could see nothing of their objectives. The German went off at the crouch on rubber-soled shoes while both groups of commandos waited.

Five minutes passed, with no sign of the volunteer scout returning. The French officer became nervous. One of his comrades vowed he had never trusted the German, whereupon another German retorted that the man had suffered in a Nazi concentration camp owing to his service with the French Foreign Legion: 'Over here the Jerries put him in that damned 361st Regiment. He hated it. They had no transport, ever.'

A few minutes before, the jovial group in the *Luftwaffe* officers' mess had been rudely startled as the door of their hut burst open to reveal a wild-looking figure in nondescript clothing with a blackened face. Before the alarmed officers could grab their weapons the stranger burst out with the most amazing warning: 'Tommies! Commandos! They're outside! They're going to blow up everything! I'll help you to catch them! *Schnell!*' Since all this news was delivered with the greatest urgency, and in German too, the open-mouthed listeners leapt to their feet and into action.

Minutes later the French lieutenant and the rest of the raiders saw figures looming up out of the darkness. In seconds there came the crash of grenades and the rattle of sub-machine guns as the two groups of raiders were ambushed from all sides. In a few minutes it was all over; every man bar one of the British group was killed or captured. Only one man ran off into the darkness of the desert; the Germans pursued him but soon gave up. Several days of trekking brought the bedraggled French lieutenant to British positions, and by then the German who had betrayed his comrades was a celebrated hero in his own camp – the 361st Regiment, the 'gypsies of the desert' as they called themselves, the ex-Foreign Legionnaires where the name of Sergeant Brockmann was toasted in whatever liquor came to hand.

After being taken prisoner by the British, Brockmann had embellished his true background, inventing the tale of suffering in a Nazi camp and eventually being accepted by the British as a genuine anti-Nazi. In fact,

Brockmann had not forgotten nor forgiven the abusive treatment he had undergone in the Foreign Legion and had no intention of changing sides.

The Unfit Ranks

The story of Britain's readiness in defence in a dangerous world following the Great War of 1914–18 is one of gross neglect, parsimony and amateurishness. Not on the part of the soldiers, airmen and sailors who had volunteered to stand guard against new aggression, but from those above them: the politicians, committee men, and above all the Treasury, who consistently refused to release the funds necessary to maintain even the basics for a realistic defence.

But after war came in 1939 it seemed as if the well-known adage was true; Britain would 'muddle through' in the far more dangerous conflict against Nazi Germany and its *Führer*. Tales of incompetence and waste seemed legion, and would never cease, though rather extraordinarily such a state of affairs never seemed to affect the outcome. Among the many jokes directed at those in charge of the nation's affairs in war were those concerning the scenes at medical examination centres, where lines of pale, nervous civilian males faced the verdict of assembled medics on their suitability to serve King and country. A few cunning malingerers managed to get through such events by feigning illnesses that were hard for the doctors to refute, but most were passed fit. And among the latter, in the war's early weeks, were a fair number who should have stayed at home.

The government's 'militia' scheme readied thousands of young men in the months before war broke out, though most remained untrained, albeit in khaki. Only when such 'soldiers' began to arrive at units was it discovered that a good proportion should never have been admitted into the forces at all. Naturally, the rush to join the colours in September 1939 swelled the numbers of recruits, but incompetence resulted in even more waste of time and taxpayers' money (something government ministries seem especially adept at).

No matter how long the volunteers and conscripted militiamen stood in line at the medical centres, in a fair number of cases their appearance before the examining doctors seemed amazingly brief. Indeed, the amateurishness of the proceedings was farcical, and is often represented rather like this:

Doctor (pressing stethoscope to man's chest): 'Feel all right?'
Recruit: 'Yes.'
Passed Grade A!

Just before Christmas 1939, the first militiamen and others were sent

Lt General Sir Frederick Pile,
chief of AA Command in
World War II.

to the still-expanding Anti-Aircraft Command. This branch of the Army was actually under the overall command of an organisation unsuitably called the Air Defence of Great Britain, a term that was soon changed but resurrected later in the war. In charge was a man who would later gain considerable fame, Air Marshal Sir Hugh 'Stuffy' Dowding, to be written up as the man who saved Britain during the air battles of 1940. However, the man actually in command of the flak guns had been appointed from the Army, and, in keeping with precedents, it was a man who knew nothing whatsoever about the job in hand.

When General Sir Frederick Pile (of Anglo-Irish stock) took up the appointment, his chief preoccupation both at home and overseas (India, Middle East) seems to have been horse riding. However, such men were usually appointed by the all-wise War Office as competent administrators; it mattered not whether Sir Frederick was acquainted with the shell velocity of the new 3.7in AA gun. In fact, Sir Frederick's main preoccupation during his first days in the job was the appalling state of his command's armoury.

There was, too, the business of the men in his force. When a fresh batch of men were posted to an AA gunsite, they were required to visit, among various offices, the sick quarters. Of twenty-five men arriving at one medical centre, the staff were astonished to find that one man had a withered arm, another was mentally deficient, one man had no thumbs, another had a glass eye which fell out whenever he moved beyond walking pace, and two more were in the advanced stages of venereal disease. To further highlight the slapdash methods of some civilian medical authorities, in 31 AA Brigade, out of 1,000 men examined on arrival, fifty received immediate discharge. Symptoms found included stone deafness, birth injuries and rheumatoid arthritis, and twenty men were classed as mentally deficient; eighteen more were clearly below even Grade B2. To General Pile's chagrin, he discovered the War Office was siphoning off his best officers and NCOs for the BEF in France, the dregs of manpower sent to him as replacements. To his greater astonishment, he found the useless specimens had already been rejected by other Commands.

General Pile's dilemma became even more acute when he was ordered to provide AA batteries to accompany the Anglo-French expeditionary corps to Norway in April 1940. 'There was great difficulty in finding the men,' he later recorded, to which he added that many so-called 'batteries' had no equipment to speak of.

The problem of manpower would continue to bedevil General Pile, as it would others, and though the commander was only one chief embroiled in difficulties owing to the bungling of those above him, he was in 1940–1 singular in being the only general in the British Army whose men were in almost daily contact and therefore battle with the enemy. This one fact should have been perfectly clear to the government and the War Office; in other words, General Pile and his command should have received massive priority in terms of personnel and equipment. Not so. When September 1940 came and it was clear the *Luftwaffe* had been stymied by day, the brunt of the battle to defend Britain fell on the anti-aircraft gunners. Dowding's few night fighters were impotent, and when it became obvious the woefully inadequate coastal divisions would not have to face invasion by sea, all attention was focused on the comparatively few gunners who blazed away at the unwelcome night visitors.

In addition, the new Prime Minister, Winston Churchill, had soon made his more vigorous presence known by minuting just about every office connected with the war effort. Thus, as the blitz developed Churchill began leaning on General Pile, and since he revelled in the sound of cannon (as he preferred to call them), the PM would often ask Sir Frederick to take him to some gunsite, usually arriving just as an 'alert' sounded. Only with difficulty could Churchill be dragged away from the blazing 'cannon' for other night appointments, such as demonstrations of the latest developments in GL (gun-laying) radar, which was in its infancy and more often than not unserviceable. Indeed, owing to official parsimony and lack of foresight the firm of Cossor Radio had entered into a private arrangement with General Pile, its star technician-scientist working all hours to perfect his contraptions which he hoped would largely take the guesswork out of gun aiming, which until that time had relied on primitive sound-detecting methods.

The PM began pressing Pile to keep him posted on how many shells were needed to knock down one German bomber. Unfortunately for General Pile, he was forced to confess that for the whole of September (1940), he doubted if the expenditure of 15,000 shells had brought down a single aeroplane! Of course Germans were being shot down, and that was the kind of result expected by both politicians and public, but both sections were woefully ignorant of the purpose of anti-aircraft fire, which was primarily concerned with (a) diverting raiders from their target, (b) breaking up formations to enable defending fighters to get at their prey more easily, and (c) forcing enemy bombers to fly higher and thus make the bomb-aimers' task more difficult. In their ignorance those outside AA Command expected results on the ground – the mangled wrecks of Nazi bombers, with or without occupants. It was not officially possible to enlighten the public at large on such matters, on either the rules governing AA defence or the ploys and tactics being tried to counter the *Luftwaffe*'s blitz.

It was the already stressed government policies as decided by count-less committees since the 1920s – and, of course, the seemingly independent, dead hand of the Treasury – which had sounded the death knell of AA defence in Britain. This resulted in extreme difficulties for General Pile when the crunch came in 1940. It was not so much the poli-ticians, and certainly not the mandarins of the Treasury, who received abusive letters by the sackload from irate members of the public demanding to know why they were being made to suffer nightly under air attack. When things became really hot in September and the night raids began, no fewer than 260,000 AA shells were sent swishing up into the sky, a fact reported to Churchill, who could hardly believe that so little seemed to be achieved at such a gross expenditure to the taxpayer.

What made it worse for General Pile was the knowledge that too many of these missiles were hurtling back to earth unexploded, because gun barrels were wearing out faster than they could be replaced from the factories. Pile would comment later that in the earlier war the guns at the front fired so many shells in fantastic barrages that their barrels became 'oval'. The 3in, 3.7in and 4.5in AA guns in use were not quite that bad in 1940, but sufficient were losing their designed shape interiors to cause the shells passing through them to malfunction. The clockwork fuses in the nose caps were designed to activate on passing through the rifled barrels of the guns; once the rifling wore out through use, the shells were discharged but inactive in the sense that they could only be det-onated by impact, which of course came when they fell back to earth, bringing more death and injury to civilians. 'We had a large number of

A British 3.7in AA gun in action, as good as the '88' but rarely used in the ground role.

duds from this cause', Pile said when recording his experiences.

So it can be seen that official errors and oversights in pre-war policy had dire effects later. The same kind of government errors prevented, as stated, sufficient men of the right calibre reaching Britain's front-line force, AA Command. Despite four million people being registered for war service by 1941, and the age limit being raised to 51, Pile continued to battle against both government and War Office who persisted in their insane policy of demoting the AA troops to a second-grade army. Typical of the parsimonious and short-sighted bungling which still prevailed even while the nation was suffering under the blitz and German invasion was expected, was a concerted attempt to cut the pay of AA 'tradesmen'. Of course, this kind of episode was and always has been typical of successive governments over many decades, who expect to have their armed forces on the cheap. From the days of Queen Elizabeth I right up to the present time, governments have tried by sometimes foul means to cut soldiers' pay and emoluments. In 1940–1 it was the gunners and other technical troops of Pile's AA Command who were the targets, men who in some cases had virtually collapsed from exhaustion following anything up to ten or twelve hours of action.

Serving the guns, sometimes under fire, was indeed exhausting and dangerous work. When vital parts of the gun loading broke down gunners loaded entirely by hand, rather than see their weapons out of action for thirty minutes while repairs were made. By dawn the hands of these loaders were bruised and bleeding. Such men, and the others involved in gunsite work (especially radar operators), were classed as skilled tradesmen, and received better pay, low though this was. It was decided to save money by declassifying them as ordinary privates, and to add insult to injury the department responsible for this particular notion made the order retrospective. Officers and men now found they actually owed the government money. This incredible move of course resulted in great bitterness and disgust among those involved, and, not surprisingly, had a knock-on effect. Troops and their officers in the AA felt they were not appreciated, despite all their great efforts; there seemed little or no incentive any more beyond doing their duty. In the event, Sir Frederick

Dame Helen Gwynne-Vaughan, ATS Controller 1940–1, who strongly opposed using her women on gunsites.

began his battle to have the order rescinded, but those responsible did not give up without a fight (needless to say, they were never in any kind of serious combat themselves).

There were no special commendations or medals to be had in AA Command, but, profiting from the Air Ministry's expertise, Pile was able to set up his own publicity unit. After the females of the ATS (Auxiliary Territorial Service) joined AA Command one publication featured an ATS band. The ladies were depicted in action, cheeks distended and apparently a fine military unit band. In fact, the whole bunch were admin and other personnel. Not one could blow a note.

And it was to Britain's womanhood that Pile turned to solve his manpower problem, a measure of the man's go-ahead ideas in the face of blimpish, diehard attitudes that did much to exacerbate his problems. In truth, the staunchest opposition came from the female camp itself – surprisingly, in view of the fact that the ATS hierarchy consisted mainly of spinsterish women's libbers. The then director-general of that force was completely opposed to anyone from the (male) War Office or any other body having any kind of power over her girls who, she felt, were entirely her responsibility. Pile persisted, until finally, and despite the director-general's continued opposition, ATS girls joined troops on gunsites, manning tracking equipment and even searchlights, apparently doing as good a job as, or even better than the soldiers, who were released to more important tasks. The girls felt they could even fire the guns, but it never quite came to that.

Beaufighter Downed

When the *Luftwaffe* began its so-called 'tip-and-run' raids on the English south coast in 1942, the defences were caught napping – not literally, of course, but deficient in certain respects. For the few German airmen involved were canny enough to fly across the Channel at low level, thereby arriving undetected by radar off seaside towns where, despite barbed wire, pillboxes and mined beaches, there were still comfortably-off old people in wheelchairs to be found soaking up the occasional sun and sea breezes.

There were very few light AA guns in place, and those gunners present had no warning. By the time their weapons were manned the speedy Messerschmitts and Focke-Wulfs had fired their guns, dropped a few small bombs and fled back across the sea. Urgent conferences took place to find solutions to the problem, and among the various measures taken was a joint Army–RAF order that to solve the crucial problem of aircraft identification no Allied plane must overfly the coast below 1,000ft. Actually, the AA gunners, including the new arrivals at hastily prepared gunsites containing 40mm Bofors and 20mm cannon, were instructed that any aircraft approaching at less than half that altitude could be considered enemy and be fired on. Obviously, in these lightning attacks by the enemy seconds counted, so the gunners needed to be on the ball with their recognition skills. Many were not. The Navy was notorious for shooting at friendly planes.

Late in October 1942, an RAF twin-engined Beaufighter, probably on routine test, its pilot either unaware of the latest crucial orders or not watching his altimeter, flew low along the coast, and on arriving off the little Kentish town of Rye was shot at by the flak gunners, and destroyed.

Hans Martin's Tale

Not one enemy prisoner of war escaped from captivity in Britain in World War II, though some tried, most notably Franz von Werra, the 'one that got away' – from Canada, that is. Plucky and courageous as he was, the boastful German fighter pilot never succeeded in his attempts to break away from England. (When von Werra submitted his experiences in writing to Goebbels with a view to publication, the propaganda minister turned it down because of certain passages that paid tribute to the British.) There were others, including the very nearly triumphant escape of two other *Luftwaffe* airmen who actually succeeded in stealing a light plane and taking flight towards the enemy-held continent. Unluckily for them they blundered by not checking the aircraft's fuel state and were forced to land again in the English countryside when its tanks ran dry.

The escape adventures of Allied (principally British) POWs from German camps have been well told in publications and films ever since the end of the war. Not so those of the other side, apart, that is, from those already mentioned and the 'Great Escape' of December 1944, designed to coincide with Hitler's last great gamble in the West, the Ardennes offensive. Arranged in Berlin, the mass escape of German prisoners in England would, so the enemy hoped, create much disruption in the Allied rear and lead to troops that could ill be spared having to deploy to combat the 'revolt'. Indeed, the Germans nourished fantastic hopes of a 'March on London' by armed POW columns who would have obtained weapons from Allied armouries and dumps in England. Most of the German POWs, well aware of the state of play, were content to sit out the last months of the war in comparative comfort and safety, eating as well as or better than the British civilian population. Unlike the Allied prisoners in Germany and Poland, these Germans stood little or no chance of being shot for escaping.

Yet there were those, principally energetic young fighter pilots similar

German *Luftwaffe* prisoners at a London rail terminus; not one escaped from Britain in World War II.

to von Werra, who just could not stand confinement of any kind, the kind of claustrophobia common to young people shut away under authority. Such a man was Hans Martin, lately pilot of a Focke-Wulf fighter shot down late in 1943. Martin had little or no hope of getting away from Britain; shut up in a camp outside Derby he longed to walk among civilians, to visit a café, perhaps even a cinema, speak to a woman, anything to get away from the cursed huts and barbed wire. He had already tried to get himself out via an outside working party, but there were no vacancies. 'I just could not stand being cooped up. I wanted to be free! Even to tour England!' Martin's CO thought him foolhardy, recommending he sit out the war in safety. But the prisoner was adamant, and once it became apparent how serious he was, the camp escape club donated a stolen map and some clothes. Martin had already saved some bread, cakes and chocolate to help sustain him once outside among the enemy. And he had two pounds in English money, plus a fair command of the language. Security seemed fairly lax in the camp and he felt quite confident of success.

It was already dusk and quite chilly as he left his billet on the evening of his attempt, the good wishes and exhortations of his comrades ringing in his ears as he slipped along the little gravel path to reach a hedge where he knew a gap existed quite large enough for him to slip through. Safely outside, he straightened up on the grass verge alongside the road, glanced anxiously about and noted with excitement that his exit appeared to have gone unnoticed. A short walk brought him to a bus stop where he found a woman waiting with a little boy. When the bus arrived the German helped the lad inside and in no time was warmly seated and asking the conductor for a ticket into town.

'Derby', Martin said, proffering a sixpenny piece.

The short journey was uneventful, and when the bus entered the most built-up area many passengers began alighting. Martin asked a man if the area was indeed Derby, and on hearing the affirmative the German alighted. Greatly excited, he glanced around. No one was paying him any attention; there were neither policemen nor troops watching, nor in fact anyone in uniform. In any case, it was a cold evening during the blackout of wartime Britain and everyone seemed intent on going about their own business. To be free was a grand tonic, to be able to walk about the streets of the English town excitement in itself. Martin began examining and gazing at the unlit shop windows, peering here and there and thoroughly enjoying himself. And when he reached a cinema he showed little hesitation in going inside.

'I checked my money and asked the pretty girl for a one-and-nine-penny seat. It was a comedy film, and I could not follow the dialogue.'

Nevertheless, Martin revelled in the comfort and his own nerve, wondering (as he put it later) what those around him would have thought had they known 'one of those horrid Nazis was among them'. The news-reel was very interesting, despite the obvious propaganda, and when the show was over Martin was reluctant to leave the comfort and security of the cinema. But he knew he had to find somewhere to spend the night, and half thought of trying to chat up a woman in an attempt to find a bed. At the very least, he had to find a lodging house, but on leaving the cinema his first thought was refreshment. He entered a mostly empty café and ordered coffee and a little cake. His excitement had worn off as he now considered his position, which was not secure by any means. The couple at another table took little notice of him, and before leaving he enquired of the woman behind the counter if she could direct him to a boarding house. She called her husband, but neither was of help.

Out in the dark, cold street again, the German's morale began to sag. There were fewer people about and he had no plan for the night. Everything would look better in daylight when he could get a bus or train out of the town, perhaps even to London. Martin toured the streets again, wondering what to do. The sustenance found in the café was wearing off but he did not plan to start consuming the rations in his pockets just yet. If only he could find a room for the night. The thought of a warm English bed with sheets, and lying awake as he planned and enjoyed some of his chocolate, kept his hopes high. But after half an hour his morale sagged once more and he soon committed an error which ruined his escapade; the hopes and plans of months, the grand 'tour' of

England, ended rather sadly and lamely in the centre of Derby.

'I saw a policeman and on a foolish impulse decided to ask him to direct me to a lodging house, or at least the railway station, where there would be a waiting room for me to rest in.'

The bobby eyed him suspiciously, asking to see his identity card. Martin was nonplussed and pretended he had left his wallet in the café. The constable took him there, and the proprietors insisted they had seen no trace of it. At this point, outside in the street again, the policeman told Martin he would have to accompany him to the station to have his identity checked. The German realised the game was up, and confessed he was an escapee from the POW camp outside the town. His 'vacation' was cut short to a few hours.

Ralf's Tale

A far more amazing escapade than that of Franz von Werra was carried out by another prisoner which, because of the fantastic security blunder by the British, deserves mention here, even though the aftermath came after the war had ended. The story is certainly little known, even though it was published about ten years after the event.

The prisoner – let us call him Ralf – was one of those Dutch youths so impressed by the German occupiers of his country that he opted to volunteer and fight for them in Russia. His motives, he explained, were because he desired to combat communism, he wanted to follow a military career, and he also had a German father.

Following some severe experiences on the Russian front in 1942–3, Ralf was returned with the remnants of his unit to Germany for rest and, as it turned out, posting as an infantry training instructor. Now a corporal, he was eventually sent to join the 16th *Panzer* Division's infantry component, which moved into France in readiness to combat the Allied invasion. By then he had acquired a German girlfriend called Erna.

When the invasion came Ralf fought on the American front, eventually being captured following the great German collapse and retreat in August 1944. He had by then been wounded and lost his girlfriend in an Allied air raid. Embittered, he reached a British POW camp and faced the prospect of repatriation to Holland and trial as a traitor. Following many hours of interrogation by the British he was permitted to settle down in a camp and act as interpreter, as his English was excellent. There were escape attempts, bungled or foiled, but after a period of outside employment on various POW work parties Ralf decided the fate awaiting him in Holland justified a determined and lone attempt to get away from England.

He chose Ireland as his goal, neutral Eire, and after making a successful escape from a workplace he did, by amazing good luck, hitch-hike his way through Wales until reaching the north-west where, after a short delay, he managed to stow away on a ship bound for Dublin. Once there, and still unchallenged, he roamed out of Dublin to find farm work and sympathisers, none of whom learned his true origins until later. But eventually, despite having made good friends, he heard that Irish police were hunting him; they were (so he was always told) working closely with Scotland Yard. So close to discovering his hideaway did the detectives come that Ralf decided to flee the country, coming up with the most fantastic and daring plan: he decided to enlist in the British Royal Air Force. After all, who would dream of searching in HM Forces for an escaped German POW?

The RAF regularly advertised for recruits in the Irish press, so Hans sent in a clipping, received application forms and in due course attended an examination across the border in Ulster. He was accepted into the Royal Air Force, having provided a copy of the birth certificate of a certain genuine Irishman called Gallagher. But during basic training provided by RAF Regiment drill instructors at Cardington in Bedfordshire Ralf was almost tripped up. He performed so well and expertly when crawling in combat training the DI decided he was no rookie at all, but a man of previous experience. Ralf got away with it, and before long was a pupil at the RAF radio school at Yatesbury, going on to become a skilled and valued radar operator on various secret installations. In fact, so well did the fugitive perform he often found himself alone on duty, surrounded by top-secret data and equipment.

The war was over, but difficulties with the Soviets were bringing about the Cold War. Ralf prospered, still undetected, finding himself posted to a base where fresh USAF personnel and nuclear bombers were arriving. He was able to go anywhere in his uniform, despite the base being infested with British and American military police. Ralf then opted for an interpreter's job on the continent, pulled back, perhaps, towards his native land. His employers were doubtless surprised to find that a supposedly simple Irish 'lorry driver' (as he had described himself) was capable of mastering tests in Dutch and German. His father, Ralf explained, had been in business in Germany and Holland before the war and had lived with him there. The RAF never asked for any proof.

As if to crown his amazing and audacious achievement, the Dutch–German escaper was so highly thought of that, having changed his mind about the interpreter's job with the forces on the continent, he was now told he rated a commission; the RAF would turn the Irishman with the unusual accent into an officer. It seems he needed but three recommendations from commanding officers, and these were already more or less available from the bases on which Ralf had performed valuable service. Yet this was only one option. Other officials, perhaps only slightly bemused by his change of heart over the interpreter's job, now suggested he might care to use his talents under the auspices of the Foreign Office – on the continent.

That an escaped German *Wehrmacht* prisoner should have reached such a level of employment in the British military was incredible. Despite being tracked to Eire by the British police and very nearly caught by the Irish authorities, here he was, apparently quite secure in the heart of the hunters' homeland, being offered plaudits and a grand job for life. The mind boggles to imagine just how far Ralf might have climbed in his new career had he not decided enough was enough.

He went 'home' on leave to Eire, rejoining Irish friends who had by then been told by Ralf of his true background. The great complication for him was ironic. He had made good friends in the RAF, one especially. He liked the service life and comradeship; indeed, it can be seen that Ralf had at last fallen into the very military career he would have us believe he had yearned for back in 1942.

Yet instead of returning to England and continuing his ascent, he decided to call an end to his charade. He wrote to the Air Ministry in London, confessing all. One can imagine the utter consternation caused when his missive reached RAF officialdom. The security implications were horrendous: a World War II POW who had had a free hand amid the latest and most sensitive equipment and affairs in Britain. Not long afterwards, Ralf 'Gallagher' surrendered to the RAF Police in Ulster, and, perhaps to his astonishment, within a short time received his discharge from the RAF – with no questions asked.

The Despair of Sqn Ldr Briggs

Following the German intervention in the Middle East in 1941, the Axis powers effectively gained control of the Mediterranean. *Luftwaffe* units based on Sicily prevented British convoys of supplies and reinforcements from reaching Malta and Egypt. Where once the Royal Navy had command of Mussolini's 'Italian Lake' (Mare Nostrum), German bombers now ruled, their reconnaissance missing nothing of note in the great naval base of Alexandria, the Malta island itself reduced and battered by bombing to near impotence. All this effort enabled Axis convoys to sail across the Med to keep Rommel's army supplied with enough men and materiel to continue the offensives.

Into this highly unsatisfactory situation arrived one Squadron Leader Briggs DFC, lately used as a flying instructor in the UK, on a supposed 'rest' following his six-month tour of duty and crack-up with No. 22 Squadron of Coastal Command. Briggs had been used as pilot of a torpedo-carrying Beaufort, a twin-engined bomber less acclaimed on its first appearance before the war than the far better-known Blenheim. Yet both emerged from the same stable, the Bristol company, and following employment in small numbers against coastal targets across the sea in daylight (suicidal for the hapless Blenheim crews), the Beaufort had been adapted to carry one torpedo. In this form the single squadron had begun anti-shipping attacks on the few German merchantmen sailing to and from continental ports. These vessels were always escorted by small craft of the German Navy, themselves soon armed with flak weapons as the RAF attacks developed. Small as these were, the enemy soon reacted by using flakships bristling with AA guns, including multi-barrelled cannon, to protect the convoys. In addition, *Luftwaffe* fighters were either on patrol in the vicinity or on standby at the coastal airfields.

These convoy supplies were far from vital to the German economy and war effort, but it would have been unthinkable for the British Air Staff to allow them to pass unmolested. The problem was that a year after the war began there were simply not the aircraft available to attack such shipping in strength. And there was another difficulty: the torpedoes supplied to the single Beaufort squadron were of an old design, prone to malfunction; they would sink, run amok off their intended course, or simply explode harmlessly in the wrong place. In any case, where submarines would fire a spread or fan of several torpedoes in the hope of obtaining one hit, a single weapon aimed virtually by guesswork from a height of exactly sixty feet in the face of fierce flak was not too likely to score a hit. Yet despite the somewhat suicidal nature of the job the Beaufort crews never gave up or saw the effort as anything but worthwhile. This was perhaps a measure of their youthful enthusiasm, but by the time Patrick Briggs left for his 'rest' following a night flying accident it had dawned on him that he was one of the very few survivors of the original squadron strength. Most had found watery graves in the North Sea.

Even so, Briggs's own love of flying, despite the odds against survival, was such that he rebelled against his instructing job, longing to get back on ops. His requests for posting back were denied, so he decided his only hope lay in the Middle East, reckoning that there he would find action in plenty. But this hope too was dashed; he was ordered to buckle down and stick with instructing. His disillusionment increased when he discovered to his dismay that there had been and still was no real policy or directing effort for the Beaufort boys. Most of Coastal Command's aircraft were used on anti-U-boat patrol and reconnaissance. The AOC (Air Marshal 'Ginger' Bowhill) would check the ops state and, it seemed, remember 22 Squadron almost as an afterthought, having his adjutant order them off against whatever German shipping happened to be available. This vague approach, coupled with small numbers and bad tactics, so infuriated Briggs that he made continued 'suggestions', with the effect that his chiefs grew weary of him and decided to get rid of him – to the Middle East.

Squadron Leader Briggs, DFC, a 'nuisance' posted to the Middle East to witness disaster.

It was customary for aircrews to fly out via Gibraltar, but by this time there was a surplus of fliers in the Middle East, though aircraft were in short supply. This was one of the first big disappointments Briggs found following his long and, for him, adventurous journey by sea, broken by the usual excellent stop-off at Durban. In Cairo it was as if no life-or-death struggle for a crucial slice of the British Empire was taking place in the desert of Libya and into the very borders of Egypt itself as General Rommel forced successive retreats on the outmanoeuvred Commonwealth Army. While everything seemed to be on almost a peacetime basis in Cairo, with abundant food and entertainment, thousands of men were being killed and maimed three hundred miles to the west.

To Briggs's dismay he found himself as one more surplus 'bod', assigned a desk job at HQ, the only Beaufort squadron (No. 39) stuck with a batch of Mk 1 aircraft in a poor state of maintenance, their Bristol Taurus engines barely capable of keeping them aloft in the hot desert air. With hordes of aggressive flies and sand constantly blowing in the breeze, heavy air filters fitted to these bombers further induced drag. Not that the new arrival discovered these technical problems until later.

Assigned the Ops 3 desk, responsible for coastal operations (in theory

The Bristol Beaufort torpedo bomber: underpowered and easy meat for enemy flak and fighters.

it proved to be passive; all action was initiated and planned by Group), Briggs found that his two officer companions, Ops 1 and Ops 2, did little or no work. The first spent his day working on racing form, with tables and calculations to help, the other sat at his desk reading old newspapers from England (having been overseas three years his only interest lay in going home). Coming from a far more active environment, Briggs's morale sagged into greater disillusionment. His requests to be posted to the Beaufort squadron were turned down flat by the Air Commodore in command. Briggs wandered the streets of Alexandria and Cairo, discovering the fabulous tropical-type sea of turquoise and deep blue off Sidi Barrani, bumping into two old Beaufort boy chums in a bar, men well able to provide all the gen since they were actually with 39 Squadron. It was late April, and they had not flown a single operation since 9 March, when both success and loss had occurred.

Briggs went to see the unit, which was twenty miles off Alexandria at Landing Ground No. 87. There, the men – aircrew and groundstaff – lived in tents; conditions were primitive, but Briggs was struck by the keenness of the men and their anxiety to get enough aircraft ready for the next op. When that would come was anyone's guess, for as Briggs found during his frequent wanderings out of his office to other departments to relieve his boredom, enemy convoys were plotted on the Operations Room map board, and most seemed to arrive safely at their African ports of Tripoli, Benghazi, or even Derna, far to the east. It became more and more obvious to Briggs that the solution lay in using Malta as an offensive base from which RAF bombers could help supplement the Navy's submarine operations, these barely able to continue owing to enemy air attacks on their moorings and facilities. He was not quite alone in seeing the wisdom of such a plan; the problem lay in getting the planes to do the job. Beauforts were routed to Malta from England via Gibraltar, but many were shot down, crashed in night landings on Malta's battered airfields, or were destroyed in the daily air raids before their crews could fly them on to Egypt. Among these were superior Beaufort Mk IIs, with better American Pratt and Whitney engines.

Briggs's irritation and frustration grew as he saw so many things wrong with the whole set-up. It seemed inconceivable that with his experience and rank he could do nothing. As convoy after convoy escaped attention and reinforced Rommel, who was steadily battling westwards towards his great prizes, Briggs fell into despair. He told any ops officers who would listen that penny-packet sorties by small groups of bombers or even single aircraft were futile, a sacrificial waste. His words seemed to fall on deaf ears. Nothing could be done. Until the new Beaufighter was fitted with a torpedo and the Wellington was adapted in the Middle East to haul two such weapons, there was nothing more they could do.

Briggs hardly noticed the fresh slip of paper attached to the map during one of his habitual visits; it noted an enemy convoy of four large freighters escorted by destroyers spotted by the routine Maryland recce plane, en route to Rommel. When he called again next day he was more attentive, for by then he had discovered Group had ordered a 'large force' to find and attack the convoy. The attack had indeed taken place, and the single Beaufort unit had with great zeal gone into action again – and suffered annihilation. Briggs stared dully at the 'ops readiness state' on another board which specified the condition of every air squadron in the Middle East. Against the strength column for No. 39 Squadron he saw a simple zero.

All of Briggs's worst fears had been justified. Blunders had cost the lives, it seemed, of all the fine, keen types he had met and spoken with at LG87, including his two chums from 22 Squadron whom he had met in the Cairo club. Briggs felt sick, sicker than he had of late since his health had taken a dive on reaching the desert climate. Yet upon further investigation he thought things were perhaps not quite so bad.

The men of 39 Squadron had worked like beavers to get nine planes into the air; now the ground crews saw it all thrown away as not one of their airmen had returned. Then, like a miracle, Briggs heard that just one Beaufort had returned, piloted by his friend Tony. He soon learned more facts. The Maryland recce crew had constantly transmitted reports of the enemy convoy, 'indiscreet' ones at that. The enemy, already alerted by the snooper, were well warned enough to summon up long-range fighter protection, and up to one hundred enemy interceptors were encountered when the nine Beauforts found the convoy. It was a serious blunder to despatch the Beauforts without fighter escort, but then no long-range fighters were available – only one or two Beaufighters had arrived. The Beaufort crews were obliged to quarter the ocean this way and that, running short of fuel, before the ships were finally sighted. Those bombers not destroyed in the convoy battle flew on to Malta, where they at once found themselves under fresh attack by enemy fighters, several Beauforts being shot down in sight of their airfield base on the island. Of the three that managed to touch down, only one remained undamaged, that flown by Briggs's chum Tony. He flew back to Egypt the next day.

'Nothing could conceal the fact that the operation had been a disaster', Briggs wrote later, adding that several of the pilots he had chatted with at No. 87 base were making their first operational flight. Briggs also noted that the errors already made were added to by the commander of the squadron when he led his planes on an overlong search, enabling the enemy ample time to prepare its defence. Indeed, the position chosen by Group for the attack was itself suicidal, for it lay within easy range of the enemy's fighters based on Sicily. The Beaufort leader could have refused to attack in such an obvious hot spot, as he could have turned for home on not finding the enemy convoy on arrival at its given position.

'All had been grave errors or misfortunes,' Briggs recorded, 'for which a high price had been exacted.'

The Stalingrad Fiasco

The blunders committed by Adolf Hitler alone were on a scale monumental in human history; he became, therefore, in a perverse sense, the Allies' greatest ally. There is no doubt that, given a free hand, his military advisers would have made the Allies' task of defeating Nazi Germany much more difficult.

In the conduct of military operations, no greater error was made by the dictator than his firm order to the 6th Army under General Paulus that it remain in the broken city of Stalingrad. 'Where the German soldier stands, he remains.' That was Hitler's supposed dictum, whereas the simple truth was he could not bear the loss of prestige which would have resulted in withdrawing that army in good time to prevent its encirclement and eventual annihilation, a drama so great it could not be hidden from the German people.

Some lesser-known episodes which resulted from Hitler's fatal decision in the first place to attack the Soviet Union comprise only a fraction of the many amazing events which overtook the doomed 6th Army in late 1942 and into the first weeks of the following year, when a little over one third of the original 334,000 soldiers were marched off into captivity by the victorious Red Army. Only about 5,000 of these would survive to see their homeland again.

It has to be pointed out when recounting some of these episodes that not even the mighty, once all-powerful *Wehrmacht* was beyond error and bungling. Its progress since September 1939 had, however, been marked by a succession of stunning victories. But an army is made up of human beings, and failings will out in some. The German soldier was far from being the fanatical Nazi automaton depicted by much Allied propaganda.

Having been committed by Hitler's decree, his military planners set about applying all their undoubted expertise to the problem of subduing the Red Army in the western USSR. On 18 June 1941, several days before 'D-day', the GSO1 (operations officer) of the 23rd *Panzer* Division took off in a Fieseler Storch light plane to make a final reconnaissance of the sector near Voronesh that his unit was to assault. Incredibly, and contrary to orders, this officer took with him complete written details of the entire corps attack. His intention was to inspect the actual terrain to be occupied by his troops as their jump-off positions on 22 June; in the event the plane overshot the zone by hundreds of yards and never returned.

Assuming that the Storch was shot down by the Soviets, the division commander ordered a fighting patrol to investigate. At this point, Stalin was playing his part and doing everything to maintain friendly relations with Hitler, despite frequent *Luftwaffe* reconnaissance probes over Soviet territory which had met with no response. But now, failing to find their missing officer in the downed Storch, the German patrol and their CO were obliged to assume the Russians had taken the man prisoner, and now knew of the impending assault. And when a careful assessment was made at staff level and the German officers found the GSO1 had also taken 'unnecessary details' of the attack, consternation spread as the implications sank in. The German officers of 23rd *Panzer* probably recalled a similar incident from 1940 when a *Luftwaffe* officer carrying Hitler's plan for the attack in the West crashed in a small plane on Belgian soil. Hitler had raged and heads had rolled. It is not known whether or not the *Führer* ever got to hear about this later blunder.

On 22 June, Operation 'Barbarossa' was launched, and 23rd *Panzer* encountered a much reinforced Russian defence of Voronesh – as if the plans had indeed fallen into enemy hands and been acted upon.

While it has been argued that Hitler's decision to 'hold fast' when the German Army was struck by the awful winter of 1941–2 was correct, no such conclusion can possibly be reached concerning the Stalingrad order. The slow death of 6th Army resulted in many an amazing episode, even though the dismal drama of those months could hardly be looked upon by the men involved as the heroic epic Nazi propaganda depicted. The Stalingrad story from the German side (if one overlooks the terrible sufferings of the remaining Russian population) is a tale which commenced in confidence, as the troops of 6th Army recovered from the shock of seeing the rout of their Italian and Romanian allies and the Red Army completing its encircling moves. They were confident because of promised relief from outside and the expectation of a break-out by themselves. Among those forces newly committed and fresh from the west on their way was the magnificently equipped *Luftwaffe* Field Division.

Following the heavy losses incurred by the German Army in its first smashing drives into Russia, the General Staff had proposed to Hitler that thousands of superfluous *Luftwaffe* groundstaff should be transferred to the Army and, once trained, sent as replacements to the eastern front. The *Führer* had agreed, and ordered Goering to commence withdrawing 46,000 men from his air force, the *Reichsmarschall* disagreeing vehemently and to such effect that his leader was forced to consider an alternative proposal. 'You can't expect me to hand these men over to the Army so that some general or other can make them attend church parade!' Goering told his chief, a pointless quip but one that highlighted the fact that such gatherings were still permitted in the *Wehrmacht*, for all the paganistic and atheistic utterings and rituals of the Nazi regime. As a result, thousands of *Luftwaffe* ground tradesmen found themselves despatched to infantry training camps where Goering made sure they received the best outfitting, from camouflage smocks to their own transport, plus, of course, supporting units including anti-tank guns. There is no doubt that once trained for ground combat the first *Luftwaffe* Field Division made an impressive showing, and they were trumpeted in the Nazi media and service journals such as the *Adler* (Eagle), the *Luftwaffe*'s own picture paper.

All that had begun in the late summer of 1942. By November, just as the Russian winter began to really bite, the new and very keen unit arrived on the eastern front (always known as the *Ostfront* to the Germans), where shabby, hardbitten veterans of the Army watched their arrival in some bemusement. The *Luftwaffe* boys called down from their vehicles, boastingly confident that their arrival signalled an end to Soviet successes. Debussing, the troops enjoyed a good meal provided by their own supply column, perhaps only a trifle surprised by the rather moth-eaten and scraggy soldiers around them. Then their officers led them off in column. To the watching soldiers the *Luftwaffe* men seemed more like a parade unit, and they were indeed Goering's latest pride and joy. Although an ex-Army man himself, the fat *Reichsmarschall*'s overweening pride in the supremacy of the air force he believed he alone had created was overwhelming, despite the reverse it had suffered in the Battle of Britain.

The fresh, green troops of the *Luftwaffe* marched off in the mistaken belief their baptism of fire would be a gentle one, as second-line troops. The Army front line and the Russkis lay before them. They vanished towards the sound of the guns that evening; twenty-four hours later, the battered remnants struggled miserably back to the rear, their faces betraying the shock of their first battle. On reaching their designated positions a few hours before the men had seen troops clad in winter outfits streaming towards them, and assumed these must be German units with-drawing after relief at the front. The ugly truth hit them at once: these were Russians. Many of the *Luftwaffe* troops were too surprised to shoot and were slaughtered in droves by the advancing enemy. Of the anti-tank battalion only twelve men survived, including its commander. That night he shot himself in his bunker, the only round to be fired from his pistol since he had arrived in Russia.

The remains of Goering's *Luftwaffe* Field Division were broken up and used as small combat groups. There would be more such divisions. None fared well, though they should not be confused with the Hermann Goering *Panzer* Division, or his parachute units.

Christmas 1942: the German Army, trapped in the jaws of the Soviet pincers, was feeling the pinch; indeed, it was beginning to starve and the first men to die of exhaustion and hunger had already been buried. The relief attempt from outside had failed. General Paulus had not left his HQ bunker and refused to give any order for a break-out, even though all preparations were made; 'a soldier's first duty is to obey', he told his staff, alluding to his *Führer*'s order.

Not long before the enemy jaws closed on 6th Army, 17,000 horses were successfully evacuated from the shrinking pocket, to live and serve another day. This left a further 12,000 animals in Stalingrad, a measure of the fact that the mighty German Army still relied heavily on horse power; by contrast, the British Army in the western theatre was completely motorised. But the sheer scale of the operations in Russia had imposed impossible burdens on the German fuel supply system; even the widespread use of horse power had not prevented the curtailment and limitation on movement among the *Panzer* divisions. And in the routes to Stalingrad the supply system with all its road and rail workings broke down. Those 12,000 horses were already emaciated, but they were eaten nonetheless, sometimes raw when there was no fuel left for cooking.

Some German battalions were ordered out of their comparatively comfortable underground bunkers, out into the wide open terrain outside the remains of the city to take up blocking positions in deep snow, where the temperature fell to thirty degrees below zero, where the earth was frozen so hard only precious explosives could make any impression as the demoralised soldiers attempted to dig foxholes and new bunkers. Normally experts, the German troops found it impossible to construct such fortifications without wood – and there was none.

When Christmas Day came those men lucky enough still to be quartered in decent shelters had a few candles to light in celebration. The Germans made a real attempt to mark this Christian festival, if only to remind themselves of the homes and loved ones they longed for. A candle stuck in an empty bottle, just for a few minutes, provided some light and warmth before being extinguished. They were too precious to burn for long. In the centre of ruined Stalingrad some troops erected

Stark images cannot convey the absolute hell of Stalingrad, where
the German 6th Army died an agonising death.

a makeshift cross from bits of wood; in another sector two men risked
their lives to fetch a small pine tree from the little wood at Gumrak, the
site of one of the *Luftwaffe*'s landing strips, now, of course, covered in
deep snow. From silver foil they cut out some stars, then made more

The Army commander. General Paulus, after surrender to the Soviets, infuriated Hitler by not committing suicide.

decorations with blackout material and any remaining oddments to hand. A few stubs of candles were added, then the 'Christmas tree' was taken to be erected on a little knoll. The candles were lit, and this amazing sight was visible over a wide area. The Russians celebrated by mortaring the tree to bits.

Despite great efforts, all normal wireless communication with 6th Army was cut off, and whatever efforts continued were jammed by the enemy. Germans manning radios who happened to tune in to Radio Moscow's German service were further depressed by the enemy's latest ploy. 'Every seven seconds a German soldier dies in Russia. Stalingrad – mass grave.' So the voice intoned over and over again, these sombre announcements punctuated only by the sound of a clock ticking out the seven seconds.

Hitler's insistence on the 6th Army remaining in possession of the ruins of Stalingrad was bolstered by Goering's promise that his *Luftwaffe* transport squadrons could keep the beleaguered troops supplied by flying in or parachuting the hundreds of tons needed daily. Despite advice from such notable *Luftwaffe* officers as von Richthofen and others that it was impossible, Goering ordered every available plane including bombers from as far afield as Sicily to begin the airlift. It was the final big blunder

221

in Goering's colourful career. A fleet of some thousand planes would not have been too many, but Goering never had them. Plane after plane was shot down or crashed, the supplies delivered were but a trickle, and those brave aircrews successfully penetrating Russian fighters and flak to land on the one or two remaining airstrips were not always laden with the essential food and ammunition so desperately needed in Stalingrad. The most curious and senseless errors were committed by the quartermaster staff loading some transport planes (one recalls the canister of red berets parachuted to the desperate troops of the British 1st Airborne in Arnhem in 1944). Four tons of marjoram and pepper were found inside one plane; Goebbels Propaganda Department in Berlin despatched 200,000 leaflets in another. The troops in Stalingrad could think of only one suitable use for such a mass of paper. When opened, another crate was found to hold protective cellophane covers for hand grenades, labels, and dried herbs. There was also cumbersome engineering equipment for which no possible use could be found. But perhaps the most foolish delivery of all consisted of thousands of contraceptives.

The incompetence continued. At the end of November the *Luftwaffe* had available 180 Ju 52s, twenty Ju 86s, and ninety He 111s. Originally, 6th Army demanded 750 tons of supplies daily; this was modified to 500 tons. Hitler ordered the following flown into Stalingrad daily: sixty thousand gallons of fuel, forty tons of bread, forty tons of weapons/ammo and a hundred tons of miscellany. The actual average daily tonnage airlifted between 24 November and 10 January was only 102 tons, though on 19 December 150 aircraft landed with 280 tons. Most days the airlifts were far below minimum; often no planes arrived at all. On 10 January the last decent airstrip in the city at Pitomnik was rendered useless, and thereafter most supplies were parachuted in, usually to individual strongpoints. The daily average fell to forty-two tons, then half that, and then only a miserable eight tons.

Too late, the Germans discovered the River Volga to be a kind of weather demarcation line. When able to, 6th Army would radio the *Luftwaffe* supply command outside the pocket: 'Good weather for egg-laying. Why no flying?' On the supply airfields the personnel could hardly see their hands in front of them for fog and snow. Conversely, aircrews, after battling through Russian fighters and flak, would arrive over the Stalingrad airstrips to find obstructions on the ground, no unloading parties in sight, or the weather impossible. They were not the only bogies to bedevil those inside and outside the city and cause bickering recriminations. The situation with the increasing number of wounded eventually led to fantastic and nightmarish scenes of horror. Long before the end came Hitler's HQ called on 6th Army to report the number of wounded so the required number of transport planes could be sent in to fly them out. The chief medical officer responded by calling urgently for medical supplies, adding, 'Thirty thousand wounded –

fifteen hundred transport planes therefore required.' This was an utter impossibility, but at first the wounded wretches were slowly but steadily flown out. The rest lay around on litters and stretchers in windblown tents or later in the open, without proper care or food and freezing to death. Their numbers grew so rapidly that before the airlifts were stopped huge numbers of those able to walk were scrambling and fighting to get aboard the few planes arriving, the twin-engined types such as the Junkers 52 and Heinkels hopelessly inadequate to hold more than a handful each, even when stripped of seats and other fittings. Men were killed as the system (such as it was) broke down completely. No vestige of German military discipline remained as these sick and wounded soldiers fought desperately to clamber aboard the flights. No words can describe the terror and horrors which occurred amid these pitiful scenes.

All of these events were some of the knock-on effects of Hitler's blunder to hold at Stalingrad. Not only did this order bring untold suffering to so many German troops, it had dire effects throughout the zone as the neighbouring armies were forced into situations on the battle-field that could have been avoided, or even rectified in good time had the *Führer* seen sense and permitted his generals to run the show in the way they knew best. The Red Army generals shook their heads in amaze-ment and certainly celebrated as they witnessed the most obvious moves in the chess game ignored by their opponent. This augured well for them. By early 1943 even the most junior officer of the Red Army had seen how the previously invincible German Army had been taken over by a man whose vacillations, crass errors and monumental blunders made all the undoubted military genius of his star generals count for nothing.

Tales of bungling were not confined, of course, to the shrinking zone occupied by 6th Army and its timid commander General Paulus, who was soon to be vilified by his *Führer* for not committing suicide rather than surrendering to the Soviets. A sergeant and ten men returning from leave stopped at the huge supply depot warehouse of 51st Corps to request sustenance before continuing their journey back to their unit, which was at the front some eighteen miles further on. On hearing its location the senior NCO in charge of the stores refused them rations as he could not be bothered with such small issues, adding, 'What sort of mess would it make of my books?' The supply staff had, unfortunately, stacked the great stocks of food between sixty drums of petrol and crates of artillery shells, smoke shells and hand grenades. That night, the sergeant and his hungry men settled down nearby, intending to continue their journey next morning, only to be woken by the sound of explosions. Turning out, fearful the Red Army had broken through on a grand scale, they realised an air raid was in progress. In fact, a single Russian light plane of the kind well known by then to the Germans was buzzing about in the darkness at a quite leisurely pace, its two-man crew dropping the occasional mini-bomb, mere ten-pounders. Normally of tiny effect, these little weapons were plopping straight into the 51st Corps supply dump, exploding and setting everything ablaze. The supply officer and his staff of twelve had retired to a cellar in haste, and did not emerge for three hours. When they did it was to find a chaos of fire and explosions, among the destruction a fiery, liquid flood from forty-five burst casks of butter. The men fled as petrol drums exploded at intervals, the grand display enhanced considerably as 16,000 shells began detonating. The fireworks continued for twenty-four hours.

But quartermasters are the same everywhere. When the huge blaze finally subsided the first thought of the officer and his senior NCO was to prepare a full report for the Army quartermaster general in Berlin. This document, duly completed in the undamaged hut office and despatched, survived in the *Wehrmacht* records. Every single item destroyed was accounted for, much of it intended for the starving 6th Army: 9,500lb of butter; 4,700lb of sugar; 28,000 tins of fish; 11,600 loaves of bread; 71 cases of pork; 22,000 iron compo rations; 8,000lb of jam; 450lb of salt; plus copious stocks of tea, coffee, chocolate and condiments. The report had, of course, begun 'Main supply depot 51st Corps Novo-Alexiyevski destroyed by enemy action.' The travelling sergeant had requested twenty-four ounces of butter, eleven tins of canned fish, four loaves of bread and less than one ounce of tea per man. He and his men surveyed the smoking ruin of the warehouse; the same supply NCO regarded them defiantly. As they chewed on their last dry crusts they watched him saunter off westwards.

Before the first week of January was out a Soviet demand for 6th Army to surrender was rejected. Whether this can be seen as an error is problematical, as most of the Germans in Stalingrad who remained alive when General Paulus did give in would die anyway. As soon as the rejection was relayed to the three Russian emissaries, someone on the German side issued an order that in future all such negotiators were to be fired on.

Two minutes after the Soviet ultimatum expired hundreds of guns opened up a terrible two-hour bombardment of the German positions. At one point this storm of steel and explosives moved forward, in the manner of a creeping barrage, only to be switched back again to complete the job of churning up the German positions. Some 14,000 Germans died on the road to Pitomnik, men desperately trying to catch planes out of Stalingrad. But of the 250 *Luftwaffe* transport machines allocated to this airlift, only seventy-five remained serviceable; at the close of the effort, 536 transports had been lost, plus 149 bombers and 123 fighters supporting, and 2,196 aircrew were killed or missing. One Viennese pilot was offered ten thousand marks by a major desperately trying to board his plane, but he was only one of around two hundred men struggling to escape. When the pilot was finally able to rev up his engines to maximum and begin the take-off run, there were still men clinging to the fuselage and the tail of the plane. The major remained.

As another transport became crammed with fugitives everything movable within its fuselage was stripped and thrown out. But there were still half a dozen wounded remaining. Somehow, one by one they were squeezed aboard. The plane was so overloaded the pilot could scarcely move in his seat. But still one German remained, squatting on his haunches in the snow, both legs broken, his head swathed in rags to keep out the bitter cold. Inside the Junkers men were lying on top of each other, but eventually three men jumped out from the plane, one of them with two broken arms. The man with useless legs was carried to the open door of the plane, which then took off, the pilot circling over the forlorn figures below who had volunteered to give up their own escape. 'Whatever sacrifices may be demanded of us as individuals is irrelevant. Victory is and always will be all that matters', as Adolf Hitler had declared three years before.

To Stalingrad gravitated men whose personal errors had put them into military custody, soldiers who had stolen, disobeyed orders, struck officers or, by various tricks, tried to feign madness to escape the Army. In short, the very same types found in most armies. Such felons ended up in the field punishment battalions, many being transported east to the Russian front; one group travelled in goods wagons, nine being found dead on arrival. The men were now designated fit for 'Labour Service East', which included lifting mines, fighting partisans and burying the dead, the last of these a never-ending task. They became expert hole diggers, and when business was at its briskest up to one hundred corpses or parts of them could be consigned to one hole, with one cross mounted above it. In some circumstances, one felon in four was allowed to bear a weapon, but eventually, as they became absorbed as replacement infantry, every man was deemed 'worthy to bear arms' again, and most if not all died in Stalingrad.

The *Wehrmacht* contained all kinds of eccentrics, men who in youth had eagerly volunteered to join Hitler's war. One lad called Fehrmann had felt his country's call in 1939 and journeyed all the way from Brazil to offer his services. Though becoming a lance-corporal, by the time he reached Stalingrad he had taken to trying to blot out the horrors around him by planning imaginary journeys round the world. To do this he had collected a batch of aids from more peaceful times: bus, rail, ship and airliner timetables, together with maps, guides and a pocket globe. He planned trips everywhere, one to a remote village in Asia, and when the Russian bomb that killed him fell, he was busily scouting a holiday trip to Japan via Vladivostok. Another man collected clocks and set up a dugout museum; two others made sport in their hole by shooting at steel helmets for wagers.

One German company was reduced to one man who hid in his hole from the cold and snow and Russian fire. During a lull he dared to emerge, to find three dead men frozen against the rough screen they had erected against the elements. Starving, and finding not one comrade alive, the soldier crawled away until reaching the cookhouse in the rear to get something to eat. The three 'cookhouse heroes' in attendance turned him away. Fifteen minutes later the same bedraggled soldier returned. He was carrying a sack, and much to the astonishment of the NCO cook in charge the man demanded five loaves of bread, ten pounds of sausage and ten tins of butter. The red-rimmed eyes of the lone applicant stared defiantly into the fat face of the cook NCO, whose own mouth opened wide, twisting into a sarcastic grin. The NCO made the mistake of refusing food once again, even though his gloved hand was slowly stirring a big pot of gruel. The beggar moved closer. He too was grinning, and as the cook rasped out his response he felt something hard jab into his overweight gut. Glancing down he saw the barrel of a big Mauser pistol thrusting into him. The beggar-soldier walked away with a filled sack, mouthing insults and waving his pistol. The cook, Paul by name, gazed after him. When the final collapse came Paul was taken prisoner by the Russians and found to be carrying 14,000 marks, which he claimed he had saved from his pay. A year after the war ended he died from typhus.

Despite all the horrendous scenes being enacted around and in the ruins of Stalingrad, the German generals still ostensibly in command of the corps and divisions refused to give up and save lives. Fresh demands arrived from the Soviets, offering to let the officers retain their side arms and swords (should they still carry them), promising honourable surrender and food and care for the wounded. By then few, if any, of these officers had any faith left in their *Führer*, but their military code and esteem forced them to err and seek the 'honourable' way out. In many cases these men declared their resolve to go down with a gun in their hands, fighting to the last; others took another course. In response to General Pfeffer's order that his IVth Corps would not surrender, the remaining men of 297th Infantry laid down their arms and marched into captivity. During the evening of 25 January, the staff of 71st Infantry Regiment gathered together in their bunker, drank a toast to each other and to Germany, and on a word of command shot themselves.

To the end Hitler's staff in Berlin continued to send stupid and mistaken orders to 6th Army; indeed, some of those still issuing from the commanding general's own bunker were blunders, and pointless ones at that. Such as that on 15 January which called all wounded to assemble at the District Command Centre: Supply Sector Three 'will be responsible for food and supplies'. By then the centre was already crammed with sick, wounded and dying. Thousands of walking (and sometimes crawling) wounded began converging on the building from all sectors, mostly men whose faces had looked young when they had reached the River Volga the previous November, in full expectation of medical treatment, food and drink, and a place of shelter. They found none of these things, for

Paulus never left his bunker. He seemed unaware of the final, desperate realities of the situation. The 'City Centre', with the Russian inscription to fallen heroes of the Revolution on its portals, was filled to overflowing with doomed men, some shirkers, scroungers and deserters. There were no beds, no medical supplies, and no food. As the newcomers arrived they tried to get past the heaps of bodies, some of them already dead, to find places or get down into the already filled cellars. In this nightmare prison the lucky ones died quickly; some shot themselves, some corpses were removed to make room for others. The job for the padres proved soul-searing. Then the building was struck by Russian shells and caught fire. As the flames took hold those inside tried to escape, including many in the cellars. Hundreds of panic-stricken men tried to reach the exits, to find their passage blocked by those unaware of the danger still trying to gain entry. Many were crushed underfoot in a long-drawn-out act of terror which went on for three whole hours. Three thousand more of Hitler's Stalingrad heroes died in the holocaust.

This kind of horror was repeated in other buildings where men sought to escape the elements and Russian fire. Such as in Simonovitch's warehouse, where some eight hundred men crouched, lay and stood awaiting a merciful end as their *Führer*'s repeated order to fight to the last man and bullet became even more insane. In the warehouse all distinction of rank had vanished; wounds and sickness saw to that. The air, fetid with the stench of untreated wounds and bodies with missing limbs, was made more excruciating by the smell given off by a single candle lying in paraffin. Here, among the horror, a morsel of stale bread was worth more than a man's life. Here were youngsters expiring from sickness such as diphtheria, not from enemy-inflicted wounds; others were covered in grey lice, disgusting little armies that moved on as each man died. No one ever left the cellar, yet outside a queue of more stricken men waited to get in.

While this kind of episode was drawing to its inevitable close, far to the west in Berlin the errors and absurdities continued. The Chief of the General Staff and the senior officers of the Operations Department put themselves voluntarily on the same scale of rations they believed were being imbibed by the troops in Stalingrad, a foolish and pointless gesture they were forced to give up after less than a week as they found it impaired their efficiency.

General Jodl, Chief of Operations, and one of Hitler's own, issued an order containing the sentence, 'The steadfastness and courage of the Army in the field derives exclusively from National Socialism.' When the end did finally come the Nazi leaders felt obliged to make a public statement extolling the heroes of Stalingrad. *Reichsmarschall* Goering's broadcast over German radio went out on the anniversary of the Nazi takeover, 30 January. During this Goering said, '. . . when you come to Germany, say that you have seen us lying at Stalingrad, as our honour and our leaders ordained that we should, for the greater glory of Germany.' An unknown source in Stalingrad responded over shortwave radio, 'Premature funeral orations are not appreciated here!'

On 17 October the ration strength of 6th Army stood at 334,000 men; of the 255,000 men remaining in the 'Fortress' after evacuations, 132,000 were killed or missing by the end of January. On 2 February the Russians took 123,000 Germans prisoner.

In 1943, Goebbels commissioned one of the German war correspondents, Heinz Schröter, to write up the Stalingrad battle as a heroic episode, extolling the Nazi spirit within it. To do this Schröter was given unprecedented access to a great number of letters, reports and other documents. Among this mass of material were hundreds of pieces of private mail, letters from Stalingrad written and despatched in one of the final airlifts. But these sacks of mail had been intercepted by the German Army's central censorship office and then taken over by Berlin for analysis to ascertain the morale of the men of 6th Army. The Army Information Department had come up with the following interesting statistic on the feelings of the Stalingrad heroes about the way Germany's leaders were running the war:

In favour	2.1%
Dubious	4.4%
Sceptical and deprecatory	57.1%
Indifferent	33.0%
Actively against	3.4%

Fewer than three weeks after this, Schröter was given the letters and other documents, including radio messages, discovering that all trace of the letter writers, names and addresses had been removed. There had been no intention the addressees should ever receive them. Schröter set to work, completing his report many weeks later. It was placed before Goebbels, who skipped through it before delivering his verdict: 'This is intolerable for the German people!'

The Turncoat Claye

Every army has its bad hats, those men who prove to be inherently unworthy of comrades, a disruptive influence in any unit. In World War II such men did not appear only among the 'other ranks': there were occasions when the Army selection boards erred in promoting candidates to hold officer rank in His Majesty's forces.

In wartime the Army boards were passing out as fit many young subalterns to lead men in battle or staff work, whether on dangerous missions or among the 'we also serve' ranks of the humble Pay Corps or other non-combat units. Such a candidate for advancement was Douglas Berneville-Claye, who was granted his commission as a second lieutenant in October 1941, and presently posted to the West Yorkshire Regiment in the Middle East. That the selecting officers in England had erred in permitting Claye to bear an officer's pips did not then seem obvious. But a year after first donning his officer's cap Claye volunteered for the Special Air Service. At this point his true merit began to emerge. As a leader of special service troops he proved quite undistinguished, so untrustworthy that veterans of hazardous SAS operations refused to accompany him on new ventures.

Nevertheless, despite misgivings, Lieutenant Claye's commanders allowed him to embark on ops, this resulting in his capture behind enemy lines. Hitler had ordered the execution of all captured commandos, but Claye was lucky and was sent first to an Italian POW camp, then to the German *Oflag* (*Offizierlager*) 79. And here Claye's true personality emerged: he went over to the enemy, becoming an informer to the German camp security staff. By January 1945 he had fully weakened to German propaganda, inviting Allied prisoners to join them in the great 'anti-Bolshevik crusade'. Claye entered the *Waffen* SS, specifically the so-called 'British Free Corps', a handful of turncoats let out of POW cages, men who succumbed to German promises of a better, more adventurous life – in reality to be used as more cannon fodder on the Russian front. Even here Claye proved a misfit, unable to agree with his fellow traitors or lead them in combat. He used his SAS training to desert his German masters, re-outfitting himself in British battledress before returning to Allied positions in the West.

Claye's past eventually became known and various charges were put to him, all of which he denied. Owing to lack of evidence he was released from custody and permitted to resume Army service, but one year later he was caught out on a comparatively small offence, that of stealing a typewriter, and was dismissed from the Army.

Polish Justice

For hundreds of Polish soldiers the years of exile in Britain were sad and bitter. Their homeland was despoiled by both Soviets and Nazis, with crimes committed wholesale.

When those Polish soldiers who were part of General Montgomery's British Liberation Army went into battle in Normandy they fought with ferocity, taking no prisoners – just as their enemy did, the Germans still believing the Nazi propaganda tales of Polish atrocities against German civilians living in the border areas in 1939.

Yet discipline among the Polish units was strict, and justice could be harsh. One Polish sergeant learned the truth of this when he erred on reaching Germany in 1945. Entering a farmhouse, he shot the farmer dead and proceeded to rape his wife. He was at once arrested, and at his court-martial pleaded he had only done what the Germans had themselves done to his own family in Poland. The presiding judge replied: 'Barbarians may behave like that, we do not.'

The sergeant was shot.

The Poor Bloody Infantry

It was perhaps among the combat soldiers at the front where errors brought the swiftest results: death or maiming. It was not without good reason that such troops were often called the 'PBI' – Poor Bloody Infantry. And it was the officer corps who paid a very high price; in one British unit almost seventy field officers were lost between D-day (6 June 1944) and their entry into Germany in January 1945. Even so, resentment against those in command often resulted because of the honours and privileges accorded officers, who always seemed to gain the best billets and conditions in the field. This the generals took for granted as the natural order of things, however much the British officer was taught to see to his men's needs. The 'them and us' feeling was on occasion furthered when those at the top erred in granting privileges to commanders that were withheld from the troops. For example, British troops, despite their tremendously hard battles in Normandy and very heavy casualties, were denied the fleshpots of Paris after its liberation. Similarly, an embargo was laid on Brussels, which did not stop officers jeeping there for lush weekends, where, incidentally, they found no shortage of good things to eat and drink.

When it came to decorations, recommendations for awards to other ranks for bravery and stalwart behaviour in the worst possible circumstances of danger and death were habitually turned away. Why this persisted is hard to fathom, especially as it engendered more resentment among the PBI who needed to respect and trust their officers in the field. One infantry officer was ashamed and disgusted over this recurring situation, noting in his diary how uncomfortable he felt as he and his officer colleagues were (it seemed) obliged to write up citations for each other for forwarding to higher authority, recommendations which were never refused. The officers who survived the war therefore emerged with suitable awards, unlike most of the men under them who went on against great odds to receive nothing by way of recognition.

It has to be admitted, in all fairness, that officers in the field were at times called upon, perhaps by tradition, to perform duties which discomforted them, such as the occasional 'church parades'. For in their wisdom, those on high firmly believed in a God-fearing armed forces, and those who were called on to kill had to receive the occasional comforting words of someone of rank, an appeasing of His wrath over what they must do. Somehow, a blessing made distasteful duties a little easier. Whether at the front or safe in some home station, it was often if not usual for the men to know that such religious occasions were compulsory duty; the alternative could be the NCO's anger or physical training instead of lying abed Sunday mornings. The sheer sense of futility and surely embarrassment present on such occasions was expressed through one officer at the front who noted the lesson he read from Chapter 53 of Isaiah must have been 'as incomprehensible to the congregation as it was to me'.

Errors of judgement with regard to the sensibilities of generals and some of their commanders were not seen in the same light by the soldiery, this working both ways in a manner of speaking. Brigadiers and lesser field commanders who had seemed splendid at home over years of manoeuvres and countless exercises went to pieces when confronted with their first battle in Normandy; they were usually quietly shipped back to England to some safer job. It was inevitable that some should fall by the wayside, those who had erred in believing themselves tough and made of the right stuff. In one case an officer vanished from his unit, only to be next seen riding back across the Channel on a landing craft; he was not, it seems, charged but survived in another post. For the lesser deserters, the PBI who ran off in terror or with nerves shattered, arrest by the military police and trial on the continent or in England resulted in terms of imprisonment. Committing desertion was a serious error but brought nothing like the terrible retributions meted out in the earlier war. A year, maybe even two, was to be served in a detention camp, usually commuted to six months or so. The calculated errors of such men paid off in the sense that they survived the war. Most of their comrades who stayed the course were killed or wounded.

Hurricanes on Salisbury Plain

The famous Hawker Hurricane fighter bore the brunt of the air battles over southern England in the summer of 1940. Though stalwart and the victor of many an air combat, it was generally considered by *Luftwaffe* fighter pilots as a far less formidable opponent than the Spitfire. In truth, the sturdy Hawker fighter was rapidly becoming obsolete. However, it proved adaptable as a fighter-bomber, and three versions were produced after 1940: the Mk IIB, C and D. The last was armed with two 40mm cannon and used effectively in the Middle East as a 'tank buster'; the

C type carried four 20mm cannon and with bombs made many raids across the Channel; the B version was produced in smaller numbers, and was armed with an incredible twelve Browning .303 machine-guns. All three variants entered squadron service in 1941.

It was Hurricane IIBs which were involved in an exercise which went terribly wrong the following year. On 13 April 1942, a rehearsal took place at Imber on Salisbury Plain, the precursor of a bigger Army–RAF manoeuvre the next day, presumably a demonstration of land–air co-operation in which the air force would prove the power of its intervention in land warfare. In this period the tactical use of air power in the British forces was still in its formative stage, far from the time when a powerful Tactical Air Force could dominate the battlefield, as it did after D-day 1944. The *Luftwaffe* and German Army had developed tactical air warfare and proved their doctrines in the blitz campaigns between 1939 and 1941. For the British, a small and limited force known as Army Co-operation Command had sufficed. But with the Dieppe raid a few months away, fresh efforts were being made to upgrade the fighter and bomber support available to the Army.

For the exercise rehearsal the troops had lined up old vehicles and tanks, together with rows of dummy 'soldiers' to represent enemy columns. Nine Hurricane IIBs from 175 Squadron led by Squadron Leader Legh would beat up this assembly, the event watched by dozens of staff officers and others who were gathered a couple of hundred yards clear of the targets. Conditions were not ideal – ground haze made observation from the air difficult – but despite this the formation leader zoomed in, and though unable to see the arrow pointing out the target, he carried out a successful attack, his twelve machine-guns raking the target vehicles and dummies with hundreds of bullets. But the following three Hurricane pilots missed altogether due to their inability to see the targets clearly. The fifth fighter, however, attacked successfully.

Then came the sixth machine, piloted by Sergeant W. McLachlan. Ground control proved inadequate, the pilot became confused by various radio messages, lost sight of the Hurricane in front and, after firing one burst which fell short, he raised the nose of his Hurricane and shot off another volley, which struck the watching spectators. One surviving officer witness has recounted how two companions either side of him suddenly collapsed. Accounts vary as to the number of casualties caused by the spray of bullets: seventeen or twenty-seven officers and other ranks killed, a further sixty-eight Army and three RAF officers wounded.

The full-scale exercise scheduled for the next day was to be attended by Winston Churchill.

The court of inquiry laid much of the blame on the unfortunate RAF

Sergeant McLachlan, who was killed in action soon afterwards, but also levelled serious criticism at the inadequate ground control arrangements.

Friendly Fire

Judging by the surly reaction of some French people in June 1944, the Allies erred in mounting the enormous D-day invasion at all. They cursed the 'liberators' for turning their farmland into a battlefield, one native sousing a British officer sitting in a jeep with a bucket of water. That kind of reception was uncommon, however, and hardly appreciated by the PBI who in one unit lost fifteen officers and 200 men in the first thirty-five days of combat.

No member of the British Liberation Army could believe their task of beating back the enemy would not have been much harder without the RAF. Yet, on 15 August the British gun lines were bombed by Lancasters; incredibly, this went on for a whole hour, an officer at 154 Brigade HQ complaining they were powerless to do anything to stop it. How this could occur after all the long experience and schooling in North Africa and at home in England is hard to understand. The Germans had righted such errors during the Polish campaign of 1939. It was the custom to post RAF liaison officers to Army field units to call in air support, but the heavies of Bomber Command seemed to operate under different rules. In fact, the only way to halt such an attack during the event was to tele-phone the RAF in England – an absurd communication blunder. The actual chain of communication was: Division to Corps to Army to Army Group to Supreme HQ to Air Ministry to Bomber Command HQ in High Wycombe, and thence to the actual bomber stations. Or so the poor Army staff on the spot believed. 'No wonder it took over an hour to stop!' one of them noted.

Unhappily, the liaison between ground and air on the tactical front in Normandy also broke down at times. One battalion commander was holding an O group briefing beside a road when planes were heard a few miles away. The meeting broke up at once, 'for everybody is scared stiff of the RAF. All day the Typhoons have been strafing the road behind us. Even generals were not immune, having to dive into ditches; one brigade HQ was destroyed and the brigade major killed. Also in August the Americans have bombed our gun lines near Caen, using forty-eight Fortresses.'

These errors, despite whatever extra precautions were put in hand, never stopped; Allied planes continued to attack their own troops right through into 1945. 'Yesterday we were bombed again by the RAF in broad daylight and perfect visibility', wrote a soldier in Germany on

22 February. The Commander Royal Engineers was struck in the head by a splinter and was not expected to live, while the Argyll and Sutherland Highlanders suffered twelve casualties. Another unit lost all its transport.

The Irish Rogues

Whatever has been recorded on the sacking and looting of towns by the enemy, the fact is that it went on among the Allies.

As one infantry officer prepared to leave a Belgian town he was met by a local deputation led by the *curé*, who proceeded to complain of the vandalism and looting by the last British unit that had recently left the area. The officer went off with the *curé* to see for himself: every single house he entered had been ransacked from top to bottom, the contents of every chest strewn over the floor. The *curé* knew the identity of the unit responsible, and passed on this information. What the officer learned came as no surprise to him as his own unit had suffered such a fate at the hands of the same Irish rogues even before they left England. They had stolen the Naafi safe and much kit from the quartermaster's stores, ransacked the officers' quarters while they were watching a boxing tournament, and finally stolen the regiment emergency fund cashbox.

Even the Germans had behaved better.

A Call to Arms

The problem of deserters was one that would never go away. In one battalion the commander discovered such people quartered in safety behind the front awaiting trial, 'an intolerable situation', he commented. He promptly had the felons marched up to occupy front positions every night. As for deserters from the enemy side, these were few in number because the families of such men would suffer as allowances for wives would be stopped and the culprits refused repatriation to Germany for twenty-five years.

This the British learned, but whether a document found on one prisoner was of German origin or just clever British black propaganda was unknown. It seems most likely to have been the latter. Both POW and his captors made an error in accepting it without question. The paper was headed the State Office for Increase of Birth Rate in Berlin, and after lamenting the loss of men through the war it told the reader the man in question was selected to service a number of German females in the 12th District of the capital, comprising nine women and seventeen girls.

Moreover, if he felt up to it he could take on a second district and become
a Breeding Officer, win a medal (1st class, with ribbon), become exempt
from all taxes and receive a pension. The document ended by promising
to send the reader a list of the females' addresses and exhorting him to
'start your fruitful work at once and report the results to this office after
nine months'.

The Luftwaffe *Reborn*

By the end of the 1944 campaign in France the Allies had written off the
Luftwaffe as a totally spent force, with virtually no planes or men left in
the once formidable bomber force. This was an error, though an understandable one as it was rare to see any German planes over the front. But
then, on 11 November, the enemy suddenly appeared over Eindhoven
in Holland, and though their bombing was puny compared to the
massive Allied blitzes, the targets could hardly be missed. For the British,
no longer fearful of enemy air attack, had not only allowed the town to
become packed out with every conceivable type of transport, but had
located their various headquarters there. The major-general of artillery
and his staff were hit, as was a brigadier of the Service Corps. Second
Army HQ was disrupted and forced to locate elsewhere, and much
damage and confusion was caused to the other units in the town.

Operation 'Gisela'

Late in the war, the *Luftwaffe* made a belated attempt to intercept Allied
bombers engaged in night operations, but not over the crumbling *Reich.*
During the night of 3/4 March 1945 up to seventy German night fighters
were despatched to infiltrate the stream of enemy planes returning to
their bases in Britain. Operation 'Gisela' was the most determined
German attempt of the war to disrupt Allied night activity in the air. With
Allied aircrews returning tired over the sea and friendly landscape, they
were at their most vulnerable. When the German fighters slipped in
among these westbound streams they became almost impossible to
detect.

On this night the German planes roamed over the eastern half of
England, from Southampton to Norfolk, even as far north as Tynemouth,
bombing and strafing every airfield showing lights to welcome home
Allied planes. In these and a later attack, Junkers 88s flew very low, one
pilot mistaking car headlights for an aircraft on the ground and opening
fire, crashing into the vehicle in the process, the driver and four Germans

being killed. Another Junkers attempted to attack an unarmed American Liberator just returning from Sweden by passing below it. The B-24 was already descending to touch down at Metfield. Spotting the intruder at 300ft, the American pilot swerved towards the Junkers, which attempted to evade but struck the ground and cartwheeled, the German crew being killed.

The Allied defences had been taken by surprise by the sudden resurgence of *Luftwaffe* activity, and as a result gunners and night fighter crews became trigger-happy. During the night of 4 March, some eighteen hours after Operation 'Gisela' (which, all told, had cost the Germans twenty-one Junkers 88s), three Allied aircraft were shot down in error: a Mosquito, an American C-46 Commando transport, and a B-17 Fortress of a night leaflet squadron. During the next night a Canadian-manned Halifax was shot down by flak, and another Mosquito by an RAF night fighter.

Bibliography

Bomber Command. HMSO 1942.

The Blitz – Then & Now. Vol. 3. Public Record Office 1990.

Bekker, Cajus (1974) *Hitler's Naval War.* Macdonald & Janes.

Blandford, E.L. (1999) *Two Sides of the Beach.* Airlife.

—— *Rogue's Regiment* (unpublished)

—— (1997) *Target: England.* Airlife.

Brissaud, Andre (1974) *The Nazi Secret Service.* Bodley Head.

Carell, Paul (1958) *Foxes of the Desert.* Macdonald.

Churchill, Winston S. (1949–50) *The Second World War.* Cassell.

Evans, A.S., *Beneath the Waves.* William Kimber.

Flower & Reeves (eds) (1960) *The War 1939–45.* Cassell.

Fussell, Paul (1989) *Wartime.* Oxford.

Galantin, Admiral L.J. (1988) *Take Her Deep.* Unwin-Hyman.

Gibbs, Wg Cdr Patrick (1992) *Torpedo Leader.* Grub Street.

Hamilton, James A. (1979) *Motive for a Mission.* Mainstream.

Hammerton, Sir John (ed.) *The Second Great War.* Amalgamated Press.

Johnson, Derek (1978) *East Anglia at War.* Jarrolds.

Kaplan, Philip & Jack Currie (1997) *Wolf Pack.* Aurum Press.

Kelso, Nicholas (1988) *Errors of Judgement.* Robert Hale.

Kessler, Leo (1991) *Betrayal at Venlo.* Leo Cooper.

Lindsay, Martin (1946) *So Few Got Through.* Collins.

Lipscombe, F.W. (1975) *The British Submarine.* Conway Maritime Press.

Liskutin, M.A. (1988) *Challenge in the Air.* William Kimber.

Marshall, Robert (1988) *All the King's Men.* Collins.

Mason, Francis K. (1969) *Battle over Britain.* McWhirter Twins.

Overy, Richard (1997) *Bomber Command.* HarperCollins.

Piekalkiewicz, Janus (1985) *The Air War.* Blandford Press.

Pile, General Sir Frederick (1949) *Ack-Ack.* Harrap.

Pitt, Barry (ed.) (1967) *History of the Second World War.* Purnell.

Price, Alfred (1976) *Blitz on Britain.* Ian Allen.

Sutton, Sqn Ldr H.T. (1956) *Raiders Approach!* Gale & Polden.

West, Kenneth (1978) *The Captive Luftwaffe.* Putnam.

White, John B. (1955) *The Big Lie.* Evans Bros.

Index